Beyond Tolerance: Gays, Lesbians and Bisexuals on Campus

Edited by

Nancy J. Evans
and
Vernon A. Wall

American College Personnel Association

Distributed by University Press of America,® Inc.
4720 Boston Way, Lanham, Maryland 20706

Cover Design by Sarah Jane Valdez

Library of Congress Cataloging-in-Publication Data

Beyond tolerance : gays, lesbians, and bisexuals on campus /
edited by Nancy J. Evans and Vernon A. Wall.
p. cm.
Includes bibliographical references.
1. Personnel services in higher education—United States.
2. Gay college students—United States.   I. Evans, Nancy J.,
1947– . II. Wall, Vernon A.
LB2343.B49   1991
378.1'94—dc20   91-23235 CIP

ISBN 1-55620-088-9 (pbk. : alk. paper)

 The paper used in this publication meets the minimum requirements of
American National Standard for Information Sciences—Permanence
of Paper for Printed Library Materials, ANSI Z39.48–1984.

CONTENTS

iii

DEDICATION

The editors dedicate this book to the ACPA Standing Committee on Lesbian, Gay, and Bisexual Awareness for their support and encouragement during the development of this very important project.

CONTRIBUTORS

Vernon A. Wall is coordinator for staffing and development, Department of University Housing, University of Georgia

Nancy J. Evans is an associate professor and coordinator, College Student Personnel Program, Western Illinois University

David C. Barnett is a staff psychologist, Counseling Center, University of Illinois at Chicago

Donna Bourassa is staff development coordinator, Department of Residential Education/Housing Services, University of Massachusetts at Amherst

Shawn-Eric Brooks is coordinator of staffing services, Office of Residential Life, University of California—Los Angeles

Maura Cullen is an educational consultant and doctoral student, Department of Organizational Development and Social Justice, University of Massachusetts at Amherst

Mark Donahue is a 1990 graduate of the University of North Carolina at Chapel Hill, BA, political science

Natalie S. Eldridge is a staff psychologist, Counseling Center, Boston University

Cheryl Hetherington is a psychologist and training consultant, Hetherington & Associates, Iowa City, IA

Michael J. Hughes is activities coordinator—fraternal affairs, California State University—Northridge

Heidi Levine is a doctoral student, counseling psychology, Temple University

Kathy Obear is a consultant, Human Advantage, Amherst, MA

Raechele L. Pope is a doctoral student, Department of Organizational Development and Social Justice, University of Massachusetts at Amherst

Amy L. Reynolds is a senior staff psychologist, Counseling Center, University of Iowa

Dick Scott is director of operations, University Student Union, California State University—Northridge

Bill Shipton is assistant director of residence life for diversity education, Department of Residence Life, Indiana University

Jim Smart is assistant director for residence services, Department of Residence Halls, University of Miami

Jamie Washington is a senior consultant, Equity Institute, Emeryville, CA, and doctoral intern, Office of the Vice President for Student Affairs, University of Maryland—Baltimore County

ACPA Media Board

FOREWORD: LETTER FROM A GAY STUDENT

This letter from Mark Donahue, a gay undergraduate student at the University of North Carolina at Chapel Hill, serves as Foreword for Beyond Tolerance: Gays, Lesbians, and Bisexuals on Campus. *His words set the tone for this book and give urgency to the material that follows. The authors support wholeheartedly the need he expresses for additional support and intervention on behalf of gay, lesbian, and bisexual students.*

This project was born out of need. The lack of available resources for dealing with gay and lesbian issues in the campus setting led to a sense of urgency among student affairs professionals, who then sought to change this condition. Through their collective experience and training, a handful of knowledgeable, determined individuals have assembled information to assist those who wish to better advocate for lesbians and gay men in the academic community. The authors of each chapter have worked diligently to develop comprehensive yet practical guides for student affairs professionals, administrators, faculty, and students.

The situations facing lesbians and gay men in the college setting are numerous and complex—deserving much more inquiry than they have received previously. Therefore, prepare to be challenged on some of the deep-seated prejudices that we all unknowingly carry with us and that can hinder our attempts at appropriate decision making. *Beyond Tolerance: Gays, Lesbians, and Bisexuals on Campus* provides you with a greater understanding of the forces at work in our society on this subject as well as encourages your supportive leadership in addressing campus concerns.

This book dispels many of the familiar stereotypes and myths about homosexuality. Although simple strategies do not exist, this work encourages you to devise solutions to the concerns of lesbians

xi

and gay men in your distinctive college environment. I hope that you act upon the proposals of the authors because they represent the convictions of leaders who have dealt with these issues firsthand in many different capacities.

You may well ask why you should select *Beyond Tolerance: Gays, Lesbians, and Bisexuals on Campus* from among the myriad books that deal with homosexuality from a social, psychological, or religious point of view. The answer is simple: This book is the only comprehensive, practical guide addressing gay and lesbian topics in campus settings in existence. Years of personal experience inform this timely, insightful resource, written specifically for campus leaders.

The controversies surrounding homosexuality are innumerable. Do gay and lesbian students have a right to organize on campus? If so, do they deserve acknowledgement and support from the administration and faculty? In what way? How should heterosexual students react to sharing living quarters or student fees with this diverse group? Whose responsibility is it to police homophobia on campus? These are all tough questions and there are no easy answers, if there are answers at all. *Beyond Tolerance: Gays, Lesbians, and Bisexuals on Campus* addresses these and other current dilemmas, and the authors try to lead you to conscientious resolutions.

I wish to extend my gratitude to the editors of this book, Nancy Evans and Vernon Wall, for taking on a very bold and innovative project. Without their urging, this book would have never materialized. The authors of each chapter deserve praise for initiating substantial dialogue and for sharing their experience. By ensuring this book's publication, the American College Personnel Association (ACPA) Media Board has performed an invaluable service for the academic community, and their constant support and feedback has been greatly appreciated. Good luck to each of you in the continuing struggle for equality and human dignity.

Mark Donahue
University of North Carolina
Chapel Hill

Introduction: Why We Need This Book

Nancy J. Evans
Western Illinois University

Since the Stonewall riots in 1969, which gave momentum to the gay rights movement, gay, lesbian, and bisexual individuals have become more open about their sexual identity and more assertive about demanding the same rights as heterosexuals. As a result, society as a whole has been forced to examine its treatment of this population. Some states and cities have established laws prohibiting discrimination based on sexual orientation; movies, plays, and books have included gay and lesbian characters and examined gay and lesbian issues; and the American Psychiatric Association (APA) no longer considers homosexuality a psychological disturbance (Bayer, 1981).

Unfortunately, at the same time that progress toward acceptance of gay, lesbian, and bisexual individuals was occurring, conservative values centering on family and disparaging alternative lifestyles became more prevalent in a large segment of American society. The AIDS (acquired immune deficiency syndrome) epidemic, affecting a large number of gay men, also became a major national and world concern. Both of these factors have been instrumental in creating a backlash against gay, lesbian, and bisexual people (Croteau & Morgan, 1989). An increase in violent acts directed against gay, lesbian, and bisexual individuals has occurred, as has a resurgence of propaganda designed to incite discrimination and oppression of this group (National Gay and Lesbian Task Force, 1987).

College and university environments are a microcosm of society. The same issues that exist in the larger community also exist in the residence halls and student organizations found on our campuses.

Issues of oppression must be addressed within college and university environments to combat their persistance in the larger society.

Although discrimination and prejudice related to racial and ethnic background are beginning to be addressed on campuses, oppression based on sexual orientation is frequently a taboo subject. In 1986, only 47 colleges and universities in this country banned discrimination based on sexual orientation (Bendet, 1986). Organizations for gay, lesbian, and bisexual students often must function without official administrative support. The need for education and intervention in the area of gay, lesbian, and bisexual concerns is critical.

The original Kinsey study (Kinsey, Pomeroy, & Martin, 1948; Kinsey, Pomeroy, Martin, & Gebhard, 1953), still the most comprehensive research on sexual behavior available in this country, indicated that, during the 1940s, 10% of the men surveyed had engaged in predominantly same-sex sexual behavior for at least 3 years. During the same time period, the reported incidence of same-sex sexual behavior for women was from one-half to one-third that of men.

Although no accurate report has been made of the numbers of gay, lesbian, and bisexual students in colleges and universities, a more recent study conducted by the Kinsey Institute (Bell, Weinberg, & Hammersmith, 1981) suggested that the college or university years are a period during which individuals are defining their orientation. If 10% of these students eventually identify themselves as gay, on a campus of 1,000 students this would mean that 100 students so identify. On a campus of 20,000 students, the number of gay students would be 2,000! Certainly, student affairs professionals must pay attention to such a significant population.

To address the needs of gay, lesbian, and bisexual students, student affairs professionals must educate themselves about the issues faced by this population. This book is designed to assist in this process. It provides both theoretical and practical information about the concerns that gay, lesbian, and bisexual individuals must address in their lives and suggests ways in which student affairs professionals can help in addressing these concerns for both students and staff who are gay, lesbian, or bisexual.

Preliminary to discussion of gay, lesbian, and bisexual concerns experienced on college campuses, a review of some of the definitional and cultural issues related to the study of homosexuality in general is useful. A historical overview of the study of homosexuality is also presented to provide a context for the material presented in this book.

DEFINITIONAL AND CULTURAL ISSUES

Definition has been a major problem in discussing homosexuality (Gonsiorek, 1982). Many definitions have focused only on actual sexual behavior and ignored emotional attachment (Shively, Jones, & DeCecco, 1984). Studies have considered homosexuality and heterosexuality to be dichotomous variables and ignored bisexuality (DeCecco, 1981; MacDonald, 1982).

Morin (1977) identified the following operational definitions of homosexuality in the research: (a) presence of homosexual behavior (e.g., Kinsey et al., 1948), (b) same-sex erotic preference (e.g., McConaghy, 1967), (c) self-reported homosexual identity (e.g., Evans, 1969), and, more recently, (d) self-reported gay identity, which, Morin (1977) noted, connotes a value system as well as designates group membership.

Another major problem has been the assumption that homosexual behavior in men and women is identical when, in fact, significant differences have been found to exist (Faraday, 1981; Golden, 1987; Henderson, 1984; Marmor, 1980). (These differences are discussed in more detail in chapter 1.)

Viewpoints on homosexuality are culture specific and influenced by the historical period during which discussion takes place (DeCecco & Shively, 1984b; Weeks, 1981). Early Western views were heavily influenced by religion and saw homosexuality as a sin. The interpretation of homosexuality as pathology developed in the 19th century. The Kinsey studies in the 1940s were instrumental in redefining homosexuality as a normal variation of sexual behavior. Finally, the civil rights and feminist movements of the late 1960s contributed significantly to the development of a positive and open gay pride movement. (See chapter 9 for a more complete discussion of these influences.)

A HISTORICAL OVERVIEW OF THE STUDY OF HOMOSEXUALITY

Researchers did not begin to study homosexuality seriously until the 1940s. That research has examined mainly male homosexuality and has been conducted primarily in the United States (Plummer, 1981a). Early studies were concerned with finding the "cause" of homosexuality, which would lead to its "cure." Several hypothetical causes were advanced: Psychoanalytic theorists postulated that the source of homosexuality could be found in early childhood experiences in the family; behavioral theorists focused on stimulus-response learning and the process of conditioning; biological theorists examined hormonal imbalance and genetic mutation. Excellent reviews of this research have been presented by DeCecco and Shively (1984a), Friedman (1986), and Risman and Schwartz (1988).

A major debate has focused on whether homosexuality is a state of being that exists at birth or a complex set of attitudes, feelings, and behaviors that any person is capable of experiencing given the right set of circumstances (Plummer, 1981b; Richardson, 1987). In-depth review of research in this area suggests that biological, family, social, and cultural factors all contribute to the development of sexual orientation (Marmor, 1980).

The psychological adjustment of homosexual individuals also has been the subject of extensive research. Unfortunately, samples often have included individuals in psychotherapy who could be expected to show some maladjustment (Gonsiorek, 1982). When appropriate research methods are used, gay and lesbian individuals have been found to be as psychologically healthy as those whose sexual orientation is heterosexual (Hooker, 1957).

During the 1970s, sociological researchers conducted a number of ethnographic studies within gay and lesbian settings. Sociologists examined interactions within the gay and lesbian community and also between heterosexuals and gay and lesbian people (e.g., Lewis, 1979; Moses, 1978; Warren, 1974). The attitudes of nongay individuals toward gay people and the effects of stigma on gay men and lesbians also have been investigated (Morin, 1977; Watters, 1986).

Recent research, particularly that conducted by psychologists, has centered on the development of a gay or lesbian identity. This work is discussed in chapter 1.

Unfortunately, almost no research has been conducted examining the experiences of gay, lesbian, and bisexual students within the college environment. Indeed, a recently published student affairs bibliography (Belson & Stamatakos, 1988) listed only 13 articles on topics related to homosexuality, most of which were not data based. Although a review of recent conference programs at the major association meetings (American College Personnel Association; National Association of Student Personnel Administrators; National Association of Women Deans, Administrators, and Counselors; and Association of College and University Housing Officers) indicates that programming related to gay and lesbian issues is receiving some attention, few of these programs are being disseminated in the literature.

THE CONTENT OF THE BOOK

This book organizes existing literature, discusses its relevance when considering the development of students, and suggests strategies for using, in student affairs settings, what we know about gay, lesbian, and bisexual individuals. Several caveats must be kept in mind, however.

First: We know very little about gay, lesbian, and bisexual students. Most of the existing research is based on older populations of self-identified gay and, to a lesser extent, lesbian people. The authors have attempted to apply existing theories and models of gay identity development, student development, and minority development to the experiences of gay, lesbian, and bisexual students, but the reader must be careful not to generalize beyond the available data.

Second: The authors cannot provide easy, cookbook answers because there are none. The authors offer their best ideas, provide resources, and propose some strategies that they or others have used. But programming about gay and lesbian concerns is a new endeavor, and little evaluation has been done concerning its impact. Often the authors write in general terms out of necessity; frequently there are no tried and true models, policies, or techniques for addressing the issues they raise. But it is important to raise these issues in the hope that someone will discover effective strategies for addressing them.

Third: An unanticipated concern arose as the manuscript was prepared. The editors discovered that although they wished to include bisexuals, few of the chapters did more that pay lip service to this need. In an effort to face the problems experienced by the editors, chapter 12, which addresses bisexuality and the dilemmas it poses for those who wish to be inclusive, has been included. The editors do not assume that this inclusion solves the problem, but perhaps it at least raises awareness levels.

Two theoretical chapters provide a basis for later chapters that focus on interventions within specific student affairs settings: In chapter 1, Heidi Levine and Nancy Evans present an overview and critique of several models of gay identity development, focusing especially on the work of Vivienne Cass. They note differences among gay men, lesbians, and bisexual men and women. This chapter addresses the questions, How do individuals develop an awareness of who they are as sexual beings? and How does this awareness affect other aspects of their self-awareness?

In chapter 2, Vernon Wall and Nancy Evans examine student development theories as they apply to gay and lesbian students and consider the unique developmental issues faced by this population. Coming out, establishing a support network, developing intimate relationships, and dealing with oppression are a few of the concerns they address.

A major problem faced by all gay and lesbian individuals is homophobia. In chapter 3, which serves as a transition from theory to practice, Kathy Obear examines the causes and outcomes of homophobia. She suggests ways of combating oppression through programming, one-on-one intervention, and policy.

Many gay, lesbian, and bisexual individuals also are members of racial and ethnic groups. In chapter 4, Vernon Wall and Jamie Washington examine the unique developmental and social issues faced by gay and lesbian students of color. They also discuss the interrelationship of the various "isms."

Chapters 5, 6, and 7 examine gay and lesbian issues specific to particular areas of student affairs practice: In chapter 5, Donna Bourassa and Bill Shipton explore the problems facing gay and lesbian students in residence halls, which include dealing with roommate conflicts, finding a support network, maintaining intimate relationships, and dealing with oppression. They discuss interventions unique to the residence setting, including staff recruitment, selection, and training strategies.

In chapter 6, Michael Hughes examines education and intervention on gay-related topics within Greek systems. He discusses the impact on chapters and on individual members of acknowledging gay and lesbian members. He also presents group interventions designed to combat homophobia and individual efforts on behalf of gay and lesbian members of fraternities and sororities.

Dick Scott addresses the purposes for and problems faced by gay student organizations in chapter 7. He discusses the dual roles of support group and political organization, funding issues, obtaining university recognition and support, programming, and developing membership and leadership.

The unique issues that face gay and lesbian students as they make career decisions are examined by Cheryl Hetherington in chapter 8. She points out that career counselors must assist gay and lesbian clients in addressing negative stereotypes, minority group status, limited role models, and issues facing gay and lesbian couples in the job search. She also presents programming and lifestyle counseling strategies.

In chapter 9, Natalie Eldridge and David Barnett take a historical look at therapeutic approaches to homosexuality and examine current philosophies. They present strategies for assisting students in exploring their identities and working through related developmental issues.

We need to remember that a significant number of our student affairs colleagues are gay, lesbian, and bisexual. In chapter 10, issues faced by these individuals are addressed by Maura Cullen and Jim Smart. They examine the decision on whether to come out to supervisors, peers, and/or students; job searches; partnerships; and legal issues.

What about individuals who are heterosexual? In chapter 11, Jamie Washington and Nancy Evans examine the process of becoming an ally, and the steps heterosexuals can take to combat homophobia and support gay, lesbian, and bisexual individuals on their campuses.

In chapter 12, Raechele Pope and Amy Reynolds tackle the issue of bisexuality and challenge student affairs professionals to find new ways of being inclusive of this population. This chapter is a fitting reminder that even the oppressed can be oppressors and that all individuals must constantly struggle to do what is right and just for all people.

For chapter 13, Shawn-Eric Brooks has amassed a comprehensive list of resources to assist student affairs professionals who wish to learn more about gay, lesbian, and bisexual individuals and ways of working effectively with this population. Books, pamphlets, articles, videotapes, and other media are included along with addresses of numerous national gay, lesbian, and bisexual organizations.

From its inception, *Beyond Tolerance: Gays, Lesbians, and Bisexuals on Campus* has been a collaborative effort involving gay men, lesbian women, and heterosexual allies. With the support and encouragement of the ACPA Standing Committee on Gay, Lesbian, and Bisexual Awareness and the ACPA Media Board, it has come to fruition. For the editors and authors it has been more than just another book. *Beyond Tolerance: Gays, Lesbians, and Bisexuals on Campus* has provided those of us involved in the project with the opportunity to share our knowledge concerning an issue about which we feel passionately. We wish to thank everyone who has encouraged and assisted us in this endeavor. We sincerely hope that our work will have a positive impact on the student affairs profession and upon the students we serve.

REFERENCES

Bayer, R. (1981). *Homosexuality and American psychiatry.* New York: Basic Books.

Bell, A. P., Weinberg, M. S., & Hammersmith, S. K. (1981). *Sexual preference: Its development in men and women*. Bloomington: Indiana University Press.

Belson, B., & Stamatakos, L. C. (1988). *The student affairs profession: A selective bibliography*. Alexandria, VA: American College Personnel Association.

Bendet, P. (1986). Hostile eyes. *Campus Voice*, 30–39.

Croteau, J. M., & Morgan, S. (1989). Combating homophobia in AIDS education. *Journal of Counseling and Development, 68*, 86-91.

DeCecco, J. P. (1981). Definition and meaning of sexual orientation. *Journal of Homosexuality, 6*, 51-61.

DeCecco, J. P., & Shively, M. G. (Eds.). (1984a). *Bisexual and homosexual identities: Critical theoretical issues*. New York: Haworth.

DeCecco, J. P., & Shively, M. G. (1984b). From sexual identity to sexual relationships: A contextual shift. In J. P. DeCecco & M. G. Shively (Eds.), *Bisexual and homosexual identities: Critical theoretical issues* (pp. 1–26). New York: Haworth.

Evans, R. B. (1969). Childhood parental relationships of homosexual men. *Journal of Consulting and Clinical Psychology, 33*, 129–135.

Faraday, A. (1981). Liberating lesbian research. In K. Plummer (Ed.), *The making of the modern homosexual* (pp. 112–129). Totowa, NJ: Barnes & Noble.

Friedman, R. M. (1986). The psychoanalytic model of male homosexuality: A historical and theoretical critique. *The Psychoanalytic Review, 73*(4), 79–115.

Golden, C. (1987). Diversity and variability in women's sexual identities. In Boston Lesbian Psychologies Collective (Eds.), *Lesbian psychologies: Explorations and challenges* (pp. 19–34). Urbana, IL: University of Illinois Press.

Gonsiorek, J. C. (1982). An introduction to mental health issues and homosexuality. *American Behavioral Scientist, 25*, 367–384.

Henderson, A. F. (1984). Homosexuality in the college years: Development differences between men and women. *Journal of American College Health, 32*, 216–219.

Hooker, E. A. (1957). The adjustment of the overt male homosexual. *Journal of Projective Techniques, 21*, 17–31.

Kinsey, A. C., Pomeroy, W. B., & Martin, C. E. (1948). *Sexual behavior in the human male*. Philadelphia: Saunders.

Kinsey, A. C., Pomeroy, W. B., Martin, C. E., & Gebhard, P. H. (1953). *Sexual behavior in the human female*. Philadelphia: Saunders.

Lewis, S. G. (1979). *Sunday's women: A report on lesbian life today*. Boston: Beacon.

MacDonald, A. P. (1982). Research on sexual orientation: A bridge that touches both shores but doesn't meet in the middle. *Journal of Sex Education and Therapy, 8*, 9–13.

Marmor, J. (1980). Overview: The multiple roots of homosexual behavior. In J. Marmor (Ed.), *Homosexual behavior: A modern reappraisal* (pp. 3–22). New York: Basic Books.

McConaghy, N. (1967). Penile volume changes to moving pictures of male and female nudes in heterosexual and homosexual males. *Behavior Research and Therapy, 5,* 43–48.

Morin, S. F. (1977). Heterosexual bias in psychological research on lesbianism and male homosexuality. *American Psychologist, 32,* 628–637.

Moses, A. E. (1978). *Identity management in lesbian women.* New York: Praeger.

National Gay and Lesbian Task Force (1987). *Antigay violence, victimization, and defamation in 1987.* (Available from author, 1517 U St., NW, Washington, DC 20009)

Plummer, K. (1981a). Building a sociology of homosexuality. In K. Plummer (Ed.), *The making of the modern homosexual* (pp. 17–29). Totowa, NJ: Barnes & Noble.

Plummer, K. (1981b). Homosexual categories: Some research problems in the labeling perspective of homosexuality. In K. Plummer (Ed.), *The making of the modern homosexual* (pp. 53–75). Totowa, NJ: Barnes & Noble.

Richardson, D. (1987). Recent challenges to traditional assumptions about homosexuality: Some implications for practice. *Journal of Homosexuality, 13*(4), 1–12.

Risman, B., & Schwartz, P. (1988). Sociological research on male and female homosexuality. *Annual Review of Sociology, 14,* 125–147.

Shively, M. G., Jones, C., & DeCecco, J. P. (1984). Research on sexual orientation: Definitions and methods. *Journal of Homosexuality, 9,* 127–136.

Warren, C. A. B. (1974). *Identity and community in the gay world.* New York: Wiley.

Watters, A. T. (1986). Heterosexual bias in psychological research on lesbianism and male homosexuality (1979–1983), utilizing the bibliographic and taxonomic system of Morin (1977). *Journal of Homosexuality, 13*(1), 35–58.

Weeks, J. (1981). Discourse, desire, and sexual deviance: Some problems in a history of homosexuality. In K. Plummer (Ed.), *The making of the modern homosexual* (pp. 76–111). Totowa, NJ: Barnes & Noble.

Chapter 1

THE DEVELOPMENT OF GAY, LESBIAN, AND BISEXUAL IDENTITIES

Heidi Levine
Temple University

Nancy J. Evans
Western Illinois University

To understand the issues faced by gay, lesbian, and bisexual people on college campuses, we must first examine the life experiences of these individuals. What it means to be gay, lesbian, or bisexual is unique to each person; but some commonalities exist as individuals become aware of their attraction to others of the same sex and integrate these feelings into other aspects of their identity.

The research that considers timing and age factors in the gay and lesbian identity development process suggests that many developmental issues occur during the traditional undergraduate years (Bell, Weinberg, & Hammersmith, 1981; McDonald, 1982). As student development professionals, we know that this is a key time for identity development in general (Chickering, 1969; Erikson, 1968; Moore & Upcraft, 1990). College and university students are faced with many areas in which they need to reconsider their self-perceptions, develop new skills, and master developmental tasks. The possibility or certainty that one is gay, lesbian, or bisexual complicates these developmental challenges and adds an additional set of complicated issues that must be resolved.

This chapter examines gay, lesbian, and bisexual identity development as it is experienced in Western society. In the next chapter, Wall and Evans more fully address the relevance of student development theory for gay, lesbian, and bisexual students and explore the wide range of developmental issues faced by gay, lesbian, and bisexual students.

Much confusion exists in the literature concerning the terms *homosexual*, *gay*, and *lesbian* as well as what the concepts of identity and identity development mean. This chapter thus begins by clarifying terms used in relation to the development of a gay, lesbian, or bisexual identity. Gay identity development models are then reviewed, with special attention given to the model proposed by Cass (1979). Distinctions are made between social and psychological models, and the advantages of Cass' psychosocial approach are noted.

Most models of development have failed to consider gender differences, and none have taken into account bisexuality. Therefore, unique aspects of lesbian identity development and special concerns of bisexual individuals are next considered to complement discussion of the major models of gay identity development. The chapter ends with a summary and critique of the work done to date related to gay, lesbian, and bisexual identity development.

DEFINITIONAL ISSUES

Researchers and theorists have paid little attention to the factors involved in the development of a gay, lesbian, or bisexual identity. Richardson (1981b) suggested that the development of gay, lesbian, and bisexual identities has been neglected for three reasons: (a) the study of homosexuality has focused almost exclusively on determining its causes, (b) homosexuality has been defined in terms of sexual acts, and (c) homosexuality has been viewed as a pathological state.

Until as recently as the 1970s, the focus of all discussions of homosexuality was etiology. Various biological and psychological causes of homosexual behavior were hypothesized, investigated, and hotly debated. The assumption in this debate was that homosexuality is a universal experience and that homosexuals are a specific type of being who exhibit predictable behaviors (Browning, 1984; Plummer, 1981). More recent writers do not assume that an individual is born with a homosexual identity but rather suggest that such an identity is socially constructed and maintained through interaction with others (Richardson, 1981a).

A number of writers have noted that homosexual *identity* must be distinguished from homosexual *acts* because individuals frequently engage in homosexual behavior without identifying themselves as homosexual (Cass, 1983–1984; Marmor, 1980; Nungesser, 1983; Richardson & Hart, 1981; Weinberg, 1978). Often, same-sex sexual activity is a precursor to developing a gay identity (Cass, 1983–1984; Weinberg, 1978).

Few writers have taken the time to define clearly the concept of homosexual or gay identity. Cass (1983–1984) identified a number of conflicting definitions in her review of the literature, including "(1) defining oneself as gay, (2) a sense of self as gay, (3) image of self as homosexual, (4) the way a homosexual person is, and (5) consistent behavior in relation to homosexual-related activity" (p. 108). She pointed out that some of these definitions are interpersonally focused, others are intrapersonal, and occasionally still others are both. The lack of clarity and agreement, as well as the difficulty in operationalizing these potential definitions, is troublesome.

Homosexual identity must be recognized as only one aspect of the person's total identity. Troiden (1984) defined identity as "organized sets of characteristics an individual perceives as definitively representing the self in relation to a social situation" (p. 102). Homosexual identity, then, is "a perception of self as homosexual in relation to a social setting" (p. 103). Minton and McDonald (1984) saw identity as including "the ascribed, achieved, and adopted roles characteristically enacted by the individual" (p. 91); sexual identity is one of these roles. They went on to define homosexual identity formation as "a life-span, developmental process that is part of the general maturational process of achieving a coherent sense of personal identity" (p. 91).

A distinction must be made between the terms *homosexual identity* and *gay identity*. Homosexual identity is a narrower term, referring to sexual behavior only, whereas gay identity suggests the total experience of being gay (Warren, 1974). The use of the term *homosexual identity* is often viewed negatively by the gay and lesbian community because it has been used as a diagnostic label by many clinicians and is often associated with a negative self-image. *Gay identity*, however, has a positive connotation within the gay and lesbian communities and is seen as encompassing emotional, lifestyle, and political aspects of life rather than being exclusively sexual (Beane, 1981).

Jandt and Darsey (1981) noted that all definitions of homosexual or gay identity have in common a shift in perception of self as a member of the majority to self as a member of the minority. Along with this change in perception comes adoption of a new set of values and a redefinition of acceptable behavior. As such, development of a gay, lesbian, or bisexual identity is mainly an internal, psychological process.

As various models of homosexual identity development are examined, the reader needs to note problems related to definition. Some theorists and researchers are careful to define their terms, but others assume the reader will know what they mean. In addition, terms such as *homosexual* or *gay identity* and labels given to various stages of gay or lesbian identity development often have different connotations in various models of development.

IDENTITY DEVELOPMENT MODELS

Models addressing homosexual or gay identity development evolved throughout the 1970s and 1980s. During this period, research started to move from a focus of "becoming homosexual" to one of "developing a homosexual identity." A great deal of overlap is evident in this research, as is some ambivalence about what is being studied.

One issue to be aware of in reviewing these models is that given their focus on gay men's development, they may not accurately reflect the perspectives of lesbian women. Similarly, there is little or no room in these models for the attainment of a healthy bisexual identity. Indeed, an inherent assumption of some is that a "healthy bisexual identity" would be a contradiction in terms! These issues are specifically addressed in later sections of this chapter.

Shively and deCecco's (1977) article on aspects of homosexual identity provided a good example of this early trend. They identified biological sex, gender identity, social sex role, and sexual orientation as the four components of sexual identity. Although the last component (orientation) encompasses physical and affectional preference, no mention is made of the establishment of identity as a gay or lesbian person.

At the same time, others were beginning to look at how a gay or lesbian identity is formed. Models based on developmental perspectives, and outlining a series of stages through which an individual moves in acquiring a homosexual identity, were proposed. These models fit loosely into two categories: those addressing social factors and those focusing on psychological changes. Many, however, encompass both areas. Those models that present specific stages of development (Lee, 1977; Coleman, 1981–1982; Plummer, 1975; Troiden, 1979; Minton & McDonald, 1984; Cass, 1979) are shown in the table.

SOCIAL MODELS

One of the first works to address the concept of gay identity was that of Dank (1971). In his study of men coming out within the gay

TABLE
Stage Models of Gay Identity Theory

Stage	Social Models		Psychological Models			Psychosocial Model
	Lee (1977)	*Coleman (1981-1982)*	*Plummer (1975)*	*Troiden (1979)*	*Minton and McDonald (1984)*	*Cass (1979)*
I. First Awareness	Signification	Pre Coming Out Coming Out	Sensitization	Sensitization Dissociation and Signification	Symbiotic Egocentric	Identity Confusion Identity Comparison
II. Self-Labeling		Exploration	Signification			Identity Tolerance
III. Community Involvement and Disclosure	Coming Out Going Public	First Relationships	Coming Out	Coming Out	Sociocentric	Identity Acceptance Identity Pride
IV. Identity Integration		Integration	Stabilization	Commitment	Universalistic	Identity Synthesis

community, Dank looked at the time lapse and (to a lesser extent) process involved in moving from first awareness of attraction to other men and then to self-labeling as homosexual. He suggested that identity development is based on the meanings that an individual ascribes to homosexuality and made clear that identification as gay and self-acceptance do not necessarily occur at the same time. Although a clear portrait of how movement through these levels occurs is not presented in this paradigm, it gave an early way to look at homosexual identity and its development.

The impact of the gay community and development of a social role have been the focus of several studies. As mentioned before, Warren (1974) was one of the first to make a distinction between homosexual and gay identities. She described gay identity as being based on the degree of affiliation that an individual has with the gay community. Generally this attachment follows engagement in homosexual (sexual) behavior and the development of a homosexual identity. In addition to the impact of the gay community, she described a "conversion effect" involved in the formation of gay identity. Through this process societal stigmas are converted into a positive identity as myths about homosexuality are encountered and challenged.

In a more radical exploration of gay identity, DuBay (1987) suggested that identity development is based on an interaction between social contacts and roles. He challenged the belief that there is an inherent, internal quality about an individual that leads to the development of a specific identity. Rather, he saw *identity* or *role* (terms that he used interchangeably) as being made up of a number of more distinct roles, which for gay and lesbian individuals serve the purpose of dealing with societal homophobia. He suggested that gay identity is made up of the merging of self-concept and sexuality, which becomes the central component in the individual's self-view. DuBay advocated dropping such roles, moving away from the concept of a gay identity, and, instead, looking at sexuality as one part of the person's total identity.

A number of writers who have approached gay identity from the social perspective focus on the coming out process. *Coming out* is an aspect of gay identity development that has been defined in various ways. In the 1960s coming out was seen as a specific occasion—a person's initial acknowledgement of same-sex attraction to another person (Gramick, 1984). Now writers stress the ongoing developmental nature of coming out, beginning when individuals start to question their sexual orientation and continuing through ongoing self-discovery and disclosure to others of their identity (Ponse, 1980; Richardson, 1981b).

Lee (1977) (see table) described coming out as one facet of a three-stage model of homosexual self-identity. His emphasis was on individuals' movement from privately recognizing themselves as homosexual to publicly sharing this identity. In the first stage, individuals self-label homosexual fantasies or experiences as deviant; then in the second stage, they begin to enter the gay culture, selectively disclose their identity, and become involved in political and social organizations. The third stage clearly builds on stage two, with individuals becoming more public in their activities and willing to be spokespersons.

Another approach that has been taken to coming out is to frame it as a developmental process encompassing both social and psychological factors. Hencken and O'Dowd (1977) suggested that there are three levels to this process: (1) awareness, (2) behavioral acceptance, and (3) public identification. At each level an individual comes out in a key area (e.g., coming out of ignorance and into awareness of feelings in the first stage), building a framework for future growth.

A more fully conceptualized model of the coming out process was offered by Coleman (1981–1982). Coleman presented a five-stage developmental model of coming out (see table), with the establishment of a gay identity centering around interpersonal relationships. As individuals progress through the stages, developmental tasks are confronted, the resolution of which determines whether movement to a new level will occur. Although such social/relational issues as seeking validation through self-disclosure, exploring sexual relationships, and establishing emotional intimacy are primary areas of focus, attention is also paid to more psychological issues. Coleman discussed ways in which these developmental tasks have impact on self-esteem and self-view, and presented stage 5 (Integration) as the point at which individuals develop a sense of both personal and interpersonal wholeness.

PSYCHOLOGICAL MODELS

Another perspective for looking at the development of gay identity focuses on the psychological (rather than social) processes involved. One of the first such models to be proposed was that of Plummer (1975) (see table). He identified four stages of identity development, moving from early awareness to the attainment of an integrated and stable identity.

Building on Plummer's work, Troiden (1979) (see table) suggested that there are four stages of gay identity acquisition. As movement through the stages occurs, feelings that the individual experiences shift from being ego-dystonic (dissonant with self-perceptions) to positively integrated and ego-syntonic (consistent with self-perceptions). As is true of several of the models discussed above, Troiden distinguished between homosexual and gay identities, with the latter reflecting involvement in a committed relationship and commitment to this identity. This last point notwithstanding, he also stated that identity is fluid and is never completely acquired in all aspects of an individual's life.

Looking at homosexual identity formation as one aspect of a lifelong developmental process, Minton and McDonald (1984) had as their foundation a nonlinear ego development model (see table). Growth is based on the interaction between the individual and societal values and beliefs. The two primary developmental tasks involved in this process are (1) forming a homosexual self-image, which culminates in attaining a positive gay identity, and (2) identity management, choosing the extent to which this identity will be shared. The goal of this model is to achieve identity synthesis (versus having a fragmented personal identity), which requires integration of all aspects of personal identity.

CASS' PSYCHOSOCIAL MODEL OF SEXUAL IDENTITY FORMATION (SIF)

To varying extents, each of the social and psychological models discussed in the preceding sections addresses the variables that have an impact on how gay identity develops. This process is a complex one, with development being affected by such diverse factors as self-image, social support, and even geography. As Troiden (1979) pointed out, gay identity evolves slowly and with some struggle. The presence (or absence) of information, resources, and a supportive community, along with such factors as family attitudes and individual personality, help determine how much struggle any one individual faces in developing an identity as a gay, lesbian, or bisexual person.

Vivienne Cass (1984) has pointed out the need for integration of the social and psychological elements of identity development and for consideration of the changes involved at the cognitive, emotional, and behavioral levels. In her model of Sexual Identity Formation (SIF), Cass (1979) fully described each of the six stages into which she divides the identity development process (see table), specifying the challenges found at each stage. Cass' model provides an exceptionally comprehensive description of gay identity development. Cass has also conducted extensive research on her theory, something which is lacking with several of the other models.

Cass' SIF model is built upon a theoretical base that addresses the interaction between psychological and sociological factors. Progression from one stage to another is motivated by incongruities felt by the individual within what Cass described as the "intrapersonal matrix." The components that make up this matrix are individuals' self-perceptions, perceptions of their behavior, and perceptions of others' response to them. At each stage, some conflict will be experienced either within or between areas of the intrapersonal matrix. This conflict is resolved either through advancement to a new stage or identity foreclosure.

The first stage (Identity Confusion) is ushered in by a growing awareness of thoughts, feelings, or behaviors that may be homosexual in nature. These self-perceptions are incongruent with earlier assumptions of personal heterosexuality and constitute the first developmental conflict of the model. How individuals perceive these characteristics or behaviors will influence the way in which they seek to resolve the incongruence, either through repression (identity foreclosure) or by moving into the second stage.

Identity Comparison (stage 2) allows individuals to begin checking out those qualities first experienced in stage 1. As they begin to gather information and seek out contacts with gay others, there is increasing congruence between self-perceptions and behaviors but increased conflict with others. As this sense of conflict heightens, individuals may move into stage 3, Identity Tolerance. This stage is marked by increased contact with the gay community, leading to feelings of greater empowerment. At this point individuals hold an increasingly strong homosexual self-image but continue to present themselves (outside the community) as heterosexual.

Moving into stage 4, Identity Acceptance, the conflict between the self and nongay others' perceptions is at an intense level. This conflict may be resolved through either passing as "straight," limited contact with heterosexuals, or selectively disclosing to significant (heterosexual) others. Those who find that these strategies effectively manage the conflict may stay at this level comfortably; otherwise the continuing conflict pushes the individual into the fifth stage of Identity Pride. In this stage the conflict is managed through fostering a dichotomized homosexual (valued) and heterosexual (devalued) world view. Stage 5 is marked not only by strong pride in the gay community and identity but also by intense anger directed toward and isolation from the heterosexual society.

How others, particularly those who are not gay, respond to the expression of these feelings influences whether individuals move into the final stage, Identity Synthesis. Movement into the sixth stage is most likely when individuals experience positive reactions from heterosexual others, creating new incongruence in their perceptions. Individuals in stage 6 perceive similarities and dissimilarities with both homosexuals and heterosexuals, and sexuality is seen as one part of their total identity. Although some conflict is always present, it is at the lowest and most manageable point in this stage.

To test her theory, Cass (1984) developed factors that describe elements of each of her six stages of homosexual identity formation. For each factor she identified the underlying cognitive, behavioral, and affective dimensions. These dimensions provided criteria for assigning individuals to one of the six stages of identity development. Cass compared participants' assignment to a specific stage according to these criteria with self-ratings on her Stage Allocation Measure (SAM). She found that individuals both matched the profile for the stage to which they had been assigned and could be placed into that same stage according to the SAM. Cass suggested these findings support the concept that individuals who perceive homosexuality to be relevant to them will have characteristics identified in her model.

SUMMARY OF IDENTITY DEVELOPMENT MODELS

The six models presented in the table approach the question of how individuals develop an identity as a gay or lesbian person from a fairly wide range of perspectives. Of these models, Lee's (1977) presentation of gay self-identification conceptualizes this process with the most narrowly social focus.

Although varying degrees of balance between personal and social factors are found across the theories, there is a general trend toward a more psychological perspective in the later models. Those theories developed earlier present coming out as a culminating event or marker, followed only by a stage of integration or further commitment. In contrast, the models of Coleman (1981–1982), Minton and McDonald (1984), and Cass (1979) place coming out very early in the process, and the latter two do not identify it as a separate stage at all.

These differences notwithstanding, there is a general pattern of developmental levels that emerges across the models. We have identified four levels, which are used as a basis of comparison in the table (in column 1). Although the models presented do not all fit into this conceptualization at exactly the same points, each passes through and refers to the tasks found in all four levels.

The level of First Awareness is a distinct component of all but one model (Minton & McDonald, 1984). At this first level individuals are becoming conscious of homoerotic feelings and behaviors, generally with no sense of these feelings being "okay." Two models (Coleman, 1981–1982; Minton & McDonald, 1984) explicitly mentioned stages before this first level, and Cass (1984) discussed assumptions about individuals' beliefs prior to entering her first stage.

The second level that we have identified is Self-Labeling. This point centers around individuals beginning to identify themselves as being gay and having early contacts with the gay community. The main distinction between the second level and the third (Community Involvement and Disclosure) is in the growing sense of acceptance of a gay identity and increasing comfort with sharing this aspect of the self with nongay others. The fourth and final level is Identity Integration, which involves incorporating gay identity into individuals' total sense of self.

LESBIAN IDENTITY DEVELOPMENT

DIFFERENCES IN IDENTITY DEVELOPMENT BETWEEN GAY MEN AND LESBIANS

Largely because of differences in the way men and women are socialized in Western society, a number of variations are evident in the patterns of identity development and lifestyles of gay men and lesbians (Cass, 1979).

The timing of events associated with the process of developing a gay or lesbian identity is different for men and women. Lesbians exhibit more variation than gay men in age at which awareness of attraction to individuals of the same sex occurs (Moses & Hawkins, 1986), and evidence suggests that gay men become aware of same-sex attractions, act on those attractions, and self-identify as gay at earlier ages than do lesbians. Men also disclose their homosexual identity earlier than women (DeMonteflores & Schultz, 1978; Sohier, 1985–1986; Troiden, 1988). Henderson (1984) proposed two hypotheses in reference to these timing variations: (1) women's sexual orientation may be more variable than men's and more tied to particular relationships, or (2) women are more likely to be influenced by societal norms that expect everyone to be heterosexual and so adhere longer to heterosexual behavior patterns and a heterosexual identity. Gramick (1984) concurred with the latter point of view.

Lesbians tend to establish ongoing love relationships earlier than gay men (Troiden, 1988) and are more likely to commit to a homosexual identity within the context of an intense emotional relationship, whereas gay men do so within the context of their sexual experiences (Groves & Ventura, 1983; Sohier, 1985–1986; Troiden, 1988). In general, emotional attachment is the most significant aspect of relationship for lesbians, but sexual activity is most important for gay men (DeMonteflores & Schultz, 1978; Gramick, 1984). As a result, lesbians tend to look for and maintain more stable, long-term relationships than do gay men (Gramick, 1984).

Although this pattern may be changing because of concern arising from the spread of AIDS, historically, gay men have been involved with many more one-time-only sexual partners than have lesbians (Kimmel, 1978; Marmor, 1980). This pattern, again, can be related to differences in the manner in which men and women are socialized; men are expected to be interested in sex before love, whereas women look for love before sex (Henderson, 1984; Westfall, 1988). Men are also encouraged to experiment sexually more than women (Coleman, 1981–1982). As one might expect given these socialization patterns, "tricking" (picking up unknown individuals for brief sexual liaisons) has been much more common among gay men than among lesbians who tend to meet others and interact in more intimate, private settings (Cronin, 1974; Gramick, 1984; Nuehring, Fein, & Tyler, 1974).

DeMonteflores and Schultz (1978) suggested that lesbians often use feelings to avoid thinking of themselves as homosexual whereas men use denial of feelings as a way to avoid self-labeling as gay. Women use the rationale that they merely love one particular woman, but men view their homosexual activity as insignificant because they are not emotionally involved with their partners.

Some researchers (Bell & Weinberg, 1978; Sohier, 1985–1986) have suggested that acceptance of homosexuality is easier for women than for men since sexual relationships between women are less stigmatized than those between men (DeMonteflores & Schultz, 1978; Marmor, 1980; Paul, 1984). The women's movement may have assisted lesbians to come out; there has been no comparable movement for men (DeMonteflores & Schultz, 1978). Also, since many lesbians become aware of their identity at later ages, they may have resolved other identity issues and be more adept at handling the coming out process than gay men who generally self-identify during their teens (Paul, 1984).

A number of writers have suggested that lesbians are more likely to view their sexuality as a choice, whereas gay men see it as a discovery (Henderson, 1984; Kimmel, 1978; Westfall, 1988). This distinction is particularly true for feminist lesbians. Feminist lesbians also identify more strongly with the political-philosophical aspects of their lifestyle, whereas gay men are more concerned with the physical-social aspects (Jandt & Darsey, 1981).

With regard to relationship development, lesbians more closely resemble other women than they do gay men (Marmor, 1980). Women, in general, are more concerned with the relational aspects of their attachments to other people and focus on establishing intimate, long-term relationships. Because they fear displeasing others, they may have difficulty breaking norms and acknowledging that they cannot accept the roles family, friends, and society have identified for them. Men, however, are taught to be independent, competitive, and autonomous. These factors appear to play an important role in the differences exhibited between lesbians and gay men.

RELATIONAL VERSUS POLITICAL LESBIANS

Great variation exists in the way lesbians describe themselves and how they come to identify themselves as lesbian (Miller & Fowlkes, 1980). And as Golden (1987) noted, feelings, behaviors, and self-identification do not always agree nor do they always remain the same over time. Two major philosophical approaches to lesbianism can be identified in the literature, however: a traditional relational viewpoint that focuses on emotional and sexual attraction to other women (Moses, 1978; Ponse, 1980) and a radical feminist perspective that views the lesbian lifestyle as a political statement (Faraday, 1981; Lewis, 1979).

A number of theorists note that a distinction must be made between women who view their lesbianism as beyond their control and those who see it as a choice (Golden, 1987; Richardson, 1981b). Generally, lesbian feminists adhere to the latter viewpoint, but relational lesbians take the former position (Richardson, 1981b; Sophie, 1987).

In a small study of 20 self-identified lesbians, Henderson (1979) distinguished three groups: (1) *ideological lesbians*, women who can be viewed as radical feminists for whom a lesbian lifestyle is politically correct; (2) *personal lesbians*, women concerned with establishing an independent identity who find homosexuality supportive of this goal and who view lesbianism as a choice; and (3) *interpersonal lesbians*, women who find themselves involved with another woman, often to their chagrin, and who experience their involvement as a discovery rather than a choice.

DEVELOPMENT OF A LESBIAN IDENTITY

Although a number of writers believe that sexual activity between women has become more acceptable as a result of the women's movement and the freeing of sexual norms (Blumstein & Schwartz, 1974; Henderson, 1979), the developmental process of identifying oneself as a lesbian is still difficult.

Many lesbians recall being "tomboys" as youngsters: a preference for "masculine" rather than "feminine" activities as a child is often the first indication that they do not fit the heterosexual pattern (Lewis, 1979). This awareness intensifies during puberty when the adolescent finds herself attracted to women rather than men. This discovery can lead to intense feelings of loneliness. Because of the difficulty young lesbians experience in finding a support group of other lesbians or identifying positive role models, this period is particularly difficult in the person's life (Sophie, 1982).

Most lesbians have a history of sexual involvement with men and, contrary to popular belief, become involved with women not because of unsatisfactory relationships with men but rather because they experience greater emotional and sexual satisfaction from women (Groves & Ventura, 1983). Indeed, women frequently identify themselves as bisexual prior to adopting a lesbian identity.

It needs to be noted that most lesbians go through a period during which they reject their identity because they are unable to deal with the stigma associated with the label *lesbian* (Groves & Ventura, 1983). Often they seek security and an escape from their feelings of isolation and anxiety in heterosexual activity or marriage (Lewis, 1979; Sophie, 1982).

Usually involvement in an intense, all-encompassing love relationship with another woman is the decisive factor in embracing a lesbian identity (Groves & Ventura, 1983; Lewis, 1979). Such an involvement often develops slowly, starting out as a friendship.

Sophie (1982) noted that it is difficult for lesbians to feel good about themselves until they reconceptualize the term *lesbian* into positive terms. This process rarely occurs in isolation. Interaction with other lesbians and other sources of information about positive aspects of a lesbian lifestyle are helpful.

Coming out, both to other lesbians and to accepting heterosexuals, is also supportive of establishment of a lesbian identity (Richardson, 1981b; Sophie, 1982). Often the individual decides to come out because it takes too much energy to maintain a heterosexual image. Usually the individual comes out first to close friends who appear trustworthy (Lewis, 1979). As the woman becomes involved in the lesbian community, pressure is often applied to come out publicly (Lewis, 1979). Doing so can be viewed as the final step in the solidification of a lesbian identity.

IDENTITY DEVELOPMENT MODELS

A number of theorists have proposed models of identity development specific for lesbians. Ponse (1980) noted three steps in lesbian identity development: becoming aware of feeling different because of sexual-emotional attraction to other women, becoming involved in a lesbian relationship, and seeking out other lesbians. This model differs from many of the gay male models in that a serious relationship is formed *before* the individual becomes involved in the lesbian community.

Gramick (1984) pointed out that in attempting to make meaning of their experiences, many lesbians reinterpret past events, feelings, and behaviors as sexual that were not perceived as such at the time they occurred. She suggested that the process of developing a lesbian identity first involves strong emotional attachment to other women leading to a feeling of "differentness" within the context of the social environment but without a recognition that this difference might be labeled as lesbian. In adolescence, heterosexual socialization patterns strongly influence all young women and often delay development of homosexual identity. Meeting other lesbians and becoming emotionally and sexually involved with another woman are usually key events in confirming and accepting a lesbian identity. In Gramick's model, supportive others, as well as sexual involvements, play a crucial role in identity development.

Lewis (1979) identified five stages in the development of a lesbian identity and focused more on the political aspects of lesbianism. Her stages include (1) experience of discomfort with the heterosexual and patriarchal nature of socialization, (2) labeling self as different from other women, (3) becoming aware of lesbianism, (4) finding and becoming involved in a lesbian community, and (5) educating self about the lesbian lifestyle.

Also writing from a feminist perspective, Faderman (1984) questioned the appropriateness of Minton and McDonald's (1984) model of identity development for lesbian feminists. She suggested that the developmental progression for these women is roughly the opposite of the model they proposed. The first step for lesbian feminists, according to Faderman, involves rejection of societal norms concerning the role of women and acceptance of a lesbian identity. This step is followed by experiences of prejudice and discrimination resulting in feelings of aloneness outside of the community of radical feminists and, finally, by sexual experiences with other women. Faderman suggested that because lesbian feminists are exposed to and accept the movement's political philosophy prior to their first homosexual experience they may not experience the guilt and shame felt by other lesbians and gay men.

In line with the two philosophical perspectives evident within the lesbian community, Sophie (1982) identified two endpoints for lesbians who have achieved identity synthesis: *integration*, that is, living as an open lesbian in both the lesbian and nonlesbian communities; and *separation*, that is, limiting one's interactions to the lesbian community as much as possible.

BISEXUAL IDENTITY

The gay rights movement has generally ignored bisexual men and women. Although Kinsey and his colleagues (Kinsey, Pomeroy, & Martin, 1948; Kinsey, Pomeroy, Martin, & Gebhard, 1953) discovered that more individuals are bisexual than strictly homosexual, later researchers and theorists have held to a rigid dichotomization of sexual behavior as either heterosexual or homosexual (Klein, Sepekoff, & Wolf, 1985). Acknowledging and attempting to understand the variation and fluidity of sexual attraction and behavior are important if we are to advance our knowledge of human sexuality and sexual identity development (Paul, 1985).

Bisexuality, particularly among women, seems to have increased in Western society, perhaps as a result of more relaxed sexual norms and the women's movement (MacDonald, 1981). A study based on a questionnaire published in *Forum* magazine found that male bisexuals outnumber female bisexuals, bisexual activity increases over the lifetime, and sexual preference changes over time (Klein, Sepekoff, & Wolf, 1985). The biased sample upon which this study was based (*Forum* readers who responded to a questionnaire) must be kept in mind, however.

Bisexuality comes in many forms. MacDonald (1982) identified four areas of variation: (1) individuals may have a preference for one gender over the other or may have no preference; (2) they may have partners of both sexes either simultaneously or sequentially; (3) they may be monogomous or have several partners; and (4) their bisexuality may be transitory, transitional, a basis for homosexual denial, or an enduring pattern. Zinik (1985) proposed the following criteria for assuming a bisexual identity: (1) being sexually aroused by both males and females, (2) desiring sexual activity with both, and (3) adopting bisexuality as a sexual identity label.

Two contrasting theories have been offered to account for bisexuality (Zinik, 1985): The conflict model suggests that bisexuality is associated with conflict, confusion, ambivalence, and an inability to determine one's sexual preference; the flexibility model hypothesizes that bisexuality is characterized by flexibility, personal growth, and fulfillment. The media tends to adhere to the former view, presenting bisexuality as a confused or conflicted lifestyle, as retarded sexual development, or as a denial of a true heterosexual or homosexual identity (Hansen & Evans, 1985).

Because the stigma attached to bisexuality is greater in many ways than that associated with homosexuality, many people who are bisexual in behavior do not identify themselves as such (Blumstein & Schwartz, 1974; Golden, 1987; Hansen & Evans, 1985; Paul, 1984; Zinik, 1985). Although some individuals are quite open about their identity, others hide it from both the heterosexual and the homosexual communities (Blumstein & Schwartz, 1977a). MacDonald (1981) suggested that bisexuals are less willing to disclose their identity than any other group because they believe that neither gays nor heterosexuals will accept them.

Bisexuals experience the same type of oppression as gay men and lesbians because society tends to group bisexuals with homosexuals. Heterosexuals assume that individuals are trying to excuse their homosexual inclinations by labeling themselves as bisexual (Blumstein & Schwartz, 1977a).

Because they do not conform to heterosexist culture, many bisexuals tend to align themselves with the gay and lesbian communities (Shuster, 1987). However, an individual's self-identification as bisexual is frequently met with skepticism in the homosexual community as well and viewed as an attempt to avoid the stigma of, or commitment to, a gay or lesbian lifestyle (Paul, 1984). The lesbian community, in particular, seems to have difficulty accepting bisexuality (Golden, 1987). Bisexuals are faced with considerable pressure to identify as homosexual and to behave in an exclusively homosexual manner (Blumstein & Schwartz, 1974; Hansen & Evans, 1985; Paul, 1985). Frequently, bisexuals respond to this pressure by pretending to be either exclusively homosexual or heterosexual depending on the social situation (Zinik, 1985).

Results of a study of 156 bisexuals conducted in the early 1970s (Blumstein & Schwartz, 1976, 1977a, 1977b) suggested that no identifiable bisexual life script exists and that identity and partner preferences change over the life course. Sexual experience and identity are not necessarily synonymous. The researchers identified several conditions that they saw as necessary for assumption of a bisexual identity: labeling, conflicting homosexual and heterosexual experiences, and contact with other bisexuals.

Zinik (1985) suggested that bisexual identity development may occur in stages similar to those proposed by Cass (1979) for homosexual identity formation. As with gay men and lesbians, the coming out process is one of both self-acknowledgement and disclosure to others (Shuster, 1987). Wide variation exists, however, in the timing and ordering of sexual experiences leading to a bisexual identification. In addition, because bisexuality lacks societal and scientific affirmation, acceptance of such an identity requires a high tolerance for ambiguity and is even harder than acceptance of a homosexual identity (MacDonald, 1981, Richardson & Hart, 1981). In most cases, bisexuals tend to identify in terms of particular relationships in which they are involved rather than with the abstract label bisexual (Shuster, 1987).

Although gay men and lesbians have formed support groups and political organizations, few such groups of bisexuals exist (Paul, 1985). As MacDonald (1981) noted, there is no "bisexual liberation movement" (p. 21). As a result, no clear bisexual identity exists, and little scientific research has examined the life experiences of bisexual men and women.

CRITIQUE AND SUMMARY

Over the past two decades a number of theorists and researchers have addressed the question of how individuals develop identities as gay, lesbian, and bisexual men and women. The shift in focus from "why" or "how" individuals "become homosexual" to understanding the process whereby they develop a gay, lesbian, or bisexual identity speaks to a more positive and healthy perspective on homosexuality. There are, however, a number of areas that need to be addressed.

One area of concern involves the datedness of some of the models discussed in this chapter. The concept of a gay identity first began to be addressed in the early 1970s, the years immediately following the Stonewall riots. The focus on coming out as a discrete step and social statement in models such as those of Dank (1971) and Lee (1977) clearly reflected the mood of the early gay-rights era. Similarly, these models are based on a social culture that has changed significantly, due in large part to the impact of the AIDS crisis, and do not necessarily describe today's realities.

Many of the models of lesbian identity development also were shaped by the political and social forces of the 1970s. The early feminist movement had tremendous influence on many of these models, leading to conceptualizations of identity centered around breaking away from patriarchal and oppressive social norms (Browning, 1984; Faraday, 1981; Lewis, 1979).

The political climate today is much different than that of 15 or even 10 years ago. There is general consensus that a conservative backlash took place during the 1980s, but we have not looked at what impact this change has had on the development and maintenance of a gay or lesbian identity. Although many (or even most) aspects of identity development have probably remained relatively constant, these models need to be reconsidered in light of a new societal context.

A second area needing consideration deals with the problems inherent in working with stage models of development. By nature, these models break the process of development into discrete, stable, and clearly discernible levels. In reality, growth is rarely so clear cut.

McDonald (1982) suggested that linear developmental models do not account or leave room for individual differences and variations in development. He found that there are clearly milestone events in the coming out process for gay men, and that these events occur in a fairly stable pattern. There is sufficient variety in the timing and direction of these events, however, to justify moving away from a linear conceptualization of the process.

Another writer who has questioned the developmental stage concept is Troiden (1984). He suggested that rather than attaining one identity, individuals develop one self-concept (or self-image) and a variety of identities that are used to assist the individual specifically in social situations. Within this framework, homosexual identity presents a way of placing self in a defined social category. The interplay between self-concept and identities shifts over time, as social contexts change, thus creating a fluid sense of identity(ies).

In the only study that has focused on women in the process of developing a lesbian identity, Sophie (1985–1986) found extensive variety in the sequence and timing of significant events. She found that events such as self-definition, contact with other lesbians, and involvement in a significant same-sex relationship occur at different points in the identity development process for different women. She pointed out that looking at this process through a linear lens is difficult and becomes more problematic as the process advances and greater individual differences emerge.

In general, there are a great needs for more research on the identity development process. For example, more research testing the models that have been (and are being) developed is needed. One of the reasons Cass' (1979) model has found wide acceptance is that she has conducted fairly extensive testing of her theory (Cass, 1984). Rather than considering external criteria as a means of validating her model, Cass compared two techniques based on her own theory for estimating level of development. Studies that contrast models or determine and measure underlying factors will add to the creation of a strong research base in this area.

As has been pointed out throughout this chapter, an area that has been severely overlooked has been identity development among lesbian and bisexual persons. Sophie's (1985–1986) study is the only one to date that looked specifically at the development of a lesbian identity, and there are no models that describe the attainment of a bisexual identity. The little research that has been conducted with these two groups clearly shows that the male-oriented models that have been developed do not adequately describe their different experiences. We need to address and fill the gaps in our understanding of these processes.

A similar gap in the research involves identity development among college and university students. Working through questions about the relevance of homosexuality or bisexuality in one's own life while also dealing with the challenges of being a college or university student adds to the magnitude of transition and potential for experiencing periods of crisis. We need to conduct research that helps us to understand the interplay between student development and the acquisition of gay, lesbian, and bisexual identities.

One issue that is of concern in all research with gay, lesbian, and bisexual people is that of obtaining truly random samples. This problem is most apparent with the *Forum* article (Klein, Sepekoff, & Wolf, 1985) mentioned earlier in this chapter. The issue of having a nonrandom sample is inherent, however, in any study that utilizes a group of individuals who self-identify as gay, lesbian, or bisexual.

The models and studies discussed in this chapter give us the foundations for this future work. We know much about college and university students and are learning about what it means to be a gay, lesbian, or bisexual person in our society. The framework is there, and our challenge is to move ahead toward expanding and bringing together these areas of understanding.

REFERENCES

Beane, J. (1981). "I'd rather be dead than gay": Counseling gay men who are coming out. *Personnel and Guidance Journal, 60,* 222–226.

Bell, A. P., & Weinberg, M. S. (1978). *Homosexualities: A study of diversity among men and women.* New York: Simon and Schuster.

Bell, A. P., Weinberg, M. S., & Hammersmith, S. K. (1981). *Sexual preference: Its development in men and women.* Bloomington: Indiana University.

Blumstein, P. W., & Schwartz, P. (1974). Lesbianism and bisexuality. In E. Goode & R. R. Troiden (Eds.), *Sexual deviance and sexual deviants* (pp. 278–295). New York: Morrow.

Blumstein, P. W., & Schwartz, P. (1976). Bisexuality in women. *Archives of Sexual Behavior, 5,* 171–181.

Blumstein, P. W., & Schwartz, P. (1977a). Bisexuality in men. In C. A. B. Warren (Ed.), *Sexuality: Encounters, identities, and relationships* (pp. 79–98). Beverly Hills, CA: Sage.

Blumstein, P. W., & Schwartz, P. (1977b). Bisexuality: Some social psychological issues. *Journal of Social Issues, 33,* 30–45.

Browning, C. (1984). Changing theories of lesbianism: Challenging the stereotypes. In T. Darty & S. Potter (Eds.), *Women-identified women* (pp. 11–30). Palo Alto, CA: Mayfield.

Cass, V. C. (1979). Homosexual identity formation: A theoretical model. *Journal of Homosexuality, 4,* 219–235.

Cass, V. C. (1983–1984). Homosexual identity: A concept in need of definition. *Journal of Homosexuality, 9*(2/3), 105–126.

Cass, V. C. (1984). Homosexual identity formation: Testing a theoretical model. *Journal of Sex Research, 20,* 143–167.

Chickering, A. W. (1969). *Education and identity.* San Francisco: Jossey-Bass.

Coleman, E. (1981–1982). Developmental stages of the coming out process. *Journal of Homosexuality, 7,* 31–43.

Cronin, D. M. (1974). Coming out among lesbians. In E. Goode & R. R. Troiden (Eds.), *Sexual deviance and sexual deviants* (pp. 268–277). New York: Morrow.

Dank, B. M. (1971). Coming out in the gay world. *Psychiatry, 34*(2), 180–197.

DeMonteflores, C., & Schultz, S. (1978). Coming out: Similarities and differences for lesbians and gay men. *Journal of Social Issues, 34*(3), 59–72.

DuBay, W. H. (1987). *Gay identity: The self under ban.* Jefferson, NC: McFarland.

Erikson, E. H. (1968). *Identity: Youth and crisis*. New York: Norton.

Faderman, L. (1984). The "new gay" lesbians. *Journal of Homosexuality, 10*(3/4), 85–95.

Faraday, A. (1981). Liberating lesbian research. In K. Plummer (Ed.), *The making of the modern homosexual* (pp. 112–129). Totowa, NJ: Barnes & Noble.

Golden, C. (1987). Diversity and variability in women's sexual identities. In Boston Lesbian Psychologies Collective (Eds.), *Lesbian psychologies: Explorations and challenges* (pp. 19–34). Urbana, IL: University of Illinois Press.

Gramick, J. (1984). Developing a lesbian identity. In T. Darty & S. Potter (Eds.), *Women-identified women*. (pp. 31–44). Palo Alto, CA: Mayfield.

Groves, P. A., & Ventura, L. A. (1983). The lesbian coming out process: Therapeutic considerations. *Personnel and Guidance Journal, 62*, 146–149.

Hansen, C. E., & Evans, A. (1985). Bisexuality reconsidered: An idea in pursuit of a definition. In F. Klein & T. J. Wolf (Eds.), *Bisexualities: Theory and research* (pp. 1–6). New York: Haworth.

Hencken, J. D., & O'Dowd, W. T. (1977). Coming out as an aspect of identity formation. *Gai Saber, 1*(1), 18–22.

Henderson, A. F. (1979). College age lesbianism as a developmental phenomenon. *Journal of American College Health, 28*(3), 176–178.

Henderson, A. F. (1984). Homosexuality in the college years: Development differences between men and women. *Journal of American College Health, 32*, 216–219.

Jandt, F. E., & Darsey, J. (1981). Coming out as a communicative process. In J. W. Chesebro (Ed.), *Gayspeak* (pp. 12–27). New York: Pilgrim.

Kimmel, D. C. (1978). Adult development and aging: A gay perspective. *Journal of Social Issues, 34*, 113–130.

Kinsey, A. C., Pomeroy, W. B., & Martin, C. E. (1948). *Sexual behavior in the human male*. Philadelphia: Saunders.

Kinsey, A. C., Pomeroy, W. B., Martin, C. E., & Gebhard, P. H. (1953). *Sexual behavior in the human female*. Philadelphia: Saunders.

Klein, F., Sepekoff, B., & Wolf, T. J. (1985). Sexual orientation: A multivariable dynamic process. In F. Klein & T. J. Wolf (Eds.), *Bisexualities: Theory and research* (pp. 35–49). New York: Haworth.

Lee, J. A. (1977). Going public: A study in the sociology of homosexual liberation. *Journal of Homosexuality, 3*(1), 49–78.

Lewis, S. G. (1979). *Sunday's women: A report on lesbian life today*. Boston: Beacon.

MacDonald, Jr., A. P. (1981). Bisexuality: Some comments on research and theory. *Journal of Homosexuality, 6*(3), 21–35.

MacDonald, Jr., A. P. (1982). Research on sexual orientation: A bridge that touches both shores but doesn't meet in the middle. *Journal of Sex Education and Therapy, 8*, 9–13.

Marmor, J. (1980). Overview: The multiple roots of homosexual behavior. In J. Marmor (Ed.), *Homosexual behavior: A modern reappraisal* (pp. 3–22). New York: Basic Books.

McDonald, G. J. (1982). Individual differences in the coming out process for gay men: Implications for theoretical models. *Journal of Homosexuality*, *8*(1), 47–90.

Miller, P. Y., & Fowlkes, M. R. (1980). Social and behavior constructions of female sexuality. *Signs*, *5*, 783–800.

Minton, H. L., & McDonald, G. J. (1984). Homosexual identity formation as a developmental process. *Journal of Homosexuality*, *9*(2/3), 91–104.

Moore, L. V., & Upcraft, M. L. (1990). Theory in student affairs: Evolving perspectives. In L. V. Moore (Ed.), *Evolving theoretical perspectives on students.* (pp. 3–23). *New Directions for Student Services*, No. 51. San Francisco: Jossey-Bass.

Moses, A. E. (1978). *Identity management in lesbian women.* New York: Praeger.

Moses, A. E., & Hawkins, R. O. (1986). *Counseling lesbian women and gay men: A life issues approach.* Columbus, OH: Merrill.

Nuehring, E., Fein, S. B., & Tyler, M. (1974). The gay college student: Perspectives for mental health professionals. *The Counseling Psychologist*, *4*, 64–72.

Nungesser, L. G. (1983). *Homosexual acts, actors, and identities.* New York: Praeger.

Paul, J. P. (1984). The bisexual identity: An idea without social recognition. In J. P. DeCecco & M. G. Shively (Eds.), *Bisexual and homosexual identities: Critical theoretical issues* (pp. 45–63). New York: Haworth.

Paul, J. (1985). Bisexuality: Reassessing our paradigms of sexuality. In F. Klein & T. J. Wolf (Eds.), *Bisexualities: Theory and research* (pp. 21–34). New York: Haworth.

Plummer, K. (1975). *Sexual stigma: An interactionist account.* London: Routledge & Kegan Paul.

Plummer, K. (1981). Going gay: Identities, life cycles, and lifestyles in the male gay world. In J. Hart & D. Richardson (Eds.), *The theory and practice of homosexuality* (pp. 93–110). London: Routledge & Kegan Paul.

Ponse, B. (1980). Lesbians and their worlds. In J. Marmor (Ed.), *Homosexual behavior: A modern reappraisal.* (pp. 157–175). New York: Basic Books.

Richardson, D. (1981a). Theoretical perspectives on homosexuality. In J. Hart & D. Richardson (Eds.), *The theory and practice of homosexuality* (pp. 5–37). London: Routledge & Kegan Paul.

Richardson, D. (1981b). Lesbian identities. In J. Hart & D. Richardson (Eds.), *The theory and practice of homosexuality* (pp. 111–124). London: Routledge & Kegan Paul.

Richardson, D., & Hart, J. (1981). The development and maintenance of a homosexual identity. In J. Hart & D. Richardson (Eds.), *The theory and practice of homosexuality* (pp. 73–92). London: Routledge & Kegan Paul.

Shively, M. G., & deCecco, J. P. (1977). Components of sexual identity. *Journal of Homosexuality, 3*, 41–48.

Shuster, R. (1987). Sexuality as a continuum: The bisexual identity. In Boston Lesbian Psychologies Collective (Eds.), *Lesbian psychologies: Explorations and challenges* (pp. 56–71). Urbana, IL: University of Illinois Press.

Sohier, R. (1985–1986). Homosexual mutuality: Variation on a theme by E. Erikson. *Journal of Homosexuality, 12*(2), 25–38.

Sophie, J. (1982). Counseling lesbians. *Personnel and Guidance Journal, 60*(6), 341–344.

Sophie, J. (1985–1986). A critical examination of stage theories of lesbian identity development. *Journal of Homosexuality, 12*(2), 39–51.

Sophie, J. (1987). Internalized homophobia and lesbian identity. *Journal of Homosexuality, 14*, 53–65.

Troiden, R. R. (1979). Becoming homosexual: A model of gay identity acquisition. *Psychiatry, 42*, 362–373.

Troiden, R. R. (1984). Self, self-concept, identity, and homosexual identity: Constructs in need of definition and differentiation. *Journal of Homosexuality, 10*(3/4), 97–109.

Troiden, R. R. (1988). Homosexual identity development. *Journal of Adolescent Health Care, 9*(2), 105–113.

Warren, C. A. B. (1974). *Identity and community in the gay world.* New York: Wiley.

Weinberg, T. S. (1978). On "doing" and "being" gay: Sexual behavior and homosexual male self-identity. *Journal of Homosexuality, 4*(2), 143–156.

Westfall, S. B. (1988). Gay and lesbian college students: Identity issues and student affairs. *Journal of the Indiana University Student Personnel Association,* 1–6.

Zinik, G. (1985). Identity conflict or adaptive flexibility? Bisexuality reconsidered. In F. Klein & T. J. Wolf (Eds.), *Bisexualities: Theory and research* (pp. 7–19). New York: Haworth.

Chapter 2

USING PSYCHOSOCIAL DEVELOPMENT THEORIES TO UNDERSTAND AND WORK WITH GAY AND LESBIAN PERSONS

Vernon A. Wall
University of Georgia

Nancy J. Evans
Western Illinois University

The development of college and university students has received significant attention in the student affairs literature during the last two decades. Numerous theories have been proposed to account for changes in the way individuals view themselves, their relationships with others, and their environment (Knefelkamp, Widick, & Parker, 1978; Rodgers, 1980). Unfortunately, most of these theories are based exclusively on the experiences of White heterosexual men. The failure of developmental theories to account for the experiences of other subpopulations of students is being recognized and corrected, however (Moore, 1990; Rodgers, 1990). This chapter adds to this effort by examining the applicability of various developmental concepts to nonheterosexual populations. Unique developmental issues faced by gay and lesbian students are also discussed along with factors that make the college or university years a crucial developmental period for these students. Challenges to researchers and discussion of interventions that can assist in development of a healthy identity for gay and lesbian students conclude the chapter.

HETEROSEXIST ASSUMPTIONS IN EXISTING PSYCHOSOCIAL THEORY

Psychosocial theorists suggest that individuals move through a number of stages throughout their lives; during each stage a specific issue takes on particular importance and must be resolved to ensure development of a healthy personality. Some theorists have discussed development across the lifespan (Erikson, 1968; Levinson, 1978; Vaillant, 1977), and others have examined stages related to identity development during the young adult years (Chickering, 1969; Havighurst, 1972; Keniston, 1971; Sanford, 1962). Each of these theories assumes heterosexuality when presenting and discussing developmental issues faced by individuals during the young adult and adult years.

Erik Erikson's pioneering work provided the basis for later psychosocial theorists. He identified eight stages of development that extend from early childhood to late adulthood. According to Erikson (1968), the central task of young adulthood is the development of identity; this task includes the integration of adult sexuality into one's personality and learning to conform to the norms and values of society. No mention is made of the possibility that one's emerging sexual identity might be nonheterosexual or of the difficulties of conforming to the societal norms if one is gay or lesbian. According to Erikson, once identity formation has been successfully accomplished, the individual possesses the capacity to develop mature intimate relationships. Erikson's heterosexist bias is most evident in his definition of intimacy: "a mutuality of orgasm with a loved partner of the other sex" (Erikson, 1977, p. 239). As Plummer (1981, p. 101) noted, "homosexuality is here defined out of the model."

Levinson (1978) conducted a landmark study of adult development based on the lives of men on the East Coast of the United States. He found critical points, which he labeled transitions, occurring at regular intervals throughout the life course. The men in his study, with one exception, were all heterosexual, and their issues included establishing love relationships with women and forming a family. As with Erikson's model, alternative lifestyles were ignored, and the impression was created that failure to follow a traditional heterosexual life path meant that one was developmentally inferior.

Chickering's (1969) vectors of development are common knowledge to most student affairs practitioners. Based on a study of Goddard College students, Chickering outlined developmental issues 18- to 22-year-old students confront. These issues include developing competence, managing emotions, developing autonomy, establishing identity, freeing interpersonal relationships, developing purpose, and developing integrity. Again, no mention is made of the possibility that students addressing these issues might not be heterosexual. To his credit, in a later article (Thomas & Chickering, 1984) Chickering indicated that his theory should be modified to account for differences in sexual orientation and gender role development, particularly as they relate to establishing identity and freeing interpersonal relationships.

Additional problems arise in applying theories of psychosocial development to lesbian women. In discussing development over the lifespan, a male model of psychological maturity usually is assumed in which increasing individuation and autonomy along with goal achievement are viewed as developmentally appropriate goals (Levinson, 1978; Vaillant, 1977). Gilligan (1982) suggested that women's identity is developed and must be viewed within the context of relationships. Societal norms, however, define accepted relational roles for women as marriage and motherhood. Lesbian women, then, fit into neither the male-oriented adult development models nor the relational model of Gilligan as it is usually interpreted (Browning, 1987).

As highlighted by these brief examples, most psychosocial theories fail to account for the development of students whose sexual identity is not heterosexual. Although all students probably face the issues presented by various theorists, concerns related to sexual identity and coming out may confound or obscure other issues (Browning, 1987). Negative experiences in a hostile environment can complicate and hinder normal psychosocial development and must be considered when examining the development of gay and lesbian students (Malyon, 1981; Remafedi, 1987). Unfortunately none of the major psychosocial theorists address this issue.

APPLICATIONS OF EXISTING THEORY TO NONHETEROSEXUAL POPULATIONS

A few investigators have attempted to test the applicability of psychosocial theory to gay and lesbian populations. Sohier (1985–1986) conducted an exploratory study using Marcia's (1966) identity interview scale (which is based on Erikson's theory) to determine the identity status of six self-identified gay men and lesbians. She found that all six had reached identity integration and that they expressed mutuality (i.e., generativity, or concern for establishing and guiding the next generation) by caring for each other and for others in both the gay and nongay community. Sohier stressed that she could not identify any signs of personality diffusion in the individuals she interviewed, although identity development was often a difficult and painful process for them. Obviously, such a small study needs replication before definitive conclusions can be drawn.

Kimmel (1978) examined the applicability of Levinson's (1978) theory of adult development for gay men and lesbian women using data from a study of gay and lesbian psychologists (Riddle & Morin, 1977). He proposed that adolescent development for gay men and lesbian women includes becoming aware of homosexual feelings, initial same-sex sexual experiences (for men), and understanding the term *homosexual*. These experiences take place between the ages of 13 and 17. The Early Adult Transition, between ages 17 and 22, includes the first sexual experience with another woman for lesbians and self-identification as homosexual for gay men. The first serious homosexual relationship occurs in the period labeled Entering the Adult World (ages 22 to 28). The Age 30 Transition (28 to 30) is marked by establishment of a positive gay identity and disclosure to parents, friends, and colleagues. Kimmel indicated that the adolescent and early adult years are particularly crucial for gay men and lesbian women and often are times of conflict and pain. For these individuals, self-identification is probably the most significant event in their lives. By contrast, Kimmel suggested that aging may be a less important issue for gay men and lesbian women than it is for heterosexuals because they are usually not as involved in crises related to the family and are a part of self-selected friendship networks that provide ongoing support throughout the lifespan. Because adult lifespan development is greatly influenced by sociopolitical factors (Levinson, 1978), replication of this study with later generations of gay men and lesbians is warranted.

In a recent study, Levine and Bahr (1989) attempted to determine the relationship of development along Chickering's vectors and sexual identity development as defined by Cass (1979b). Students contacted through gay student organizations completed the Student Development Task Inventory II (SDTI-II) (Winston et al., 1981), which is designed to assess a student's level of development on three scales (Developing Autonomy, Developing Purpose, and Developing Mature Interpersonal Relationships) based on Chickering's vectors. They also completed the Sexual Identity Formation Scale, a modified version of the Stage Allocation Measure (Cass, 1979a). Students in the early stages of sexual identity formation scored higher on the SDTI-II than students in the middle stages of sexual identity formation; however, SDTI-II scores of students in later stages on the sexual identity model were higher than those in the middle range, suggesting that students "catch up" in other developmental areas once their sexual identity issues are resolved. This study warrants replication, particularly in light of its small sample size (N = 87).

Vargo (1987) used concepts from Gilligan's (1982) theory to examine issues that arise in lesbian couples. She noted that lesbians, like other women, are socialized to be passive, dependent, and other-oriented. These traits can lead to the inability of lesbian women to establish lives separate from their partners. In addition, since identity is viewed in relation to others, preservation of self is often tied to maintenance of one's partnership. These hypothetical connections deserve study.

Unfortunately, these few preliminary attempts to study the utility of psychosocial theory for understanding the issues faced by gay and lesbian individuals are all that could be found in an exhaustive review of the literature. The potential for further study is obvious.

We can, however, examine specific developmental issues facing gay and lesbian students and use this information to guide our study of the applicability of developmental theory to this population. Some issues are similar to those faced by all students but have particular salience for gay, lesbian, and bisexual students, although other concerns are unique to nonheterosexual individuals.

DEVELOPMENTAL ISSUES OF GAY AND LESBIAN STUDENTS

The college or university years are years of extreme change. Students are confronted with a variety of issues. Each issue is dealt with differently—based on the student's maturity and the experiences that he or she has had. As a result, the student who may be struggling with his or her sexual identity may have a more difficult task as these issues appear.

For example, many activities during the undergraduate years encourage students to develop self-esteem and a distinct identity (Chickering, 1969). For the gay or lesbian student, answering the question "Who am I?" can be especially difficult (Schneider & Tremble, 1986). Homosexuality continues to be a subject that is looked upon with disgust by many people and is not widely accepted as a healthy orientation. As a result, gay and lesbian students begin the "self-esteem battle" a few steps back from heterosexual students. They may question their self-worth and wonder where they fit into society and the university community. Also, the majority of social activities during the undergraduate years are heterosexually based. Whether it is attending a social function or dating, the gay or lesbian student can experience extreme anxiety as he or she decides how to "play the game." Coupled with this issue is the fact that most gay and lesbian students do not discover a community with which to connect initially. For many students this discovery does not occur until the later years of college, and for some this discovery does not occur at all. As a result, gay and lesbian students may feel even more isolated than heterosexual students.

During the college or university years many students also begin to make decisions concerning the part religion will play in their lives. For lesbian and gay students, coming to terms with their religious beliefs can be a difficult task in light of the fact that homosexuality is not accepted in most religious environments (Ritter & O'Neill, 1989). These students may attempt to ease their sexual orientation conflicts through misinterpretations of various biblical readings. The conflict becomes "Can I be gay and also have religious beliefs?" Other issues that the gay and lesbian student may find particularly challenging are the development of career goals (see chapter 8) and health-related issues such as coping with AIDS and the fear that almost always accompanies it. It is important also to point out that the issues discussed in this chapter are impacted by the environment. Both the size of an institution and the type of institution (e.g., rural or urban; public, private, or religiously affiliated) can influence the extent to which gay and lesbian students feel comfortable during their developmental process (Henderson, 1984).

All students experience challenges during their college or university years. However, there are some additional concerns faced only by nonheterosexual students. To be successful in working with gay and lesbian students, student affairs professionals must be aware of and sensitive to their unique issues.

In looking at the developmental issues unique to gay and lesbian students, one must remember that this population is diverse. Gender, age, cultural background, and experience are four factors that combine to create very distinct gay identities and experiences (Westfall, 1988). As mentioned earlier, and discussed at length in chapter 1, there are several general differences between gay men and women. Among them is the process of identifying oneself as lesbian or gay. Men seem to become more concerned and anxious about the possibility that they *might* be gay than women (Westfall, 1988). Once this identification is made, men view it as a "discovery" in that they have finally "admitted" their homosexuality. Women, however, "reconstruct" the past by examining and emphasizing their significant friendships/relationships with other women (Henderson, 1984). Men also tend to involve themselves in same-gender sexual experimentation to a greater extent than women during the college or university years (Henderson, 1984).

Dillon (1986) and Sophie (1982) both compiled lists of issues of concern for young lesbians and gays. One issue listed, "grieving loss of membership in the dominant heterosexist culture and entry into a permanently stigmatized group" (Dillon, 1986, p. 38), is worth exploring further. The experience of being a minority, especially an invisible minority, can be powerful in shaping one's life (Westfall, 1988). Unlike other minorities that are more easily identified (e.g., African Americans, Hispanic Americans, disabled students, Asian Americans), lesbian and gay students frequently have no family support or role modeling to help them deal with this new-found status. As a result, lack of peer support and isolation can become almost overwhelming to newly self-identified lesbian or gay students (Crooks & Baur, 1987).

COMING OUT

Coming out is a term used to describe the process of, and extent to which, one identifies oneself as lesbian or gay (Crooks & Baur, 1987; Miller 1980; Sophie, 1982). Sophie (1982) detailed coming out as a two-part process: coming out to oneself and coming out to others. Coming out to oneself is perhaps the first step toward a positive understanding of one's homosexuality. This process not only includes the realization that one is homosexual but also accepting that fact and deciding what to do about it. Coming out to others is an experience unique to gay and lesbian students. The decision to come out to another person involves disclosing one's sexual side, which is, for the most part, viewed as being a private matter. Some gay and lesbian students are afraid of being rejected, but others worry that their sexual identity will be the "overriding focus" in future interactions between themselves and the other person. However, coming out does not always result in negative consequences. Dillon (1986) was quick to point out that coming out to others also can develop "relief and a sense of closeness" (p. 38). Other issues related to coming out are decisions about the extent of the revelation (should everyone know that one is gay or should disclosure be selective?), timing, and anticipated consequences.

The decision not to come out to others is called *passing*. Our culture tends to assume heterosexuality (Edelman, 1986), and lesbian or gay persons who do not actively correct the heterosexual assumption are considered to be passing as heterosexuals. College or university students who are gay or lesbian may believe that passing as heterosexual is preferable in an environment built on heterosexual events such as dances, dates, and parties. These students, however, usually experience some conflict as they make decisions on when to pass and when to be open about their sexuality. The students may also experience some hostility from individuals who are open about their homosexuality and feel that these students who are passing are not being honest with themselves and others.

One final issue in the development of gay and lesbian students is homophobia and homohatred. Homophobia is an irrational fear of homosexuality in others and/or homosexual feelings and behaviors in oneself (Crooks & Baur, 1987). Kirk and Madsen (1989) coined the term *homohatred*. Whereas homophobia describes an irrational fear, homohatred describes violence against gay and lesbian persons. In essence, both words are part of a continuum. In the minds of the authors, "homohaters" are ones who "act" on their exaggerated fears. Our current culture is biased against homosexuals, and many negative stereotypes concerning gays and lesbians exist. Homophobia and homohatred can be major stumbling blocks to the development of gay, lesbian, and bisexual students. It is important to point out that homophobia and homohatred are not limited to the heterosexual population. Gay and lesbian persons can also exhibit these behaviors. Homophobia and homohatred on the part of the lesbian or gay student can result in self-loathing, loss of esteem, and behavior inconsistent with one's true feelings but consistent with heterosexual societal expectations (Groves & Ventura, 1983; Sophie, 1982). The impact of homophobia is discussed in more detail in chapter 3.

CHALLENGES FOR RESEARCHERS

The lack of research to support developmental theory is a problem of which student development specialists are well aware. The problem is even greater when one is seeking information specifically concerning the development of various subgroups, including ethnic, racial, differently abled, or age-specific populations. The problem is particularly severe for gay, lesbian, and bisexual populations because of the invisibility of these individuals.

A difficult problem arises when attempting to study gay, lesbian and bisexual populations: that of obtaining a representative sample. Because of the stigma attached to being gay, lesbian, or bisexual in this society, many individuals choose to hide their identity. As a result, identifying a random sample of this population is impossible. Researchers, of necessity, must sample those individuals willing to identify as gay, lesbian, or bisexual. These persons are usually those who are most comfortable with their sexual orientation and probably at a higher level of development. It is most difficult to find out what those individuals who are at the earliest stages of development are thinking and feeling.

As a result, investigators usually rely on the reports of gay, lesbian, or bisexual individuals concerning their early experiences. Unfortunately, memory is always selective, particularly when experiences have been painful. Routinely gathering information about sexual orientation when anonymously collecting data concerning human development might provide a start in better understanding individuals in the early stages of gay identity development.

Most researchers who are seeking a sample of gay men or lesbians look to gay or lesbian organizations or to patrons of gay or lesbian establishments (e.g., bars, bookstores). These sources tend to bias the sample in favor of more activist and open gays and lesbians while limiting the numbers of more conservative individuals, bisexuals, and, again, individuals at lower stages of gay identity development. At the very least, researchers must clearly identify the characteristics of their samples demographically and idealogically.

To provide a picture of the development of gay, lesbian, and bisexual individuals across the lifespan, in-depth, longitudinal case study is a technique that must be considered. This type of qualitative study will allow researchers to investigate the interaction of gay identity development and other aspects of development such as career development, development of interpersonal relationships, and maturity. Changes in the importance of developmental issues over time will clear, and theoretical concepts can be tested.

All psychosocial theory must take into account the historical conditions existing at the time it was written and tested. Because of the very significant issues facing the gay and lesbian communities during the last two decades (e.g., AIDS, the increasing conservative backlash, increased violence), current and ongoing study of these populations is particularly important. A study published in 1990 may reveal significant differences from the same study conducted a decade earlier.

We must as well consider differences among members of the gay and lesbian communities. As we have noted, the scant research in existence suggests that lesbians and gay men are quite different with regard to their developmental paths and the issues they face. These differences must be explored further. Bisexuals have rarely been studied; research on this population is crucial. And we must examine the impact of double or triple minority status on gay, lesbian, and bisexual individuals.

The undergraduate years have a significant impact on the lives of young adults who are beginning to develop their identities. Being away from home—often for the first time—these students are forced to make many decisions on their own. Relationships with peers become more and more important. For some, opposite and same-sex relationships are clarified for the first time. Addressing the issue of sexual identity along with the other issues facing college and university students can complicate the developmental process. Therefore, it is important that information gained through the implications of various student development theories be utilized to design environments in which students who are gay or lesbian can learn and grow.

MAKING A DIFFERENCE

How can student affairs staff effectively meet the needs of lesbian and gay college and university students? Robert Schoenberg, at the University of Pennsylvania is currently researching the development of lesbian and gay college and university students. Through interviewing self-identified gay juniors and seniors at three different institutions, Schoenberg (1988) has concluded that student services have a significant impact on students who are exploring and discovering their sexual orientation. He has compiled a list of 13 suggestions for administrators to help improve the campus environment for gay and lesbian students:

1. *The establishment of a nondiscrimination clause to protect the rights of gay and lesbian students.* An institutional commitment to protect gay people (as we protect other minorities) is vital for affirming the presence of gay people on our campuses.

2. *A sensitivity statement and training for staff and faculty* working with students. People need to become aware of and educated about gay people and their experiences.

3. *A university statement against homophobia,* letting people know that hostility toward gay people will not be tolerated.

4. *Staff screening against homophobes* to prevent biased people from harassing or harming gay and lesbian students.

5. *Intolerance of antigay or heterosexist language.* This is a form of discrimination, just as is racist and sexist language.

6. *A campus liaison between gay and lesbian staff and students and the administration* to help communicate the specific needs and perceptions of gay people to those who shape policy.

7. *Increased gay and lesbian library resources* so people have the chance to learn as much as possible and read literature that speaks to the gay and lesbian experience.

8. *Orientation activities for gay and lesbian students* to help acclimate these students to their new environment and to let them know of resources that may be of use to them.

9. *Literature to prospective students about gay and lesbian organizations* to let students know what activities are available.

10. *Invitation and action to meet the needs of gay and lesbian students.* We need to seek out needs and stop merely reacting to occasional student complaints.

11. *Retention study of gay and lesbian students.*

12. *Carefully trained and sensitized security people.* Careless comments or actions by law enforcement people can be particularly damaging to people. The better sensitized law enforcement people become, the more constructively they can deal with gay and lesbian students.

13. *Availability of gay publications.* Gay and lesbian students need to have publications available that address their sexuality and resulting issues.

Although these suggestions are very specific, the underlying message is that we in student affairs need to be informed and sensitive to the needs of lesbian and gay students. This process begins with the student affairs staff member. First, gather as much information as you can. Increase your knowledge about the topic of homosexuality. The resources chapter at the end of this book is an excellent start. Second, examine your values and beliefs. Knowing where you stand on specific issues and having a willingness to be "stretched" can be extremely beneficial. Third, remember that each gay and lesbian student is an individual, each with different experiences and each at his or her own level of development.

Roughly 10% of your campus population is gay or lesbian (Kinsey, Pomeroy, & Martin, 1948; Kinsey, Pomeroy, Martin, & Gebhard, 1953; Henderson, 1984). On most campuses, this group will be your largest minority. The authors hope that this chapter has shed some light on issues facing gay and lesbian students. It is through understanding that student affairs professionals can begin to aid in the establishment of college and university environments that support gay and lesbian students and challenge attitudes that are not congruent with the ideals of diversity appreciation.

REFERENCES

Browning, C. (1987). Therapeutic issues and intervention strategies with young adult lesbian clients: A developmental approach. *Journal of Homosexuality, 14*(1/2), 45–52.

Cass, V. C. (1979a). *Cass stage allocation measure (SAM).* Unpublished manuscript.

Cass, V. C. (1979b). Homosexual identity formation: A theoretical model. *Journal of Homosexuality, 4,* 219–235.

Chickering, A. V. (1969). *Education and identity.* San Francisco: Jossey-Bass.

Crooks, R., & Baur, K. (1987). *Our sexuality* (3rd ed.). Menlo Park, CA: Benjamin/Cummings.

Dillon, C. (1986). Preparing college health professionals to deliver gay-affirmative services. *Journal of American College Health, 35* (1), 36–40.

Edelman, D. (1986). University health services sponsoring lesbian health workshops: Implications and accessibility. *Journal of American College Health, 35* (1), 44–45.

Erikson, E. H. (1968). *Identity: Youth and crisis.* New York: Norton.

Erikson, E. H. (1977). *Toys and reasons: Stages in the ritualization of experience.* New York: Norton.

Gilligan, C. (1982). *In a different voice: Psychological theory and women's development.* Cambridge, MA: Harvard University Press.

Groves, P. A., & Ventura, L. A. (1983). The lesbian coming out process: Therapeutic considerations. *Personnel and Guidance Journal, 62,* 146–149.

Havighurst, R. J. (1972). *Developmental tasks and education* (3rd ed.). New York: David McKay.

Henderson, A. (1984). Homosexuality in the college years: Developmental differences between men and women. *Journal of American College Health, 32,* 216–219.

Keniston, K. (1971). *Youth and dissent.* New York: Harcourt Brace.

Kimmel, D. C. (1978). Adult development and aging: A gay perspective. *Journal of Social Issues, 34,* 113–130.

Kinsey, A. C., Pomeroy, W. B., & Martin, C. E. (1948). *Sexual behavior in the human male.* Philadelphia: Saunders.

Kinsey, A. C., Pomeroy, W. B., Martin, C. E., & Gebhard, P. H. (1953). *Sexual behavior in the human female.* Philadelphia: Saunders.

Kirk, M., & Madsen, H. (1989). *After the ball: How America will conquer its fear and hatred of gays in the 90s.* New York: Doubleday.

Knefelkamp, L., Widick, C., & Parker, C. A. (Eds.). (1978). *Applying new developmental findings. New Directions for Student Services*, No. 4. San Francisco: Jossey-Bass.

Levine, H., & Bahr, J. (1989). *Relationship between sexual identity formation and student development.* Unpublished manuscript.

Levinson, D. J. (1978). *The seasons of a man's life.* New York: Knopf.

Malyon, A. K. (1981). The homosexual adolescent: Developmental issues and social bias. *Child Welfare, 60*(5), 321–330.

Marcia, J. E. (1966). Development and validation of ego identity status. *Journal of Personality and Social Psychology, 3*, 551–558.

Miller, R. (1980). Counseling the young adult lesbian. *Journal of the National Association for Women Deans, Administrators, and Counselors, 43* (3), 44–48.

Moore, L. V. (Ed.). 1990. *Evolving theoretical perspectives about students. New Directions for Student Services*, No. 51. San Francisco: Jossey-Bass.

Plummer, K. (1981). Going gay: Identities, life cycles, and lifestyles in the male gay world. In J. Hart and D. Richardson (Eds.), *The theory and practice of homosexuality* (pp. 93–110). London: Routledge & Kegan Paul.

Remafedi, G. (1987). Male homosexuality: The adolescent's perspective. *Pediatrics, 79*(3), 326–330.

Riddle, D., & Morin, S. (1977, November). Removing the stigma: Data from individuals. *APA Monitor*, pp. 16, 28.

Ritter, K. Y., & O'Neill, C. W. (1989). Moving through loss: The spiritual journey of gay men and lesbian women. *Journal of Counseling and Development, 68*, 9–15.

Rodgers, R. F. (1980). Theories underlying student development. In D. G. Creamer (Ed.), *Student development in higher education: Theories, practices, and future directions* (pp. 10–95). Cincinnati: American College Personnel Association.

Rodgers, R. F. (1990). Recent theories and research underlying student development. In D. G. Creamer (Ed.), *College student development: Theory and practice for the 1990s* (pp. 27–79). Alexandria, VA: American College Personnel Association.

Sanford, N. (1962). Developmental status of the entering freshman. In N. Sanford (Ed.), *The American college: A psychological and social interpretation of the higher learning.* New York: Wiley.

Schoenberg R. (1989, April). *Unlocking closets in the ivory tower: Lesbian/ gay identity formation and management in college.* Paper presented at the meeting of the American College Personnel Association, Washington, DC.

Schneider, M. S., & Tremble, B. (1986). Training service providers to work with gay or lesbian adolescents: A workshop. *Journal of Counseling and Development, 65*, 98–99.

Sohier, R. (1985–1986). Homosexual mutuality: Variation on a theme by E. Erikson. *Journal of Homosexuality, 12*(2), 25–38.

Sophie, J. (1982). Counseling lesbians. *Personnel and Guidance Journal, 60*, 341–344.

Thomas, R., & Chickering, A. W. (1984). Education and identity revisited. *Journal of College Student Personnel, 25*, 392–399.

Vaillant, G. E. (1977). *Adaptation to life.* Boston, MA: Little, Brown.

Vargo, S. (1987). The effects of women's socialization on lesbian couples. In Boston Lesbian Psychologies Collective (Eds.), *Lesbian psychologies: Explorations and challenges* (pp. 161–173). Urbana, IL: University of Illinois Press.

Westfall, S. B. (1988). Gay and lesbian college students: Identity issues and student affairs. *Journal of the Indiana University Student Personnel Association*, 1–6.

Winston, R. B., Jr., Miller, T. K., Hackney, S. T., Hodges, J. L., Polkosnik, M. C., Robinson, J. A., & Russo, B. A. (1981). Assessing student development: A developmental task approach. *Journal of College Student Personnel, 22*, 429–435.

Chapter 3

HOMOPHOBIA

Kathy Obear
Consultant, Human Advantage

In sharp contrast to the popular stereotypes and myths, gay, lesbian, and bisexual people are as diverse as the society at large. They are in every occupation and geographic region, every neighborhood and ethnic/racial group, every economic class and religious organization. There are bisexuals, lesbians, and gays of all ages and physical and mental abilities, from all kinds of homes, and with every kind of lifestyle. Yet they have at least one thing in common: They all experience homophobia and heterosexism on a daily basis. This chapter reviews some of the manifestations of homophobia and heterosexism in society and on college and university campuses, and examines some of the causes and "correlates" of homophobic attitudes. A final section reviews and identifies some specific strategies for combating homophobia and heterosexism on university campuses.

Homophobia is the irrational fear, hatred, and intolerance of people who are gay, lesbian, or bisexual (Pharr, 1988). These intense prejudicial feelings often result in the belief in powerful negative stereotypes and discriminating actions against people who are gay, lesbian, or bisexual. When gays, lesbians, and bisexuals are socialized in the same homophobic cultures as heterosexuals, they often internalize these negative stereotypes and develop some degree of self-hatred and low self-esteem, a form of internalized homophobia (Weinberg, 1972).

Stereotypic attitudes translate into oppressive behaviors in societies that use cultural and institutional power to support prejudice. Racial prejudice combined with cultural and institutional power equals racism. Sexist attitudes plus cultural and institutional power to enforce these attitudes becomes sexism. Homophobic prejudice

plus cultural and institutional power results in heterosexism: a belief in the inherent superiority of heterosexuality and, therefore, its
right to dominance (Lorde, 1983).

Homophobia and heterosexism are manifested through actions
and behaviors in three different, yet interrelated, components of
society: the cultural, the institutional, and the individual. The following sections explore specific examples in each of these areas.

MANIFESTATIONS OF HOMOPHOBIA: THE CULTURAL LEVEL

Heterosexism and homophobia are manifested at the cultural level
through a societal belief system that creates norms and values that
promote heterosexuality and perpetuate negative stereotypes and
homophobic myths (Morin & Garfinkle, 1978). The societal attitudes
of the majority culture in this country do not recognize the legiti-
macy of the lives and lifestyles of lesbians, gays, and bisexuals.
These attitudes impact many cultural norms, including the definition of family and traditional gender roles (Ritter & O'Neill, 1989).
This cultural belief system is used to justify discrimination against
and harassment of people who are lesbian, bisexual, or gay.

Numerous studies document the prevailing homophobic attitudes
in our culture. In a 1983 study, over 50% of college students who
responded labeled homosexuality more deviant than murder and
drug addiction (Pogrebin, 1983). In a 1983 *Newsweek* survey, less
than one-third of those polled felt that homosexuality was an acceptable alternative lifestyle (Morganthau et al., 1983); and in a
1985 poll, three-fourths of the respondents stated they believed that
"homosexual relations" between consenting adults were always wrong
(National Opinion Research Center, 1985). A recent Gallup poll
taken in the fall of 1989 showed a small increase in the support for
gay rights, but 53% of all adults who responded still did not agree
that relationships between consenting adults of the same gender
should be legal, and 29% said gays and lesbians should not have
equal job opportunities (Salholz et al., 1990).

The cultural belief that heterosexuality is the only legitimate
pattern of intimacy is reinforced every time people listen to a "top
40" radio station or read a mainstream magazine. On billboards and
in commercials, movies, and television shows, there are visual reminders that the only "normal" and "healthy" family is one that is
both heterosexual and nuclear. This limited definition of family is
supported by a wide variety of laws, policies, and cultural practices

that are used to discriminate against people who are gay, lesbian, or bisexual.

Many cultural images provide powerful messages that prescribe strict traditional gender roles for all men and women. There are numerous cultural stereotypes that reinforce the myths that heterosexuals adhere to traditional gender roles and that people who cross these lines must be gay, lesbian, or bisexual. The fear of being labeled as gay, lesbian, or bisexual keeps many men and women of all sexual/affectional orientations adhering to traditional gender roles. By restricting their behaviors and activities, both men and women may limit their educational and economic opportunities and fail to reach their full potential as human beings (Pharr, 1988). The effect of sexism in maintaining strict gender roles is a critical component for understanding the manifestations of homophobia and heterosexism in society. This relationship among gender roles, sexism, homophobia, and heterosexism is explored in further depth in the "correlate" sections.

MANIFESTATIONS OF HOMOPHOBIA: THE INSTITUTIONAL LEVEL

Homophobia has such incredible institutional power in our society that it "is great enough to keep 10 to 20% of the population living lives of fear (if their sexual identity is hidden) or lives of danger (if their sexual identity is visible) or both" (Pharr, 1988, p. 2). Gay, lesbian, and bisexual people experience homophobia and heterosexism in myriad situations through all of the institutions in our society, including governments, the legal system, health care systems, religious organizations, the media, and education institutions.

People who are lesbian, bisexual, or gay do not have legal protection for their civil rights at the federal level or in 48 states in this country. Only Wisconsin and Massachusetts and a few cities have passed civil rights legislation that prohibits some forms of discrimination based on sexual/affectional orientation. Without civil rights protection, lesbians, bisexuals, and gays—with little to no recourse—can be barred from a variety of jobs, harassed at work or fired, dishonorably discharged from military service and the ROTC, and discriminated against when trying to buy or rent housing, use public accommodations, or immigrate into this country (Goodman, Lakey, Lashof, & Thorne, 1983).

Legal recognition of marriage vows between two people of the same gender does not exist; therefore, gay and lesbian couples cannot receive the many benefits that heterosexual couples receive from health and life insurance plans, tax codes, social security and pension regulations, joint credit policies, tuition waivers, bereavement leave policies, and inheritance laws. In addition, gays, lesbians, and bisexuals are subject to due process violations; and many juries and judges have handed down lighter sentences for murderers and rapists when the victims are known to be lesbian, gay, or bisexual (Blumenfeld & Raymond, 1988).

One of the most frightening manifestations of homophobia and heterosexism in the legal system involves the issues of parenting. Many lesbians, bisexuals, and gay men have children from previous or current heterosexual relationships. Others choose to become parents through adoption or alternative insemination. Many cases have been reported in which lesbians and gays have lost child custody battles based solely on their sexual/affectional orientation. Lesbians, bisexuals, and gays have been denied the right to adopt or to become foster parents because many of those in power believe that children should be placed in "normal" and "traditional" homes, even though there is solid evidence that over 92% of cases of child abuse, including sexual abuse of children of the same gender, are perpetuated by heterosexuals (Blumenfeld & Raymond, 1988).

Health care systems continue to promote homophobia and heterosexism. When lesbians, bisexuals, and gays are in need of medical attention or want to enter a therapeutic relationship, they often encounter medical and mental health professionals who maintain that homosexuality is a mental sickness or a state of arrested development. Many bisexuals, lesbians, and gays believe that it is far too risky to come out, to disclose their sexual/affectional orientation, to doctors and nurses for fear there might be a notation on their permanent records that could be subpoenaed by insurance agencies, the courts, or their employers. In addition, lesbians, gays, and bisexuals in same-gender partnerships are not legally recognized as family members and can be denied visitation rights in hospitals.

Religious organizations have long been a source of blatant homophobia and persecution of people who are gay, lesbian, or bisexual. Bisexuals, lesbians, and gays who look for support from most traditional religious groups are told they have sinned and violated God's will. Although a few religious organizations are reevaluating and changing their official policies on these issues, many are not.

In October 1986, the Vatican issued a decree that reiterated the Catholic Church's stance on homosexuality. It warned that homosexual inclination tends "toward an intrinsic moral evil" and "must be seen as an objective disorder" (Ostling, 1989). One fact is painfully clear: When respected role models and authority figures espouse homophobic attitudes and values in the name of a Higher Power, they play a powerful role in the socialization and education of a vast number of people in this country.

Scholars continue to argue over the accuracy of interpretations of various translations regarding homosexuality from the different major religious documents (McNaught, 1981). There is not enough space in this chapter to discuss the complex and emotional controversies surrounding homosexuality and religion. The work of McNaught (1981), Boswell (1980), and McNeill (1988), and the chapter on religion in Blumenfeld and Raymond (1988), are useful resources.

Homophobic images are perpetuated by the media. In one night of television viewing, children and young adolescents are bombarded with "fag jokes" on shows and in commercials. When bisexual, lesbians, and gays are portrayed in film, television, literature, and theater, their characters are often stereotypic and only serve to reinforce societal prejudice. It is extremely rare to find healthy and satisfying relationships between same-gender partners portrayed in the mainstream media.

In a similar fashion, mainstream news rarely covers events and issues of importance to the gay, lesbian, and bisexual communities. For example, the three largest national news magazines (*Time*, *Newsweek*, and *US News & World Report*) failed to cover the October 1987 March on Washington, despite the fact that it was one of the largest civil rights demonstrations in this nation's history ("Articles," 1988). The few stories that are reported are often sensationalized and full of misconceptions and misinformation.

As an example of how homophobia is manifested in the news media: By October 5, 1982, 634 people in the United States were reported to have AIDS, the "gay disease," and 260 had already died. In New York City, home to half of these cases, the *New York Times* had written only two stories about the epidemic in 1981 and only four more in all of 1982, none of which had been on the front page. In contrast, during the Tylenol poisoning incident of 1982, there were 54 articles printed in the *New York Times*, of which 4 appeared on the front page. The total number of reported deaths due to Tylenol poisoning was seven (Shilts, 1987).

Because of homophobia, AIDS has been labeled a gay disease. For years the vast majority of government officials refused to provide critical financial resources, and as a result, tens of thousands of people died and hundreds of thousands were needlessly infected. President Reagan did not even say the term *AIDS* in public for the first 7 years of his presidency. He finally mentioned it in a speech

6 years after AIDS had been declared a national epidemic (Shilts, 1987).

The same neglect, omission, and distortion found in the media are reflected in school systems across the country. As for other groups that are targets of oppression, the history/herstory of lesbians, gays, and bisexuals has been ignored, altered, and manipulated to meet the needs of the majority culture. The invisibility and lack of availability of accurate information perpetuate negative homophobic stereotypes and deny gay, lesbian, and bisexual students access to the vast cultural resources and systems of support that exist outside of the mainstream culture.

In many ways colleges and universities are microcosms of the larger society. Homophobia and heterosexism are manifested at the institutional level at colleges and universities by the invisibility and denial of the issues and concerns of bisexual, lesbian, and gay students, faculty, and staff. What are some of the critical areas? What questions can be asked to identify possible sources of institutionalized heterosexism on college and university campuses?

Most college and university nondiscrimination policies and codes of student conduct specifically prohibit discrimination based on gender, age, ability, nationality, and race, but only a small number include any reference to eliminating harassment and discrimination based on sexual/affectional orientation. Many personnel benefits packages and policies provide health care, insurance, and other benefits for the spouses of heterosexual staff and faculty, but few colleges or universities offer similar programs for the life partners of staff and faculty who are gay, lesbian, or bisexual.

At many colleges and universities there are either specific offices or individual staff or faculty whose primary role is to develop programs and provide services and safe spaces to meet the needs of students from different subgroups of the campus population, such as women, students of color, international students, students with disabilities, athletes, Greeks, and nontraditional-aged students. *A question to ask key administrators is, Is there a similar program with comparable staffing and financial resources to meet the needs of the gay, lesbian, and bisexual students who most likely represent between 10 and 20% of the student population?*

Most college and university policies, programs, and services are designed to meet the needs of students without considering the specific needs of those who are gay, lesbian, or bisexual. The assumption that all students are heterosexual may be evident in the lack of attention to the specific issues of gay, lesbian, and bisexual students in a wide variety of areas, including career counseling, academic advising, health services, campus ministry, residence life, family housing, new student orientation, athletics, student leadership development, and mental health.

The area of discipline and policy enforcement provides an example of how homophobia and heterosexism might be manifested on college and university campuses. *A question to ask is, Are the discipline procedures, institutional response, and sanctions for students who are perpetrators of homophobic incidents similar to those of alleged perpetrators of racial or sexual harassment and violence?* In addition, many colleges and universities have developed and publicized a comprehensive reporting structure and support system for victims of sexual assault and of racial and sexual harassment. *Another question to ask is, Is there a parallel system for the targets of homophobic harassment and violence?*

Many colleges and universities provide training for staff, faculty, and student leaders on the issues of racism and sexism. *The question to ask is, Are there similar programs required on the issues of homophobia and heterosexism?* In addition, many faculty are working to combat sexism and racism by redesigning their course curricula and materials to eliminate sexist and racist materials and to better represent the contributions and issues of White women and people of color. *The question to ask faculty and academic deans is, Are you equally committed to eliminating homophobic materials and to accurately representing the contributions and issues of people who are lesbian, gay, or bisexual?*

Societal institutions create and perpetuate cultural values and norms that promote heterosexuality and condemn homosexuality. This is specifically evident on college and university campuses. Individuals internalize these negative homophobic stereotypes and prejudices, which, in turn, shape their actions and attitudes toward people who are gay, lesbian, or bisexual. Manifestations of individual homophobia are explored in the following section.

MANIFESTATIONS OF HOMOPHOBIA: THE INDIVIDUAL LEVEL

People who are gay, lesbian, or bisexual are often victims of hate crimes: They are verbally harassed, threatened, intimidated, physically assaulted, raped, and murdered. They are victims of arson, vandalism, and police abuse. The National Gay and Lesbian Task Force published a study in 1984 that reported that of the 2,000 lesbians and gay men in their research pool from eight major U.S.

cities, over 90% had experienced some form of victimization because of their sexual/affectional orientation (National Gay and Lesbian Task Force, 1984). Gays and lesbians are seven times more likely to be the victims of crimes than the average citizen. Hate crimes against gays, lesbians, and bisexuals have nearly tripled in recent years. A report issued in 1987 by the National Institute of Justice concluded that lesbians and gays are probably the most frequent victims of hate crimes (Zuckerman, 1988). Though the number of reported cases of all types of harassment and violence is dramatically increasing, it would be safe to suggest that the vast majority of incidents involving homophobia are never reported to the police for fear of public exposure (National Gay and Lesbian Task Force, 1984).

Given the intense institutional pressures and the power of cultural stereotypes, it is no wonder that so many individuals on college and university campuses are actively homophobic: Their actions merely reflect the attitudes and values of the larger society. According to Kevin Berrill, director of the Anti-Violence Project of the National Gay and Lesbian Task Force, students on campuses across the nation have experienced a wide variety of forms of harassment and violence: threatening phone calls, death threats, verbal abuse, and physical assault. They have found harassing notes inside their locked cars and watched as fellow students have paraded by wearing "fag-buster" T shirts (Berrill, 1989).

Four different surveys conducted recently on university campuses asked gay, lesbian, and bisexual students to describe the types of abuse they had experienced because of their sexual/affectional orientation. Between 45 and 65% of respondents reported having experienced verbal insults, 22 to 26% reported being "followed or chased," and 12 to 15% noted they had been sexually harassed or assaulted. Threats of physical violence were reported by 16 to 25% of those surveyed, and 35 to 58% said they feared for their safety. Others experienced having objects thrown at them, having their property damaged, receiving threats of public exposure, being spat upon, and being physically assaulted with weapons. Over 90% expected to experience further acts of homophobic harassment while in college (Berrill, 1989).

Most people are shocked and angered once they learn about the harsh realities of homophobic hate crimes. However, there is far less understanding of the damage and danger of the more subtle form of homophobia that is popular across the nation: homophobic name-calling. Such off-handed jabs as "Hey you faggot!" or "What a fag!" or "She's such a dyke!" are often heard while walking among a crowd of college students or through a residence hall lobby. Most students, faculty, and staff do not understand how these seemingly innocuous comments are actually powerful oppressive tools that create and reinforce fear and contempt toward lesbians, gays, and bisexuals and remind everyone of the negative consequences for those who cross over socially approved gender role behavior. Students clearly learn the difference between acceptable and unacceptable behavior on campus when they hear faculty, coaches, administrators, and hall directors confront racist jokes and sexist comments but not homophobic slurs.

Most students who experience homophobic harassment do not report these incidents to the police or the student affairs division. They may fear the consequences of public exposure in the campus newspaper or from a violation of confidentiality. They may also want to avoid a negative response from the staff with whom they have to work throughout the reporting process. In addition, reports and rumors of acts of individual harassment and abuse may provide warnings to other bisexuals, lesbians, and gays to "stay in the closet." The threat of potential violence is an effective tool that keeps many people from living a more open lifestyle and from organizing to work in coalition to combat homophobia and heterosexism in the public arena. As a result, most college administrators, residence hall staff, and faculty do not understand the severity of the problems of homophobia and heterosexism on their campus.

It is socially acceptable to be actively homophobic in many public arenas. It is rare to find people who will confront these forms of oppressive behavior. Staff, students, and faculty may hesitate to interrupt homophobic comments for a variety of reasons. The fear that their own sexual/affectional orientation may be called into question is a critical force that silences many potential allies. Many college students do not have the self-confidence or assertiveness skills to challenge and interrupt the homophobic actions of their peers, much less their professors.

The manifestations of homophobia and heterosexism at the cultural, institutional, and individual levels deny gay, lesbian, and bisexual people access to many of the rights, resources, and services they need to live full and productive lives in society. These manifestations create a climate of fear, harassment, and discrimination that forces many to live their lives as second-class citizens.

HOMOPHOBIA: CORRELATES

While researchers argue over the etiology or "causes" of homophobia, several studies have identified a series of correlates of negative homophobic attitudes. Herek (1985) summarized much of the empirical research on attitudes toward gays and lesbians and concluded that people with negative homophobic attitudes also tend to have similar attitudes and behaviors that correlate with their beliefs about homosexuality. Herek found that people who are homophobic are less likely to have had personal contact with lesbians and gay men, more conservative toward sexuality, more likely to be older and less educated, more likely to attend church regularly and subscribe to a more conservative political ideology, more likely to support traditional and restrictive gender roles, and more likely to manifest high levels of authoritarianism and related personality characteristics (dogmatism, rigidity, intolerance of ambiguity). In addition, according to Herek, heterosexuals tend to have more negative attitudes toward gays and lesbians of their same gender, and more negative homophobic attitudes are manifested by men than women.

Correlates to these negative homophobic attitudes include limited experiences with people who are gay, lesbian, or bisexual; adherence to traditional gender roles; cognitive development; self-esteem; and internalized homophobia.

CORRELATE: LIMITED EXPERIENCE WITH PEOPLE WHO ARE GAY, LESBIAN, OR BISEXUAL

As a result of cultural, institutional, and individual homophobia and heterosexism, the majority of gay, lesbian, and bisexual people choose to live in the closet and lead a double life by trying to pass as heterosexual in public. The lack of visibility of the majority of gays, lesbians, and bisexuals has a profound effect on heterosexuals. Most people have no idea of the number of bisexuals, lesbians, and gays on their campus and in this country, and severely underestimate the total figure.

In a 1983 *Newsweek* poll, only 25% of the respondents said that they had friends who were gay or lesbian (Morganthau et al., 1983). Because there are so few publicly visible role models, most heterosexuals have very few opportunities to have any personal contact with people who they know are gay, lesbian, or bisexual (Gochros, 1985). It is a vicious cycle: Many people live very closeted lives to avoid harassment and abuse; therefore, fewer people have the opportunity to have positive personal interactions that might give them new information that would challenge them to change their attitudes (D'Augelli, 1989; D'Augelli & Rose, 1990; Morin & Garfinkle, 1978).

Most people seem to fear what they do not understand and come to rely on what they "know," that is, stereotypes, to create some sense of order in their world. Research has clearly demonstrated that an increase in knowledge reduces homophobic attitudes and values (Wells & Franken, 1987). These changes in homophobic attitudes also happen when students and staff have the opportunity to have personal interactions with gays, bisexuals, and lesbians whom they believe to be similar to themselves in backgrounds and social status (Morin & Garfinkle, 1978).

CORRELATE: ADHERENCE TO TRADITIONAL GENDER ROLES

One of the most critical forces that perpetuates homophobia is our compulsive societal adherence to traditional gender role stereotypes. Homophobia adversely affects men and women of all sexual/affectional orientations because it is deliberately used in our society to enforce the rigid gender roles that maintain the patriarchical system of oppression (Steinem, 1978). The fear of being called a "sissy" or a "tomboy" keeps many boys and girls constantly monitoring their behavior in order to abide by the strict societal gender roles (Pharr, 1988). As a result, few are allowed access to their full range of behaviors or to develop as whole and centered human beings.

If young boys and men successfully fulfill their socially prescribed gender roles, they are often rewarded with economic and educational opportunities and with access to power over women and children. If men or boys step too far afield and violate traditional gender roles, they may become targets of harassment and ridicule. If they are too gentle and sensitive, or cry too often, or choose to work in a nontraditional (that is, women's) field, their sexual/affectional orientation may be questioned. If they choose to not fight or participate in other violent activities, or if they do not play organized sports, they may at any point be called a "faggot" or "queer." This homophobic labeling can make them as vulnerable as gay men to losing many of their heterosexual and male privileges (Pharr, 1988).

The perpetrators of violence against gays and lesbians tend to be White males in their teens and early twenties (Blumenfeld & Raymond, 1988). It is curious to consider the possible connections between homophobic violence and the extreme social pressure most young males experience to fit into the traditional macho male stereotypes. How many men go "fag bashing" in an attempt to prove they are "real men"?

Young girls and women who obediently fit into their prescribed roles are often rewarded with a wide variety of other kinds of perceived heterosexual privileges: social approval, family and community support, men who are supposed to protect and take care of them, and a sense of purpose. Most women and girls know that if they step too far outside the realm of acceptable gender role behavior by asserting their rights and preferences, by demanding equality and equity, by organizing to end violence against women and children, by demanding the right to control their own bodies, or by refusing to caretake the needs of others at their own expense, they may lose these perceived heterosexual privileges and become victims of homophobic harassment (Pharr, 1988).

Lesbian and gay baiting is an incredibly powerful tool that works to maintain the status quo (Pharr, 1988). How can people defend themselves against accusations that question their sexual orientation? How can they prove their heterosexuality? Without sexism there is no need to enforce the adherence to traditional gender roles. Without traditional gender roles, is there a need for homophobia?

CORRELATE: COGNITIVE DEVELOPMENT

People with negative homophobic attitudes tend to manifest high levels of authoritarianism and demonstrate an intolerance of ambiguity (Herek, 1985). These data suggest a possible connection between homophobic attitudes and a person's level of cognitive development. People who think in dualistic ways tend to believe that things are either right or wrong, superior or inferior, and good or bad (Perry, 1970). Most dualists want to be among those who are right, superior, good. It is difficult for them to tolerate differences, multiple truths, and alternative realities. This is a rich area for futher research and analysis.

CORRELATE: SELF-ESTEEM

Self-esteem may be one of the most critical correlates to address in developing interventions to minimize and eliminate homophobia. When people have a low self-concept, they are desperate to find ways to compensate for their negative self-image and prove that they are competent and capable (Beattie, 1987). People who are homophobic can find some false sense of esteem from believing that they are superior to people who are gay, lesbian, or bisexual. If they have a high need for social approval and peer acceptance, they may actively participate in homophobic harassment and violence in an attempt to be a part of a peer group and earn the respect of others. But people who have a solid self-esteem and a positive identity are less likely to promote or believe prejudices and far more likely to let go of stereotypes once they are confronted with contrary evidence (Blumenfeld & Raymond, 1988). If people feel confident and worthwhile, they have little need to put others down or to feel threatened by those who are different from themselves.

CORRELATE: INTERNALIZED HOMOPHOBIA

Internalized homophobia is another possible correlate for those who are actively homophobic. People who are trying to deny or suppress their gay, lesbian, or bisexual orientation may choose to try to prove they are not one of "them" by actively participating in homophobic harassment and abuse. Smith (1983) argues that gay, lesbian, and bisexual people are unlike most other oppressed groups because their identity is not apparent at birth. Internalized homophobia and the powerful social pressure to be heterosexual keep many gays, lesbians, and bisexuals from acknowledging and acting on their sexual/affectional orientation for many years. In an attempt to repress their own gay, lesbian, or bisexual orientation, individuals may become vigilant in their efforts to deny the rights of other gay, lesbian, or bisexual people.

There is insufficient empirical data to explain how and why individuals form and maintain their negative homophobic attitudes (Herek, 1985). Further research and analysis of the correlates of homophobia may provide clues for how to develop educational interventions that effectively minimize and interrupt homophobic prejudice and harassment.

RECENT CHALLENGES AND CHANGES

Groups have been organizing and challenging homophobia and heterosexism for over 100 years, but many people claim that the modern gay rights movement began the night of June 27, 1969, when the patrons of the Stonewall Inn in Greenwich Village rioted and fought back during a police raid (Weiss & Schiller, 1988). During the past two decades the modern gay rights movement has exploded across the nation. National organizations coordinate efforts to bring about change in educational systems, the courts, and the Congress. In almost every major city, dozens of groups and organizations provide a wide variety of social services, political pressures, cultural events, and economic supports. Scores of different national and local newspapers and magazines provide updated and accurate information in the alternative press. Marches and rallies bring millions of lesbians, gays, bisexuals, and heterosexual allies out each year to celebrate and advocate for political change. These grassroots movements have forced some legislators to pay attention to the needs and issues of gays, lesbians, and bisexuals and to work to pass civil rights legislation that prohibits discrimination based on sexual/affectional orientation.

The AIDS crisis has deeply affected the gay rights movement. Some believe that out of the immeasurable devastation and despair have risen very powerful grassroots coalitions working in every geographic region for civil rights and social change. Many state that this crisis has placed the issues and concerns of gay, lesbian, and bisexual people in all of the living rooms and classrooms across the country because programs educating the public about AIDS often also address the issues of homophobia and heterosexism.

Others suggest that the energy and resources within the gay, lesbian, and bisexual communities have been focused almost exclusively on the issue of AIDS and that there has been a loss of momentum on such other pertinent issues as child custody rights; domestic partnership laws; civil rights legislation; racism, sexism, agism, ablism, religious intolerance, and classism within the communities; human sexuality curricula; and homophobic education programs. One further perspective is that people have used the myth that AIDS is a "gay disease" as one more reason to scapegoat the gay, lesbian, and bisexual communities and to further "justify" homophobia and heterosexism.

The gay rights movement experienced a major setback in 1986 when the Supreme Court upheld the constitutionality of the Georgia sodomy laws that prohibit consensual, private adult sexual acts commonly associated with homosexuality. In response to this and other heterosexist events, people across the nation have mobilized in even greater numbers to bring about equity and equality for gay, lesbian, and bisexual people. One critical step on the road to justice has been to lobby for national legislation that prohibits discrimination based on sexual/affectional orientation. In February 1990, the Senate passed a bill that requires the Justice Department to publish statistics of hate crimes, including homophobic incidents (Salholz et al., 1990). These data may provide the stimulus to convince federal and state legislators of the need for civil rights legislation to include sexual/affectional orientation.

In the years since the 1969 Stonewall riots, many things have changed. There are currently 50 openly gay and lesbian elected officials around the country (Salholz et al., 1990). During the 1988 presidential election, the Human Rights Campaign Fund, a gay lobbying group, was the ninth largest independent political action committee (PAC). Seven cities have "domestic partnership" laws that grant lesbians and gays many of the legal spousal rights of married couples. Wisconsin and Massachusetts have passed laws banning discrimination against gays and lesbians, and several other states are involved in a similar legal process. At least seven same-sex couples have been recognized as legal parents and granted permission to adopt a child, and gays and lesbians are able to adopt children as single parents in many states (Monagle, 1989).

Today there are gay, lesbian, and bisexual professional organizations in every field imaginable. There are gay-, lesbian-, and bisexual-owned businesses, athletic teams, cultural and musical events, and support groups. Lesbian, gay, and bisexual people have organized political groups within almost every political movement and work in coalition with heterosexuals to combat oppression in every form.

Numerous groups affiliated with traditional religious organizations meet the spiritual needs of many gays, bisexuals, and lesbians: Metropolitan Community Church (MCC), some Jewish synagogues, Integrity (Episcopal), Dignity (Catholic), Lutherans Concerned, and Presbyterians for Lesbian and Gay Concerns. Other religious denominations have moved toward the acceptance of lesbians, gays, and bisexuals: Quakers, Unitarian Universalists, Disciples of Christ, and the United Church of Christ (Blumenfeld & Raymond, 1988; Nugent & Gramick, 1989).

In October 1987, over 650,000 lesbians, gays, bisexuals, and their allies marched together through the nation's capital to demand their civil rights and to focus international attention on the AIDS crisis. There have been numerous positive changes in the past two decades. It is critical that this momentum and progress continue in the years to come.

INTERVENTION STRATEGIES

This section provides an overview of some of the types of interventions that student affairs professionals can implement to minimize and eliminate individual, cultural, and institutional homophobia and heterosexism on college and university campuses. There is little research and few published works documenting successful antihomophobia interventions. The ideas here are intended to stimulate new thinking and creative action, to represent a vision of what can be, to provide an introductory overview of possibilities for interventions by student affairs staff. Additional detailed suggestions and intervention strategies for specific areas and departments are included in many of the chapters that follow. Student affairs professionals at some colleges and universities may not have the resources or authority to implement some of these suggestions: Types and numbers of interventions may be limited by the size, financial stability, and religious or political affiliation of a specific institution.

An invaluable resource for further reference is *In Every Classroom: The Report of the President's Select Committee for Lesbian and Gay Concerns* published by the Office of Student Life Policy and Services, Rutgers, The State University of New Jersey, (201) 932-7255. (Copies are available for $10.00 from the following address: 301 Van Nest Hall, Old Queens Campus, Rutgers, The State University, New Brunswick, NJ 08903.)

A. STRATEGIES TO FOCUS UNIVERSITY ATTENTION

1. Mission statement. The mission of every institution of higher education needs to state clearly the campus community's commitment to create and maintain "an environment in which all members of our community, and specifically lesbian and gay students, are able to participate and develop intellectually and emotionally, free from fear, violence, or harassment" (Nieberding, 1989, p. 8). The statement can identify as one of the primary goals of a college or university education student development of the necessary skills, knowledge, and attitudes to live and work effectively in a pluralistic world.

2. Campus-wide task force. The president or chancellor can appoint a commission to address the issues of homophobia and heterosexism on campus. To be most effective, the membership of this commission needs to reflect the diversity within the community and include members who are gay, lesbian, and bisexual, or heterosexual allies who represent a variety of class and ethnic backgrounds and who are actively working on various levels to combat homophobia and heterosexism and other forms of oppression. This commission needs to be a legitimate institution and have the power and resources to conduct a thorough assessment of the current campus climate for lesbian, gay, and bisexual students, staff, and faculty. Its recommendations for changes and interventions need to be endorsed by the various college or university governing bodies before they are publicized throughout the college or university community and in college or university publications.

This commission can then change its focus and become the coordinating body that oversees the implementation of the various policies, programs, and changes. It can invite different professional staff, faculty, student staff, and student leaders who represent all sexual/affectional orientations to work in coalition to develop short- and long-range plans for designing system-wide interventions.

B. STRATEGIES FOR TRAINING AND DEVELOPMENT

The level of awareness and acceptance of the student affairs professionals, faculty, administrators, and student staff is critical on any campus. Every student affairs division, each individual academic department, and all college and university offices that serve students, alumni, staff, and faculty need to sponsor regular training programs exploring homophobia and heterosexism on their campus. In addition, the issues of homophobia and heterosexism need to be included in almost every type of training session available to staff and faculty throughout the year. Articles can be distributed to help staff and faculty stay current on the issues. Monies can be allocated to develop and maintain a comprehensive resource library containing books and subscriptions to periodicals and newspapers that address the issues of lesbian, gay, and bisexual people. Staff and faculty can be encouraged to develop personal networks with people who are gay, bisexual, and lesbian so that they can learn firsthand about these issues and concerns. They can be allocated travel monies to attend conferences and workshops for further training, after which they can develop in-service programs in order to share their new insights with colleagues.

C. STRATEGIES FOR POLICY DEVELOPMENT

After the professional and student staff have had some basic awareness training, it will be helpful to have them work together to reexamine related policies, procedures, and practices, and to identify each area that might in some way perpetuate homophobia and heterosexism. Staff need to explore policy enforcement and sanctioning, particularly concerning homophobic-related harassment and assault, as well as policies and procedures that address the college or university nondiscrimination policy; the sexual harassment policy; the reporting of homophobic incidents; students and staff who test HIV positive; staff selection and employment; advertising policies; how funds are allocated; the live-in policies for hall directors; room changes; benefits packages for staff, faculty, and their life partners and family members; and policies governing who can live in graduate student housing and "family" housing.

D. STRATEGIES TO COMBAT HOMOPHOBIC VIOLENCE AND HARASSMENT

Every college and university needs to expand its affirmative action statement and student conduct codes specifically to prohibit any harassment, abuse, or discrimination based on sexual/affectional orientation. These policies need to be widely publicized and regularly endorsed by the top administrators and faculty leaders. The areas responsible for policy enforcement need to have the power and jurisdiction to develop and impose appropriate sanctions that are designed both to hold students and staff accountable and to increase their awareness and understanding of the devastating effects of homophobia.

E. STRATEGIES FOR EDUCATIONAL PROGRAMMING

Educational programming opportunities need to be provided for different specific target groups, such as homophobic heterosexuals; open-minded heterosexuals; closeted gays, lesbians, and bisexuals; and "out" gays, lesbians, and bisexuals. It may be helpful for trainers and presenters to review different social identity development models as they design their interventions to meet the specific needs of each group. Many campuses already have effective programming intervention models and speakers bureaus that are designed to address other critical issues, such as sexual assault, AIDS awareness, racism, and alcohol abuse. A similar structure can be developed in which a core of skilled presenters gains further training on how to design and facilitate seminars on combating homophobia on college and university campuses. They can then develop different curricular guides for the various groups across the campus.

The issues addressed in programs for heterosexual and mixed audiences need to include what is homophobia; how has socialization perpetuated negative homophobic stereotypes; how is homophobia manifested on college and university campuses and in society; what are the myths and facts surrounding homophobia; what it is like to be lesbian, gay, or bisexual on this campus; what are the connections between sexism, heterosexism, and homophobia; strategies for minimizing and interrupting homophobia and heterosexism on an individual, cultural, and institutional level; and how to be an effective ally against homophobia and heterosexism.

Programs designed specifically for students, staff, and faculty who are gay, lesbian, and bisexual need to include such additional topics as coming out; internalized homophobia; the stages of identity development for people who are bisexual, lesbian, or gay; the consequences of using different survival and collusion strategies on campus; the trade-offs for choosing to live more openly on campus; how to develop supportive networks and support systems; the issues to consider when choosing a career; other forms of oppression within the gay, lesbian, and bisexual communities; issues of multiple oppressions for people who are lesbian, gay, and bisexual; how to combat biphobia, the fear and hatred of people who are bisexual, within the majority culture and within the gay and lesbian communities; building coalitions among gays, lesbians, and bisexuals; and wellness and health issues.

While staff and faculty work to educate about homophobia and heterosexism at all levels, they also need to develop learning opportunities that challenge students to develop the basic "building blocks" of valuing diversity: positive self-esteem, a strong sense of personal identity, relativistic thinking, openness to new ideas, a belief in the right of all people to human rights and civil rights, a sense of personal power and self-efficacy, the ability to stand up for what they believe and to question authority, a commitment to androgyny, assertiveness and listening skills, and a sincere commitment to lifelong learning and self-actualization. These skills and attitudes can be taught and reinformed while staff and faculty are interacting with students in their roles as advisers, disciplinarians, counselors, educators, and role models.

F. ADDITIONAL STRATEGIES FOR SPECIFIC STUDENT AFFAIRS DEPARTMENTS

There are a number of offices on college and university campuses that need to reexamine how effectively their services and programs meet the needs of students, staff, and faculty who are lesbian, gay, or bisexual; and to develop additional interventions that combat homophobia and heterosexism and challenge students, faculty, and staff to value diversity.

1. The student affairs office. The top administrator in student affairs can play a powerful role in developing a department mission statement that emphasizes the goals of valuing diversity and combating homophobia and heterosexism. Many colleges and universities have staff members who provide services and programs for different groups who are targets of oppression, such as students of color, students with disabilities, women, and international students. It is critical to have at least one staff member whose job responsibilities specifically include providing support and advocacy for gay, lesbian, and bisexual students on campus.

2. Health center. The health center staff need to explore their policies and procedures to ensure that all information and records are completely confidential. The medical staff may need regular in-service training seminars to stay current on the different medical needs of gays, lesbians, and bisexuals. Some students may request a physician who is gay, lesbian, or bisexual, and so, if at all possible, the health center staff need to compile a referral list of college or university and community health care workers.

Health educators provide a wide variety of programs for the heterosexual campus community that address many issues of interest to gay, lesbian, and bisexual students as well, for example, developing healthy relationships, safer sex, wellness lifestyles, alcohol and drug abuse, and time and stress management. These programs need to be expanded to include sections that focus on the needs of lesbians, gays, and bisexuals, and that specifically explore the issues of homophobia on campus.

3. Counseling center. All of the counseling center staff who do intake sessions and work with clients need to be thoroughly trained in all aspects of homophobia and heterosexism. In addition, if it is feasible, there needs to be at least one counselor in the center or who is available for referrals in the local community to provide services to students who specifically request someone who is gay, lesbian, or bisexual.

Counselors can facilitate outreach seminars and support groups designed to explore a variety of critical areas, such as coming out, how to handle harassment and homophobic behaviors, dealing with anger, living with multiple oppressions, self-empowerment, developing healthy relationships, alcohol and drug abuse, coming out to parents, violence in relationships, healthy sexuality, the roles of women, the roles of men, AIDS education, and being HIV positive.

Staff members can deliberately manage the physical environment to communicate an acceptance of all sexual/affectional orientations by placing posters, pamphlets, and books in visible places that specifically address the issues of lesbians, gays, and bisexuals. In addition the counseling center staff need to work collaboratively with other student affairs professionals, security officers, and faculty to develop a system to provide support and advocacy for the victims of homophobic harassment and violence that is similar to those provided for the survivors of rape, sexual assault, and racial harassment.

4. Career services. The staff in the career center can provide a wide variety of information to gay, lesbian, and bisexual students that may help them as they decide on their course of study and career direction. It will be helpful to keep current lists of the companies and organizations that include sexual/affectional orientation in their affirmative action policies and those that provide training on homophobia for their managers and employees.

Articles exploring the various choices and dilemmas around coming out on the job can give students the chance to better understand the realities of homophobia and heterosexism in most work places in this country. Alumni who are gay, lesbian, and bisexual can be asked to serve as mentors or sponsors for students. They can talk on panels about their lives and experiences at work. They can help develop internships and cooperative education experiences in businesses and organizations that work to combat homophobia and heterosexism in the work place and in the larger community.

5. Financial aid. Some gay, lesbian, and bisexual students are disowned by their families and receive no financial support. The financial aid staff needs to be able to work with these students effectively and be willing to find creative ways to meet their needs. In addition, they can actively seek donors for scholarships that are awarded to students who work to combat homophobia and heterosexism on campus.

6. Admissions. The staff of the admissions office need to be aware of the campus and community services and programs for gay, lesbian, and bisexual students and discuss these in their marketing materials, high school presentations, and campus tours.

7. Housing and residence life. The resident assistants can be powerful role models and educators around the issues of homophobia. They need to receive training that helps them develop techniques for interrupting the wide variety of homophobic comments and behaviors that may occur on their floors. They need support for working with roommate conflicts that involve the issue of sexual/affectional orientation and for developing social programming activities that are not heterosexist. In addition, the staff in residence life can take the lead in efforts to include the needs and issues of students who are lesbian, gay, or bisexual in orientation activities and resource guides for new students.

8. Off-campus housing. Staff can develop a listing of landlords of apartments and houses that are supportive of gay, lesbian, and bisexual students. They can keep a separate book for lesbian, gay, and bisexual students who are looking for roommates. In addition, the staff can provide advocacy support and mediation for students who are having problems with the homophobic landlords and work with local government officials to change any homophobic housing laws and regulations.

9. Student leadership/campus activities. Campus activities staff and other advisers of student groups play a critical role in helping students develop programs and services that meet the needs of the diverse student population. They can provide antihomophobia awareness and sensitivity programs for student leaders, pledges, and officers and members of student organizations. These interventions can help students understand how most graphics and pictures on advertisements and bulletin boards reflect only the heterosexual experience, and how most social and recreational activities are designed primarily for heterosexuals, for example, dances, formals, escort dinners, co-ed sports teams, parties, and dating games.

Student groups and Greek organizations can play an active role in combating homophobia by providing films, concerts, theatre productions, speakers, and activities that do not perpetuate heterosexism. They can share their financial resources and work in collaboration with the student groups for gay, lesbian, and bisexual students to both sponsor and advertise educational and social programs for the entire campus community. In addition, campus activities and student union staffs can sponsor distinguished lecturers series, posters and films series, and theatre, art, and music presentations that specifically explore issues of homophobia and heterosexism.

The campus activities staff can play a crucial role in the allocation process of student fees to student groups. Often, some homophobic members of the student government try to deny official recognition and funding to the bisexual, gay, and lesbian student group. Staff members can provide needed advice and counsel as the students work to resolve this conflict.

10. Security/campus police. Officers and staff need to receive training on how to respond appropriately to incidents of homophobic harassment and violence. There needs to be at least one officer who is designated to work as the advocate for victims of homophobic violence. Members of the police/security force need to develop a close relationship with members of all campus and community groups who provide services and programs for victims of homophobic harassment and violence, including the counseling center, the women's center, health services, the local police department, the local battered women's shelters, and the student group for gay, lesbian, and bisexual students. They can initiate efforts to develop a hotline service and to work with other campus and community agencies to develop a support program for victims of homophobic hate crimes similar to those provided for victims of sexual assault and racial harassment. In addition, they can coordinate the documentation and publication of all forms of hate crimes.

11. Campus ministry. Students who are struggling to understand how to integrate their sexual/affectional orientation with their religious and spiritual needs may seek out the campus minister or other religious/spiritual staff for guidance. It is critical that these staff members and faculty understand the varying opinions within different organized religions regarding sexual orientation. If they cannot discuss these issues with students in an open and supportive way, then they need to refer them to other staff and community leaders who can be more accepting and helpful.

G. STRATEGIES FOR WORKING WITH FACULTY AND OTHER CAMPUS GROUPS

Student affairs staff can create changes throughout the campus by working directly with other departments and groups. They can work with faculty to help them develop new curricula and identify textbooks and articles that provide accurate and up-to-date information about the lives, her/history, and cultures of lesbians, bisexuals, and gays. They can provide antihomophobia training for academic advisers, new faculty, and teaching assistants. They can work collaboratively with faculty to develop a visiting professors or a distinguished scholars program that selects faculty to teach interdisciplinary courses that specifically explore issues of homophobia and heterosexism.

Student affairs staff can work with the campus newspaper and radio station to encourage them to cover the events and issues of gay, lesbian, and bisexual students and staff, and to eliminate all comments, pictures, music, and advertising that perpetuate homophobia. They can work with the library and the campus bookstore to develop and maintain a thorough and current collection of books and periodicals. They can assist the audiovisual staff in acquiring more film and media resources for classroom and co-curricular instruction.

H. INDIVIDUAL INTERVENTIONS AND ROLE MODELING

RAs, hall directors, student group advisers, and other student affairs staff can play a critical role in challenging homophobia because they work directly with a wide variety of students on a daily basis. Positive role models have incredible power to influence the values and actions of students who revere and respect them. The cognitive dissonance created when homophobic students are challenged by someone they trust and admire can be one of the most significant tools for combating individual homophobia.

There are also a wide variety of interventions individuals can make every time they interact with a student, faculty, or staff member. What books are on your shelves? What posters are on your walls? What button and T shirts do you wear? What seminars do you present? How often do you assume students and staff are heterosexual? On which committees do you serve? Which issues do you champion in your daily conversations? How often do you include examples using gays, lesbians, and bisexuals in all of your other seminars and classes? What journals does your office order and have available in the waiting area? What comments do you confront? Which ones do you leave unchallenged? About which issues do you write letters to the editor? What articles do you circulate? What educational activities do you encourage? Which campus programs do you attend, and which students, faculty, and staff do you invite to join you?

Heterosexual staff members can be powerful allies and use their privilege to combat individual, cultural, and institutional homophobia and heterosexism. The choices are not always easy, and many allies may experience rejection, harassment, and loss of organizational power when they choose to take a stand. Yet, at these moments, they may begin to understand a little about what it is like for many gay, lesbian, and bisexual people who choose to be visible, positive role models each and every day of their lives.

Many people who are gay, lesbian, or bisexual struggle over the decision of when, how, or if to come out on campus. The documented stories of discrimination and abuse toward those who chose to come out work effectively to keep many in the closet living in fear of disclosure. It has never been truly safe in this society to come out and publicly affirm sexual/affectional orientation, and many would argue that the circumstances and crises of the 1990s make it even more difficult and potentially dangerous.

The question of whether and when to be public about sexual/ affectional orientation must continue to be one of personal choice and discretion. However, one of the most powerful ways to combat homophobia and heterosexism is for bisexuals, lesbians, and gays to refuse to collude with their oppressors and to come out of their collective closets. Invisibility helps to do the work of the oppressor. It is important for lesbian, gay, and bisexual staff and faculty to break the silence and choose visibility in every possible situation. Every time they do not turn their heads in shame, by their actions they make heads turn and create one more opportunity to combat homophobia and heterosexism.

CONCLUSION

Only about one-quarter of this nation's youth complete a college or university education and move on to assume leadership roles in businesses, schools, social service and government work, religious organizations, the judicial system, the medical profession, volunteer efforts, and myriad other influential organizations. The college or university experience may be the first and last time most students have the opportunity to learn about homophobia and heterosexism and how they collude within this system of oppression.

How prepared are our students and staff to become effective leaders in a world that is becoming increasingly diverse and in which the interconnectedness of global issues is taking center stage? College and university administrators, student affairs staff, and faculty can help shape the future by giving the students who move through colleges and universities the building blocks to truly value diversity. They can impact the quality of life for generations to come if they work to combat homophobia and heterosexism and all other forms of oppression within their spheres of influence.

This chapter has explored some of the manifestations and correlates of homophobia and heterosexism and identified a wide variety of strategies to combat homophobia and heterosexism at the cultural, institutional, and individual levels on university and college campuses.

There is no hierarchy of oppressions, and no one can afford the luxury of fighting only one form of discrimination (Lorde, 1983).

They are all interconnected and interrelated. This society will survive or perish together. The choices are getting clearer every day.

The often quoted comments of Pastor Martin Niemoller, a survivor of a Nazi death camp, continue to provide inspiration for millions (Bartlett, 1980):

> In Germany they first came for the Communists and I didn't speak up because I wasn't a Communist. Then they came for the Jews, and I didn't speak up because I wasn't a Jew. Then they came for the trade unionists, and I didn't speak up because I wasn't a trade unionist. Then they came for the Catholics, and I didn't speak up because I was Protestant. Then they came for me and by that time no one was left to speak up.

The Nazis also "came for the homosexuals and the lesbians" and tens of thousands were brutally tortured, mutilated, and murdered alongside all of the other victims (Plant, 1986), but neither of these groups is mentioned in this passage or in most other historical references to the Nazi Holocaust. This "oversight" is illustrative of the pervasive invisibility that gay, lesbian, and bisexual people still experience today. The work of student affairs professionals, faculty, and staff can help to create a different ending to this passage and, hopefully, a new beginning for us all.

REFERENCES

Articles & News. (1988, January). *Lesbian Connection, 11*(3), 3.

Beattie, M. (1987). *Codependent no more: How to stop controlling others and start caring for yourself.* New York: Harper/Hazelden.

Bartlett, J. (1980). *Familiar quotations* (15th ed.). Boston: Little, Brown.

Berrill, K. (1989, March). *Combating homophobia.* Presentation at the annual meeting of the American College Personnel Association, Washington, DC.

Blumenfeld, W. J., & Raymond, D. (1988). *Looking at gay and lesbian life.* Boston: Beacon.

Boswell, J. (1980). *Christianity, social tolerance, and homosexuality.* Chicago: University of Chicago Press.

D'Augelli, A. R. (1989). Homophobia in a university community: Views of prospective resident assistants. *Journal of College Student Development, 30,* 546–52.

D'Augelli, A. R., & Rose, M. L. (1990). Homophobia in a university community: Attitudes and experiences of heterosexual freshmen. *Journal of College Student Development, 31,* 484–491.

Goodman, G., Lakey, G., Lashof, J., & Thorne, E. (1983). *No turning back: Lesbian and gay liberation for the '80s*. Philadelphia: New Society.

Gochros, H. L. (1985). Teaching social workers to meet the needs of the homosexuallly oriented. In R. Schoenberg, R. S. Goldberg, & D. A. Shore (Eds.), *With compassion toward some: Homosexuality and social work in America* (pp. 137–156). New York: Harrington Park.

Herek, G. M. (1985). Beyond homophobia: A social psychological perspective on attitudes toward lesbians and gay men. In J. P. De Cecco (Ed.), *Bashers, baiters, and bigots: Homophobia in American society* (pp. 1–21). New York: Harrington Park.

Lorde, A. (1983). There is no hierarchy of oppressions. *Interracial Books for Children, 14*(3–4), 9.

McNaught, B. (1981). *A disturbed peace: Selected writings of an Irish Catholic homosexual*. Washington, DC: Dignity.

McNeill, J. (1988). *The church and the homosexual* (3rd ed.). Boston: Beacon.

Monagle, K. (1989, October). Court backs two-mom family. *Ms.*, p. 69.

Morganthau, T., Coppola, V., Carey, J., Cooper, N., Raine, G., McCormick, J., & Friendly, D. T. (1983, August 3). Gay America in transition. *Newsweek*, pp. 30–40.

Morin, S. F., & Garfinkle, E. M. (1978). Male homophobia. *Journal of Social Issues, 34*(1), 29–47.

National Gay and Lesbian Task Force (1984). *National anti-gay/lesbian victimization report*. New York: Author.

National Opinion Research Center (1985). General social surveys. *1972–1985: Cumulative codebook*. Chicago: University of Chicago.

Nieberding, R. A. (Ed.). (1989). *In every classroom: The report of the president's select committee for lesbian and gay concerns*. New Brunswick, NJ: Rutgers University Press.

Nugent, R., & Gramick, J. (1989). Homosexuality: Protestant, Catholic, and Jewish issues: A fishbone tale. *Journal of Homosexuality, 18*(3–4), 7–46.

Ostling, R. N. (1989, November 13). The battle over gay clergy. *Time*, pp. 89–90.

Perry, W. G. (1970). *Forms of intellectual and ethical development in the college years*. New York: Holt, Rinehart, & Winston.

Pharr, S. (1988). *Homophobia: A weapon of sexism*. Little Rock, AR: Chardon.

Plant, R. (1986). *The pink triangle: The Nazi war against homosexuals*. New York: Henry Holt.

Pogrebin, L. C. (1983). The secret fear that keeps us from raising free children. *Interracial Books for Children, 14*(3–4), 10–12.

Ritter, K. Y., & O'Neill, C. W. (1989). Moving through loss: The spiritual journey of gay men and lesbian women. *Journal of Counseling and Development, 68*(1), 9–15.

Salholz, E., Clifton, T., Joseph, N., Beachy, L., Rogers, P., Wilson, L., Glick, D., & King, P. (1990, March). The future of gay America. *Newsweek*, pp. 20–25.

Shilts, R. (1987). *And the band played on: Politics, people, and the AIDS epidemic.* New York: St. Martin's.

Smith, B. (1983). Homophobia: Why bring it up? *Interracial Books for Children, 14*(3–4), 7–8.

Steinem, G. (1978). The politics of supporting lesbianism. In G. Vida (Ed.), *Our right to love: A lesbian resource book* (pp. 266–269). Englewood Cliffs, NJ: Prentice-Hall.

Weinberg, G. (1972). *Society and the healthy homosexual.* New York: St. Martin's.

Weiss, A., and Schiller, G. (1988). *Before Stonewall: The making of a gay and lesbian community.* Tallahassee, FL: Naiad.

Wells, J. W., & Franken, M. L. (1987). University students' knowledge about and attitudes toward homosexuality. *Journal of Humanistic Education and Development, 26*(2), 81–95.

Zuckerman, L. (1988, March 7). Open season on gays. *Time*, p. 24.

Chapter 4

UNDERSTANDING GAY AND LESBIAN STUDENTS OF COLOR

Vernon A. Wall
University of Georgia

Jamie Washington
University of Maryland—Baltimore County

University campus life may be a challenging experience for students, but it is manageable as long as there are places to go to get the support and service needed. For gay and lesbian students, these supports often are underground, overworked, or nonexistent. And when they do exist, particularly on predominantly European-American campuses, the services and supports for gay and lesbian students often do not meet the additional needs of ethnic-minority students.

Much of what is in print about the gay and lesbian experience in the United States has been written from a European-American perspective. Although this perspective is important in order to understand the experience of lesbian and gay persons, it is not complete. One of the challenges in writing this chapter is the lack of written information on the topic. Therefore, much of the information is based on interviews conducted with gay and lesbian members of three ethnic communities: African American, Latino/Hispanic American, and Asian American. Quotes from these interviews are an important part of this chapter. The students attend the University of Georgia, the University of Maryland, Georgia Tech, Emory University, and the University of Maryland—Baltimore County.

Another challenge in writing a multiethnic and multiracial chapter is what language to use. Words are important; and the authors wish to be inclusive and not offensive. Therefore, for the purpose of this chapter, the authors ask that the readers accept *people of color* as the term for representing the three populations that are addressed. We recognize that some of the information in this chapter is more subjective and qualitative than quantitative; however, this information gives the reader a greater sense of how better to serve and support lesbian and gay students of color.

WHERE DO WE BEGIN?

When an individual is both a person of color and a gay or lesbian person, that individual may feel that only one part of his or her identity can be important. As a result, sexual orientation is often underemphasized. For many, it is difficult to strike a balance that allows them to be empowered and liberated in both of their oppressed identities. Multiple oppressions affect their lives because:

1. They feel that they do not know who they are.
2. They do not know which part of themselves is more important.
3. They do not know how to deal with one part of themselves oppressing another part of themselves.
4. They do not have anyone to talk to about the schism, the split in personality, they feel.
5. They feel radical and, more often, misunderstood by each group if and when they say that both parts are of equal importance.

As college and university educators attempting to create environments that are supportive of the learning and growth process for all students, recognizing the differences in the experiences of people of color is an important factor.

On college campuses, offices have been charged with providing support and services for underrepresented or targeted groups. To say that most of these offices only deal with one aspect of a person's identity is not a criticism; it is a reality. As a result, students often are forced to choose where to go on the basis of which part of their identity needs servicing or support.

The experience of each racial or ethnic group depends upon cultural norms and traditions as well as such usual factors as the environment in which the individual grows up, experience of other family and friends with gay and lesbian issues, and personality style and type. In the sections that follow, the experiences of specific ethnic minorities are discussed. Information gathered from students of color as they discussed their own experiences is presented. Among these specific student experiences are some common themes that are addressed in the conclusion.

IDENTITY DEVELOPMENT FOR GAY AND LESBIAN STUDENTS OF COLOR

To establish a foundation for understanding gay and lesbian students of color, we must first examine current studies on identity development for ethnic-minority lesbians and gay men. Identity development of ethnic-minority lesbians and gay men has previously examined identity development in the context of ethnic minority and lesbian and gay identity models (Espin, 1987; Wooden, Kawasaki, & Mayeda, 1983).

Both studies used the theoretical model of homosexual identity formation (Cass, 1979) as a model for understanding the six stages of development involved in developing an integrated identity as a homosexual person. As discussed in chapter 1, the six stages are Identity Confusion, Identity Comparison, Identity Tolerance, Identity Acceptance, Identity Pride, and Identity Synthesis.

In her study on identity development among Hispanic/Latina American lesbians, Espin (1987) also used the Minority Identity Development Model (Atkinson, Morten, & Sue, 1979) as a model for understanding Hispanic/Latina American identity. This model has five stages:

1. *Conformity.* An individual prefers dominant cultural values over his or her culture.
2. *Dissonance.* An individual experiences cultural confusion and conflict and challenges accepted values and beliefs.
3. *Resistance and Immersion.* An individual actively rejects the dominant society and culture and endorses only minority-held views.
4. *Introspection.* An individual questions the too-narrow restrictions of the previous stage and feels conflict between loyalty to his or her own ethnic group and personal autonomy.
5. *Synergetic Articulation and Awareness.* An individual experiences a sense of self-fullfillment with his or her cultural identity and accepts or rejects cultural values on the basis of individual merit or prior experience.

As Espin (1987) noted, these models of identity development are similiar in describing a process that begins with embracing negative or stigmatized identities and moves gradually from a rejected and denied self-image to embracing an identity that is finally accepted as positive. Both models describe one or more stages of intense confusion and at least one stage of complete separation from and rejection of the dominant society. The final stage for both models implies the acceptance of one's own identity, a commitment against oppression, and an ability to synthesize the best values of both perspectives and to communicate with members of the dominant groups (Chan, 1989).

Although these models present a means for understanding identity development of either homosexual identity *or* ethnic-minority identity, they do not examine how an individual who is gay or lesbian *and* a member of an ethnic-minority group comes to terms with identity issues. In the next sections, issues that contribute to the development of the gay, lesbian, or bisexual person of color are discussed.

AN AFRICAN-AMERICAN PERSPECTIVE

For those who grow up in an African-American home, it is difficult not to have some connection with a religious institution through parents, grandparents, or others in the extended family. Few people dispute that in many African-American communities the role of family and religion is central not only in families that consider themselves "religious" but also by people who seldom, if ever, participate in any type of traditional religious practices (Icard, 1986).

Much of the heterosexism and homophobia that is experienced or felt is justified first by religious teachings. Thus many young African-American gay and lesbian persons grow up believing that they are going to die and go to hell and as a result spend a great deal of energy and effort trying to change their sexual orientation (Icard, 1986). This is not unlike the experiences of many White gay and lesbian persons with strong religious influences. In the African-American community, however, the Christian church has for many years been one of the central places of truth, goodness, and solidarity. Many of the leaders of the civil rights movement came out of the church. Much of the organizing against racism still occurs in the church.

In the African-American community the minister continues to be an important figure held in high regard. Behaviors of questionable morality are denounced and scorned by the minister. When the young African-American person hears homosexuality condemned by this person overtly, covertly, and regularly, he or she learns quickly that there is neither support nor solitude in the place traditionally of most importance to many African-Americans in times of trouble (Icard, 1986).

In African-American families, as in most families, there is little to no discussion of homosexuality. However, the existence of "these people" in the community is recognized; they are most often teased and put down, but interestingly, at other times they are treated with respect and dignity, particularly if they are extremely open and stereotypical members of the gay or lesbian community. These people are somehow less threatening; perhaps because they are extremely masculine or feminine and do not call into question the heterosexual's own sense of sexuality and self—unlike the gay male football player and the lesbian fashion model, who may cause individuals to wonder if they, too, could be gay, lesbian, or bisexual (Icard, 1986).

- One African-American University of Maryland student said this: "My family certainly knows I'm lesbian, but we would never talk about it. Since junior high school, I can remember being called a dyke, and I knew I was; but I didn't want anyone else to know, so I never said anything. I know that my mother knew because she never asked me about boyfriends like she did with my sisters."

- An African-American University of Maryland—Baltimore County student stated this: "My family still does not know. I didn't even fully know 'til I got to college. I thought that if I just didn't think about it or do anything that God would take these desires away; but I found that they didn't go away—they got stronger. I returned to campus after being home for Christmas during my sophomore year and realized I had left a male magazine under my mattress. I was terrified. About 2 weeks later, I started getting letters and phone calls from my mom asking me about girlfriends and giving me scriptures to read that condemned homosexuality. It was awful."

For African-American students as well as students of most other ethnic groups, the approval and support of the family can have a profound impact on the development of a positive identity. Noteworthy is that in many churches people are taught that their family can be wrong, that people need to be an example as a Christian; thus, if more churches were understanding of homosexuality, many people would feel more empowered to deal with family attitudes and behaviors (Icard, 1986).

Many lesbian and gay African Americans do not feel that coming out beyond themselves and other close gay and lesbian friends is necessary—or even smart. The small numbers of men and women of color who feel that they can take leadership in the lesbian and gay rights movement make this apparent (Loiacano, 1989). More gays, lesbians, and bisexuals of color are speaking up and coming out in the work place today, but dealing with the alienation from the community of African Americans that often accompanies such openness as well as with the racism of the White community is still difficult.

"Support networks are often small and private. Members are usually only brought into groups by other already established members," said one African-American University of Georgia student. There is often a more open network of support for White gays and lesbians through campus organizations or support groups. This can be a doubly difficult experience for African-American students: Some feel as if they have to deny the African-American part of themselves and only be gay or lesbian in those settings, and then go to their own community and just be African American and not gay or lesbian (Loiacano, 1989).

For many African-American gays or lesbians, initimate relationships often occur in sporadic ways. For the student on a predominantly White campus, the experience can be extremely chilling and revealing.

- One University of Maryland African-American student told us this: "I was in love with this White Italian man. We had a great relationship, I thought; we enjoyed being together. It wasn't until one night that I went to a bar where he was out with other White gay friends, and all he did was say hello to me from across the room; and when I approached him and his friends, he acted as if I was some casual acquaintance. I was crushed. When I later confronted him, he said he was a little drunk and that his friends really wouldn't understand."

- One University of Maryland—Baltimore County African-American lesbian shared this: "I had a White lover for 3 years of college, and we were doing fine until I started taking some courses in African-American studies. She couldn't understand what more I needed to know since I was already Black."

As is sometimes the case with heterosexual relationships, dating across racial lines appears not to be widely accepted within the gay and lesbian community. In larger cities, the community can be fairly segregated; some bars and other establishments are predominately African American and others deny entrance to non-White gay and lesbian persons.

- One African-American University of Georgia student made these comments: "One particular bar seemed blatantly racist to me.

It was a private club—membership only. I would stand in line and watch everyone pay their money and get in. When I would reach the door, I was always asked for my ID and membership card. When I inquired as to why no one else was asked to show a membership card, I was told that the doorman knew 'these people.'"

In looking at the differences between men and women, it is evident that women of color often struggle with triple oppression issues. It is difficult to decide which banner gets the most time or if some banners deserve any. The women's movement for many years was, and in some cases still is, seen as the White women's quest for independence and voice. Within this movement African-American women have often been unheard. Therefore, the issue of race seems to override the issues of sex, and African-American women often have put more energy or felt more support along the lines of racial identity. Because many of the White lesbian community support feminist views, African-American women have formed their own communities of support. These communities or networks are closely knit, and although these groups certainly are not vehemently separatist, men often are not comfortable in these circles.

African-American men struggle with being respected as a "man" within the community. There is a great deal of pressure for successful African-American men to produce. This means finding a good African-American woman, raising a family, and being a good role model for African-American boys. Once an African-American man is suspected of, or identified as, being gay, he may no longer be seen as a viable contributor to the African-American community. This is one reason African-American gays often maintain "heterosexual appearing existences" (Icard, 1986).

AN ASIAN-AMERICAN PERSPECTIVE

Chan (1989) has developed what is probably the most revealing research on gay and lesbian Asian-American persons to date. This section is based on this research and amplified by quotes from the interviews conducted by the authors. Chan surveyed 19 women and 16 men between the ages of 21 and 36 who identified themselves as being both lesbian or gay and Asian American. Based on the survey, Chan concluded that overt acknowledgement of homosexuality may be even more restricted by Asian-American cultural norms than it is in mainstream American society. Asian-American families view homosexuality as "shame put upon the family." As one Asian-American student commented, "The family is your identity, and if you are rejected by the family you're isolated." This belief makes it difficult for students to make decisions about their sexuality. In Asian cultures being gay or lesbian is frequently viewed as a rejection of the most important roles for women and men—that of being a wife and mother for women and that of being a father carrying on the "family line":

> The family is valued as the primary social unit throughout a person's life, and the most important obligation, especially as a son, is the continuation of the family through marriage and the bearing of children. If a daughter or son is lesbian or gay, the implication is that not only is the child rejecting the traditional role of wife-mother or son-father but also that the parents have failed in their role and that the child is rejecting the importance of family and Asian culture. (Chan, 1989, p. 17).

Given the importance of family and community relationships in Asian cultures, it is likely that Asian-American lesbians and gay men have not come out to their parents because of the overwhelming fear of rejection and stigmatization. As one Asian-American student observed, "I wish I could tell my parents—they are the only ones who do not know about my gay identity, but I am sure that they would reject me. There is no frame of reference to understand homosexuality in Asian-American culture." Some Asian-American lesbian and gay students choose to remain closeted not only among their families but also in the Asian-American community as well because homosexuality is such a taboo in Asian cultures.

Do Asian-Americans who are gay and lesbian prefer one identity to another? Chan found that more respondents identified themselves as lesbian or gay than as Asian American. However, others refused to choose because making a choice would mean denying an important part of their identity. As one Georgia Tech Asian-American student reported, "There aren't many Asian-American students on this campus—so, you can imagine how many gay Asian-American students there are." Thus Asian-American gay and lesbian persons find themselves in a position of not feeling comfortable in either community. This information can be used to discuss support networks for lesbian, gay, and bisexual Asian-American students.

Asian-Americans sometimes experience frustrations as they attempt to develop intimate relationships. Some feel discrimination from the European-American gay community. As one Asian-American Emory University student stated, "No matter how hard I try

to ignore it, White gays sometimes see me as Asiar
It's almost as if I've invaded 'their' space." Asian-/
lesbian persons must deal with these feelings as the
veloping intimate relationships.

The differences between men and women within the culture a
similar to those in European-American society. The difference occurs
in the triple minority status that Asian-American lesbians experience. This status usually produces greater discrimination and hostility.

A HISPANIC/LATINO-AMERICAN PERSPECTIVE

In discussing persons of color whose primary language is Spanish,
it is important to point out there are several terms that can be used
to describe ethnicity. These terms tend to vary by geographic region.
For this section, the authors use the term *Hispanic/Latino American.*

In her study of 16 Latina lesbians, Espin (1987) found that her
respondents expressed a desire to identify as *both* Latina and lesbian,
with varying degrees of success. She concluded that Latina lesbians
face a fundamental dilemma: "the conflict of the fear of stigmatization in the Hispanic community as lesbians versus the loss of
support for their identity as Hispanics in the mainstream gay community" (p. 42).

The family is the basic unit within Hispanic/Latino societies. Most
Latin-American cultures place a strong emphasis on the importance
of the family. This emphasis encompasses much more than the immediate family. Grandparents are considered an integral and important part of the family. Aunts, uncles, their children, and even
more distant relatives are also considered part of the extended family
(Carballo-Dieguez, 1989).

Catholicism is widespread among Hispanics/Latinos and strongly
influences the culture. This religion, based on conservative and traditional values, strongly rejects gay lifestyles (Suro, 1988). Hispanic/
Latino-American gays and lesbians who consider religion an important and integral part of their lives may feel alienated from their
culture as a result of these strong religious values. It is not surprising that most Hispanic/Latino-American gays and lesbians experience deep rooted feelings of guilt (Carballo-Dieguez, 1989). As
one University of Georgia student put it, "I knew whatever I was
doing wasn't right and that I was going to hell for sure."

In Hispanic/Latino culture, coming out does not always happen.
As a matter of fact, a great many Hispanic/Latino persons *never*
identify themselves as gay. As one Georgia Tech student stated,

"There's a special kind of attachment to the masculine and the female in our culture. It makes it more difficult to be self-accepting." In traditional Hispanic/Latino society, the sexual roles of men and women are clearly defined. Men must be macho, women must be pure (Carballo-Dieguez, 1989). A man who has an opportunity for a sexual encounter must not overlook it, or he will risk being considered dumb. Sexual urges of men are said to be "difficult to control." Within this logic, men who satify their "urges" through homosexual encounters are "forgiven" (Carballo-Dieguez, 1989).

As with the other ethnic groups mentioned in this chapter, Hispanic/Latino American gay and lesbian persons also seem to have difficulty finding a support network. As one Hispanic/Latino-American University of Georgia student commented, "I am so afraid that my Hispanic friends will tell my family that I am gay. Our families are so connected. I meet my family every Sunday for dinner at Grandma's—and every Sunday I meet a new family member who knows someone on my campus."

There also seems to be a definite difference in societal norms in relation to males and females. Within the Latin-American culture, for instance, male and female sex roles are extremely strong. Males are seen as providers, whereas women are to "stay with the children." Issues that conflict with this norm—including homosexuality—are usually looked at negatively.

FOSTERING A SUPPORTIVE ENVIRONMENT

We often think of people as having one majority identity with everything else secondary or mattering little if at all. Living with multiple oppressions causes an individual either to choose the important one or ones or to live a life of being a different person in different settings and never feeling whole—never really feeling accepted, respected, and understood for his or her own total life experiences.

As the issues of racism, sexism, and heterosexism are addressed, it is important that we address issues of diversity. Ways that gay, lesbian, and bisexual persons are alienated or included on our campuses are as follows:

Ways to Alienate	*Ways to Include/Support*
Being only closet supporters of gay, lesbian, and bisexual rights or views	Being vocal and open supporters

Having a minority affairs office (whose true mission is to serve the needs of all minority students) but not clearly considering gays, lesbians, and bisexual people in this group	Insuring that this office is inclusive or other supports are in place
Supporting actions that demonstrate harassment of racial minorities only is unacceptable	Supporting actions and policies that demonstrate harassment of gay, lesbian, and bisexual persons is also unacceptable
Producing publications, flyers, and handbooks that assume heterosexuality	Producing publications, flyers, and handbooks that take into account sexual orientation differences
Telling or laughing at jokes that make fun of gay, lesbian, or bisexual persons	Not supporting jokes that put down any group of people
Requiring 3-hour training session on minority students' needs (excluding gay, lesbian, or bisexual persons) for resident student staff	Requiring equal training time for this topic
Assuming that there are no gay, lesbian, or bisexual persons on the campus or staff in the residence halls who need support	Showing them that, whether they need it or use it, support is available
Assuming all gay, lesbian, and bisexual persons are European Americans.	Demonstrating a willingness to look at each person as an individual taking into consideration their ethnic background.

How supportive is your campus environment for gay, lesbian, and bisexual students of color? Most important is that the campus needs to be inclusive. Remember that as we investigate various theories of gay, lesbian, and bisexual identity development, there is another component that impacts all stages: ethnicity. Continue to keep a check on language and behavior. Are you making assumptions that all gay, lesbian, bisexual persons are of European-American heritage? In all we do it is important to remember that it is impossible to ignore race or ethnicity and that it is equally impossible to "take off" or "turn off" sexual orientation. We cannot continue ignoring multiple oppression issues. Racism must be addressed in all White support groups. Heterosexism in the Korean Student Association, in the Latino American Society, and in African-American courses as well as in women's studies must be addressed. As long as any part of us is oppressed, we are totally oppressed.

REFERENCES

Atkinson, D. R., Morten, G, & Sue, D. W. (1979). *Counseling American minorities.* Dubuque, IA: Brown.

Carballo-Dieguez, A. C. (1989) Hispanic culture, gay male culture, and AIDS: Counseling implications. *Journal of Counseling and Development, 68,* 26–30.

Cass, V. C. (1979). Homosexuality identity formation: A theoretical model. *Journal of Homosexuality, 4,* 219–235.

Chan, C. S. (1989). Issues of identity development among Asian-American lesbians and gay men. *Journal of Counseling and Development, 68,* 16–20.

Espin, O. M. (1987). Issues of identity in the psychology of Latina lesbians. In Boston Lesbians Psychologies Collective (Eds.), *Lesbian psychologies: Explorations and challenges* (pp. 35–51). Urbana, IL: University of Illinois Press.

Icard, L. (1986). Black gay men and conflicting social identities: Sexual orientation versus racial identity. In J. Gripton & M. Valentich (Eds.), [Special issue of the *Journal of Social Work and Human Sexuality, 4* (1/2)] *Social work practice in sexual problems* (pp. 83–93). New York, London: Haworth.

Loiacano, D. K. (1989). Gay identity issues among Black Americans: Racism, homophobia, and the need for validation. *Journal of Counseling and Development, 68,* 21–25.

Suro, R. (1988, January). Vatican and the AIDS fight: Amid worry, papal reticence. *New York Times,* p. A23.

Wooden, W. S., Kawasaki, H., & Mayeda, R. (1983). Lifestyles and identity maintenance among gay Japanese-American males. *Alternative Lifestyles, 5,* 236–243.

Chapter 5

ADDRESSING LESBIAN AND GAY ISSUES IN RESIDENCE HALL ENVIRONMENTS

Donna Bourassa
University of Massachusetts at Amherst

Bill Shipton
Indiana University

The current climate on college and university campuses reflects widespread negative attitudes toward lesbians and gays in every setting studied (D'Augelli, 1989b). Campus climates tend to mirror the values and patterns of acceptance that exist in the larger society. Presently, societal trends continue to include subtle and overt forms of intolerance based upon sexual orientation. Campus incidents ranging from verbal harassment to "queer-bashing" are on the rise nationwide (National Lesbian and Gay Task Force, 1988).

Several articles (Bendet, 1986; "Fight over," 1984) draw attention to the specific difficulties that gay and lesbian students who live in residence halls face:

> The social climate is chilly at best on college campuses; occasionally it is downright hostile. Where it's possible to do so, many gay students prefer to live off campus—in houses, apartments or university co-ops—since dorm life is a particular problem. "It's like living in a fishbowl," says Jane, a Texas lesbian who has lived in the dorms for 3 years because it is less expensive and more convenient than renting an apartment. "Everyone knows what everyone else is doing all the time. It's hard not to let them see that other part of me". ("Fight over," 1984, p. 10)

Other personal accounts by gay and lesbian students highlight difficulties that range from dealing with heterosexual roommates to being the target of physical violence within the residence halls ("Fight over," 1984). Bendet's (1986) report on homophobia on American campuses detailed the personal account of two gay male students living in a residence hall. Their personal story begins with an isolated incident of verbal harassment in the form of name-calling:

> But the incident would soon become more than an unprovoked insult. Over the following months, at least 20 young men in the dorm participated in a deliberate and escalating campaign of harassment. Scores of other students witnessed the abuse and did nothing either to curb it or offer support to the victims. And no one seemed to notice that anything was wrong—no one, that is, but Steve and Dennis. (Bendet, 1986, p. 32)

Accounts such as these are too familiar to today's lesbian and gay students either because they have experienced some form of harassment themselves or they live with the constant fear of being targeted. Evidence from one recent study of antigay and antilesbian reactions at a major university showed these fears to be warranted (D'Augelli, 1989a). In this study, nearly three-fourths of the lesbian or gay students surveyed reported that they had faced verbal insults directed at them, and nearly one-fourth had been threatened with physical violence. More than half reported they were occasionally afraid for their personal safety, and over one-third changed their daily routine to avoid harassment.

The impact of homophobic harassment on gay and lesbian students encompasses a broad range of responses. Bendet (1986) reported on the differing responses of the two gay male students:

> By spring, Dennis was coping with his dormmates' relentless animosity by planning a move to off-campus housing at the end of the semester. But Steve was feeling the heat. His grades began dropping. His concentration was diffused by vague depression. No matter what he tried, he just couldn't keep the climate of hostility from seeping into and corroding even the little pressures of his daily life. Maybe, he thought, he should just drop out of school. (p. 36)

Clearly, the literature reflects that homophobic attitudes, beliefs, and behaviors are pervasive inside residence hall communities. The coping strategies developed by lesbian and gay students often include not disclosing their sexual orientation. D'Augelli (1989b) found that most gay and lesbian students conceal their status. Findings indicated that 80% conceal their gay or lesbian status from roommates, 89% from other undergraduates, 65% from faculty, and 70% from job supervisors. Thus, residence halls may not only be unresponsive to the needs of gay and lesbian students, but they may also have the potential to be viewed as places where there is significant harassment if not outright danger. For this "invisible minority," residence halls may not be a viable living option unless residence hall administrators actively respond to the needs of lesbian and gay students.

This chapter provides residence hall administrators with an overview of the critical issues lesbian and gay students face in residential settings and provides suggestions for addressing these issues through a broad range of educational and programmatic interventions. The first section primarily discusses the specific developmental challenges that living in a rigid, heterosexist environment poses for lesbian and gay students, but the issues heterosexual students face are also included.

The second section focuses on strategies for adequately preparing residence hall staff to respond to the needs of gay and lesbian students. Those who work in residence halls are often the first resource persons a gay, lesbian, or bisexual resident turns to for emotional support or assistance with a difficult situation. Numerous studies, including those of Bowles (1981) and D'Augelli (1989a), document the importance of designing and implementing effective staff training programs.

The third section describes some successful educational programs that have been instituted by residence hall staff on various campuses. Programs aimed at various developmental levels and populations are identified; specific programs aimed at the majority as well as the targeted population are emphasized. In summary, the authors provide practitioners with some overall strategies for operating from a position of strength in addressing these issues on their respective campuses.

ISSUES FACING GAY AND LESBIAN STUDENTS

The issues and concerns faced by lesbian and gay students have their roots in the very rigid assumptions of heterosexuality that pervade the residence hall environment. Although the same assumptions are made in society at large, the close quarters of a residence hall, combined with young adults searching for a sexual identity, usually "turn up the volume" in a heterosexist environment.

A glance at a calendar of activities in a residence hall provides many examples of the ways we assume that all of our population is heterosexual. From dating game programs to dinner exchanges, we send a message to everyone in the community that the needs and interests of lesbian and gay students do not matter, that these people do not really exist. The sense of alienation and invisibility that results should not be hard for heterosexuals to understand. Yet it happens over and over again.

Some of the specific issues and concerns for gay and lesbian students in the residence halls are as follows:

Coming out. As has been discussed in previous chapters, the process of accepting and validating oneself as gay or lesbian is a frightening process. To come out in a rigid heterosexist residence hall setting can be absolutely terrifying. Because of the homophobia in the environment, the coming out process can be even more painfully slow and wrenching than usual. Lesbian and gay students are in for a lonely experience unless they are fortunate enough to know staff, faculty, or students who are open and trusted.

Lack of privacy. Most students complain about the lack of privacy in a residence hall setting. But for gay and lesbian students who have a "secret" that they can admit to only a few trusted friends, the privacy issue becomes even more troublesome. One of the many messages that society conveys to these students is, "If you have to be who you are, at least don't flaunt it . . . be discreet." How can persons truly celebrate who they are discreetly?

Nevertheless, discretion becomes the name of the game. Because there is so little privacy, most gay and lesbian students go to great lengths to hide who they are. As much as the gay male might like to have posters of men in his room, he either settles for no posters at all or decides to bury his feelings and puts up posters of women. The lesbian wants to have the picture of her lover on her desk but instead hides it, and herself, in the closet.

Roommates. The issue of privacy is, of course, related to having roommates. Students who have gone through most of the coming out process and are comfortable with themselves usually resolve the roommate issue by either finding a single room or finding a roommate who is not homophobic. This, however, is easier said than done. Often it is the resident assistant who is in the best position to ease or resolve roommate issues.

Lack of activities. Most lesbian and gay students feel very alone and isolated in a residence hall environment. Both formal and informal activities are designed for a heterosexual world. Most often these students must find social outlets and other lesbian and gay students outside the residence hall, if they find them at all. The result is that they usually live "on the edges" of the environment, not really feeling a part of the community.

Also, in spite of the myth, all lesbian and gay students do not know each other. For example, it is not uncommon for a student who is gay or in the process of coming out to learn years later that there was another student just down the hall dealing with the same issues and feeling the same isolation. These sad situations will continue as long as there are no activities designed to validate the lives and experiences of lesbian and gay students.

Dealing with harassment. Physical, verbal, and emotional abuse of gay and lesbian students in residental settings is common. What is not common is the reporting of these incidents (Bendet, 1986; D'Augelli, 1989a). And why should it be? How can we expect students to report these incidents to people and offices who give no indication whatsoever that they believe gays, lesbians, and bisexuals exist, let alone deserve dignity and respect? Why should lesbian and gay students trust an institution that will not include sexual orientation in its nondiscrimination statement?

It is fairly obvious that these issues and the "veil of heterosexuality" make life difficult for lesbian and gay students. What is less obvious is that heterosexual students pay a price for living in a solely heterosexist environment. Such an environment allows homophobia to flourish and feed on itself. It creates a sense of judgment and hatred that dehumanizes not only the victim but also the oppressor. It denies to heterosexual students the reality of lesbian and gay orientations, which have been with us through recorded time and will not, in spite of any effort, go away. It deprives *all* students and makes all of us a little less than who we are.

STAFF SELECTION AND TRAINING

There is no possibility of adequately responding to the issues and concerns faced by gay, lesbian, and bisexual students in the residence halls without a carefully selected professional and paraprofessional staff that has experienced a thorough and ongoing educational program. This process occurs in three parts: recruitment, selection, and training. All three parts interrelate, and any one part done well makes it more likely all steps in the cycle are effective. For example, a strong, successful training program makes recruitment easier, which results in better selections.

RECRUITMENT

A strong recruitment program seeks and attracts (1) lesbian, gay, and bisexual applicants and (2) applicants who understand the importance of celebrating diversity, including sexual orientation. Probably most important for this recruitment effort is the development for the department and/or institution of clear and specific statements of diversity that include sexual orientation as one component. An example of such a statement is the following *Housing Services: A Statement on Sexual Orientation* from the University of Massachusetts at Amherst (revised and reissued 7/82; reissued 5/89):

> The University community of students, faculty, and staff can be seen as a microcosm of the Commonwealth. As a state university, its population represents the rich diversity of the population of Massachusetts. It also shares the Commonwealth's complex task of creating an environment where people of different backgrounds and interests can interact in safe and humane ways. As an educational institution, the University is ideally suited to the task of making life in a diverse community a positive, educational experience. In order to accomplish this, the University must remain responsive and sensitive to the needs of all its members.
>
> As gay men and lesbians become more visible nationally and in the Commonwealth, more concern about homosexuality/lesbianism on campus is manifested by legislators, taxpayers, and parents of students. Gay men and lesbians have always been a part of the University community, just as they have always played a part in every aspect of national life as legislators, taxpayers, and parents of students as well as University faculty, staff, and students.
>
> The issue for the University is not that lesbians and gay men are becoming part of the community but rather that they may choose to become a much more visible and vocal part. Housing Services has long held and continues to hold the position that basic rights must and will be extended to all members of the community. Acting upon this position involves eradicating certain misconceptions as well as espousing certain assertions.

First, Housing Services asserts that a person's sexual orientation should not be a criterion in employment decisions; rather, demonstrated competence must be the major criterion.

Second, Housing Services further asserts that lesbian and homosexual students and staff are entitled to an environment which is nonoppressive. Harassment based on sexual orientation is not acceptable and will be addressed through appropriate administrative action as well as educational programming.

Third, role modeling and professional competence are not affected by sexual orientation any more than they are by any other personal characteristics such as race, sex, or handicap. The chance for students to get to know gay and lesbian staff, faculty, and students can be an important part of the educational process.

Fourth, the University community and those who are concerned with its welfare must not confuse demands for human rights with proselytizing and sexual aggression. The University has a responsibility to protect students from all forms of sexual aggression; it also has a responsibility to respond positively when members of the community request to participate fully and openly in the life of the community.

Fifth, requests that lesbians and homosexuals be recognized as complete human beings cannot be equated with advocacy that everyone should be homosexual or lesbian. The confusion of these two very different ideas often leads to an unnecessary defensiveness on the part of heterosexuals.

Housing Services' support of homosexual and lesbian students and staff reflects its belief that the University must accept and integrate the Commonwealth's diverse population into its educational community in ways that are responsible both to the University and the Commonwealth.

A second example is a *Department of Residence Life Statement on Diversity* from Indiana University—Bloomington:

The Department of Residence Life is professionally and personally committed to celebrating the rich diversity of people who live in our residence hall and family housing communities. We believe that our living environments must foster freedom of thought and opinion in the spirit of mutual respect. All of our programs, activities, and interactions are enriched by accepting each other as we are and by celebrating our uniquenesses as well as our commonalities.

The diversity of our communities takes many forms. It includes differences related to race, ethnicity, national origin, gender, sexual orientation, religion, age, and ability. We believe that any attempt to oppress any individual or group is a threat to *everyone* in the community. We are guided by the principle that celebrating diversity enriches and empowers the lives of *all* people.

Therefore, everyone who chooses to live in or visit our residential communities must understand that we will not tolerate any form of bigotry, harassment, intimidation, threat, or abuse, whether verbal or written, physical or psychological, direct or implied. Alcohol or substance abuse, ignorance, or "it was just a joke" will not be accepted as excuses. Such behavior will be dealt with appropriately through the disciplinary process.

Our residence communities are rich, alive, and dynamic environments that are designed to enable all individuals to stretch and grow to their full potential. Only by understanding and celebrating our diversities can we create an environment where innovation, individuality, and creativity are maintained. We pledge ourselves to this end.

Although there are many questions regarding the legality of enforcing standards of behavior and speech in relation to issues of diversity, this debate need not delay such statements of diversity that are designed to express the value that a department or institution places on recognizing and celebrating differences. Such statements can be prominently featured on all written documents and materials, including recruitment flyers, application forms, recommendation forms, manuals, handbooks, and evaluation forms. If properly emphasized, such statements say clearly to all potential candidates, "We will not compromise on the value we place on celebrating diversity in our residential environments." They speak particularly to gay and lesbian candidates, who may have reasons not to trust departments or institutions. Such statements may make the organization appear to be a more welcome setting for employment.

Actively recruiting lesbian and gay candidates is a uniquely challenging task. Because most choose to be invisible and are not often affiliated with specific gay and lesbian professional, political, or social organizations, one needs to hope that well-designed recruitment materials will entice applications from these candidates. And if the intent and action of the department are sincere, it is likely this will happen.

At Stanford University, for example, the Office of Residential Education explicitly encouraged RA applications from gay and lesbian students (Yuh, 1987). The purpose is to attract candidates from diverse sexual orientations who will promote openness to issues of sexuality and sexual orientation. Hiring some openly gay and lesbian students who are comfortable with themselves can go a long way toward promoting discussion and alleviating fear.

Of course, recruitment materials need to be widely distributed to gay and lesbian organizations on campus. Sending a representative from the department to speak at a meeting of one of these organizations is highly recommended. But even more important, taking the opportunity at all recruitment meetings to discuss the value of diversity, with specific mention of sexual orientation, makes it more likely that people who are homophobic will not apply.

Finally, when bringing paraprofessional or professional candidates to campus for interviews, it is important not to make the assumption that all candidates are heterosexual. For example, when providing information to candidates about campus and community organizations and activities, include information about organizations and activities designed to assist and support gay and lesbian people. Not only does this provide valuable information to gay and lesbian candidates and give them names and phone numbers to call to learn about the campus/community climate, but it also makes a statement to heterosexual candidates about departmental values and makes it more attractive to candidates who share these values.

SELECTION

Most of us can cite many examples of staff who displayed alarming homophobia in responding to incidents that occurred in a residential setting. We usually end up asking ourselves, "How did these people get hired?" The answer, of course, is that our selection process did not effectively screen out candidates who were homophobic.

One reason for this may be that the interviewers who assess the potential of candidates do not understand the importance of hiring nonhomophobic staff. If, indeed, openness and responsiveness to issues of sexual orientation are of value to the department, this must be clearly and emphatically communicated to the interviewers. Some sort of training session for interviewers, especially student interviewers, must be scheduled, and it needs to include information and training that will enable them to make judgments about attitudes of candidates with regard to issues of diversity.

Another reason for failure to screen out homophobic candidates is that our techniques are inadequate. Sometimes only one brief question is asked of the candidate regarding "attitudes toward gays and lesbians." The question is usually couched in simplistic terms that make it obvious to the candidate what the interviewers want to hear. Thus, a response along the lines of "gays and lesbians have the right to live their own lives" can be interpreted by an interviewer as a satisfactory response. But how do we know the candidate is telling the truth? And more importantly, if the candidate is speaking the truth, what does the response mean? Could it mean "gays and lesbians have the right to live their own lives, just not around me"?

Probably the best technique for understanding a candidate's attitudes about issues of diversity is to talk to the candidate for a long enough period of time to reach below the surface. The conversation needs to be free-floating in the sense that the interviewer's questions take the dialogue to deeper levels and uncover the candidate's feelings. We learn much more when we elicit responses out of a person's "guts" than we do when we elicit responses out of a person's "head." Useful questions include the following:

- Tell me about your feelings towards gays, lesbians, and bisexuals.
- But what about your *feelings*?
- How would you *feel* if your brother or sister told you he or she was gay/lesbian?
- Would you want them to tell your parents? Why? Why not?
- Where do you think homophobia comes from?
- What is the best way to deal with homophobia?
- Do you think heterosexuals pay a price for homophobia?
- Some people think that affirmative action guidelines should include sexual orientation. What do you think?
- Tell me about the fears you have in dealing with gay, lesbian, or bisexual students; in dealing with homophobia.
- How would you feel if you discovered your roommate or close friend was gay, lesbian, or bisexual?

Another technique involves a role play that can be adapted from Wesleyan University's "Coalition for Lesbian and Gay Awareness" workshop (Diffloth, 1987). The role play begins by instructing the candidate that for the next several minutes he or she is to assume the role of a gay or lesbian student. Based on his or her own life experiences, responses to some questions about being gay or lesbian must be made. The candidate is told that if he or she is gay, lesbian, or bisexual, he or she can either share real life experiences or make up things. Once the role play begins, questions such as the following can be asked:

- How does it feel being gay, lesbian, or bisexual?
- Does your roommate know?
- Do your parents know?
- Do you have a significant other?
- How do you protect your privacy?
- What do you need from your resident assistant?
- How do you deal with harassment?

At the end of the role play, the candidate is asked to report on his or her feelings. Though this technique can be risky and needs to be conducted by a skilled interviewer, it can yield a wealth of information about the candidate's attitudes.

TRAINING

There are many techniques that can be used to educate staff effectively about different sexual orientations; examples include role plays, sentence completion exercises, fact sheets, case studies, student panels, and audiovisual materials.

Prior to choosing specific techniques, it is helpful to think of the process of training on diversity issues as occurring in three phases: (1) awareness, (2) information, and (3) action. Though these phases are not necessarily separate and distinct, they are helpful in organizing an effective training program.

In choosing the content for a training program, techniques need to be selected that enable participants to answer questions in all three phases. Trainers need to avoid the common trap of focusing on the action phase before adequately dealing with the awareness and information phases.

The questions to be answered in each phase are:

1. *Awareness.* What are my attitudes, opinions, and feelings about being gay, lesbian, bisexual, and heterosexual? Where did these attitudes, opinions, and feelings originate? How did I acquire them? What is my emotional response to words like gay, lesbian, faggot, dyke, queer, heterosexual, homophobia, bisexual? Why am I sometimes fearful about discussing or thinking about these issues? How did I learn homophobia?

2. *Information.* What are the statistical data about numbers of gays, lesbians, and bisexuals? How is sexual orientation really a

continuum instead of an either/or situation? What are some of the experiences and feelings of gays, lesbians, and bisexuals on our campus? In our residence halls? What causes people to be gay, lesbian, and bisexual? What causes people to be heterosexual? What is homophobia? What is coming out?

3. *Action.*   What can I and will I do to deal with my own homophobia? How can I help others combat their homophobia? How can I be supportive of gay, lesbian, and bisexual residents? How can I help students who are coming out? What resources and referral agencies are available on campus to assist gay, lesbian, and bisexual students? How can I model nonhomophobic behavior to students? What specific programs and activities can I promote to educate residents on this topic?

Finally, there is one trap that we often fall into when dealing with issues of diversity. We think people of color should teach us about racism; women should teach us about sexism; Jews should teach us about Jewish oppression; students with disabilities should teach us about ablism; and gays, lesbians, and bisexuals should teach us about homophobia and heterosexism. Although we have much to learn from the victims of oppression, we have at least as much to learn from those who perpetuate and feed oppression, especially those of us who do so unwittingly. All people benefit if we can someday live in a world free from homophobia, heterosexism, and all other forms of oppression. Therefore, it is imperative that heterosexuals share responsibility for facilitating training programs on heterosexism.

RESIDENCE HALL PROGRAMMING

Residence hall administrators who are actively engaged in developing programming strategies to further their commitment to appreciation of differences in sexual orientation need to begin by assessing the attitudes and beliefs of their residence population. The results of such an assessment will suggest the level and types of intervention needed to enhance the environment.

Nyberg and Alston (1977) found that a majority of college students hold the belief that homosexuality is wrong and admit to disliking gays and lesbians. Goodwin and Roscoe (1988) studied student acceptance of homosexuality and found that the majority of students are highly nonaccepting (45%) and only 5% fit into the most accepting quadrant. However, these studies did not discuss whether these assessments of student attitudes are used to assist in developing programming strategies.

Similar findings were reported in a Quality of Life Survey conducted at the University of Massachusetts at Amherst in fall 1989. The survey was administered to all students living in the residence halls. One of the survey statements was "I would feel comfortable with a roommate of a different sexual orientation." Respondents checked strongly agree, agree, disagree, or strongly disagree. The return rate was 80% (approximately 8,000 residents); 71% checked either disagree or strongly disagree; 52% of those respondents were male and 43% were female.

Although the University of Massachusetts at Amherst has a long-standing history of offering many programming interventions in this area, these results suggest that the university is a long way from breaking down homophobic attitudes among students and replacing them with attitudes that allow students to be comfortable with different sexual orientations. At the least, the results indicate the need for continued priority in programming interventions dealing with sexual orientation.

Results from this study also indicated that residence hall staff need to develop multiple interventions that take into account the various developmental needs of the majority and targeted population. Student development theories stress the importance of balancing the developmental variables of challenge and support. This basic theoretical construct suggests that programs aimed at the majority population need to focus primarily on challenging members to become sensitized, aware, and willing to unlearn prejudicial attitudes and beliefs. Programs designed for lesbian, gay, and bisexual students, however, need to focus primarily on support issues and enable members to achieve a sense of pride regarding their identity.

Several developmental models are cited in the literature that can assist student development educators in determining the appropriate level and type of programming intervention needed to achieve an environment that truly embraces diversity. Hughes (1987) invited student development educators to evaluate their campuses based on developmental levels that campuses must respond to in order to achieve diversity. Her model identified six hierarchical levels: "(1) negative valuing of diversity, (2) exploring the meaning of diversity and creating learning opportunities, (3) gaining acceptance and increasing tolerance for diversity, (4) creative testing for principles of diversity, (5) positive valuing of diversity, and (6) building human community" (p. 544). Clearly, programming interventions need to coincide with the developmental level assessed as characteristic of the overall campus climate.

Body (1986) designed a developmental stage model specifically aimed at programming interventions related to gay, lesbian, and bisexual issues. Adapted from Hersey and Blanchard's Situational Leadership Model, Body's model refers to the stages as (1) anchoring and awareness, (2) educate and sensitize, (3) personalize and humanize, and (4) support. In utilizing this model, during the first stage members are introduced to the concept of sexual preference and sexual orientation as well as issues gays, lesbians, and bisexuals face; programs with films and speakers that give attention to the issues faced by gays, lesbians, and bisexuals are useful. In the second stage, the focus is on dealing with one's own homophobia; workshops and experiential opportunities that allow members to examine their own belief systems are effective.

At the third stage, the focus is on creating opportunities for gay, lesbian, and bisexual members to feel empowered and part of the community; activities at this stage include gay, lesbian, and bisexual awareness days; programs to train gays, lesbians, and bisexuals to be members of a speakers bureau; and coalition-building activities with other groups. The final stage focuses on providing continuous support and nurturance; programming possibilities include networking activities, support groups for gay, lesbian, and bisexual RAs and/or residents; and courses on gay studies in the residence halls.

Many of these program examples fit into more than one stage; there is a degree of overlap in the objectives and outcomes of each of the stages. The critical issue for residence hall programmers is ensuring that program offerings cover all developmental levels. Too often the majority of programs address only one or two stages, with the emphasis tending to be on creating awareness and providing education. Providing students with opportunities to move beyond basic awareness is essential but often overlooked (Bourassa & Cullen, 1988).

The importance of awareness and educational interventions needs to be underscored because these interventions serve as the foundation for further learning. A National Lesbian and Gay Task Force publication (1984) titled *Student Organization Packet* states:

> There are many ways to begin to educate the straight community. Many lesbian/gay groups consider their educational programs to be at the top of their priority list. Three good methods are (1) zap sessions, (2) a resource center, and (3) campus-wide events. Zap sessions can be an effective

source of gay awareness education in the classroom, the dorms, and for resident advisers' orientation workshops. (p. 4)

In essence, a zap session consists of a panel of gay, lesbian, and bisexual students who discuss their own coming out experiences and prejudices they have encountered and field questions. This publication stresses that zaps in residence halls are an excellent way of letting gay, lesbian, and bisexual first-year students know that there is an organization out there for them. Gay, lesbian, and bisexual student organizations that provide a speaker's bureau have been instituted on many campuses. An essential ingredient for ensuring the program's success is adequate training for the speakers. Training usually consists of rehearsing, anticipating and role playing possible questions, and working through one's own internalized homophobia.

In sponsoring these sessions, residence hall staff need to be sensitive to the limitations of relying on members of this group to be solely responsible for educating others. First, it is emotionally demanding for gays, lesbians, and bisexuals to tell their stories. Second, panelists speak from their own personal experiences; they do not speak for all gays, lesbians, and bisexuals. Therefore, they cannot do justice to the breadth of diversity that exists within each cultural subgroup. Finally, such sessions create the risk of heterosexuals believing that they can only learn about these issues through direct contact with gays, lesbians, and bisexuals. Thus, although these sessions are extremely valuable, they should be used with caution and preferably in conjunction with other programs.

In describing the need for a resource center, the National Lesbian and Gay Task Force (1984) stated that such a center "is not only important to the straight student body, but [it is] also a way for gay students to learn more (probably than they thought they could) about their 'heritage' " (p. 4). Ideally, space needs to be allocated within the residence halls for such a center to exist. In addition to providing a functional area where programs and events can be held, the space can also function as a safe place for students to network informally, build community, and provide each other with support. At the University of Massachusetts at Amherst, the Program for Gay, Lesbian, and Bisexual Concerns is located in a residence hall; the space contains a resource library for student and staff use.

Sponsorship of campus-wide educational programs and cultural activities is a way for the entire community to demonstrate its commitment to increasing understanding on campus and fostering appreciation of gay, lesbian, and bisexual culture. It is important that residence hall staff attend such events to serve as role models and to demonstrate their support. In addition to providing programs specifically on gay, lesbian, and bisexual issues, it is essential that all campus-sponsored events are screened for sensitivity to these issues. For example, if a campus invites a comedian or comedienne to perform, staff need to check to insure that the program content does not include humor derogatory toward gays, lesbians, and bisexuals. In sponsoring film series, staff need to be certain that films depicting gays, lesbians, or bisexuals do not reinforce stereotypes.

SUMMARY

Professional and paraprofessional staff in residence halls have a unique opportunity to sensitize and educate residents about issues related to sexual orientation. Staff have an obligation to prepare students to live in the "real world," a world that includes people along the entire continuum of sexuality.

To summarize and reiterate:

1. Staff must constantly remind themselves not to assume that all students and staff are heterosexual. Staff must be mindful of those cues in the environment that might perpetuate this veil of heterosexuality. As a small example, take a look at the residence life office. Can someone assume from looking at the books on the shelves, the posters on the walls, and the magazines on the table that this is a place where gay, lesbian, and bisexual students and staff are welcome? And when social activities are planned, are people invited in a way that allows gays, lesbians, and bisexuals to feel comfortable bringing a same-gender guest or partner?

2. It is important to provide programs and activities that appeal to the gay, lesbian, and bisexual population. In addition, institutions have an obligation to plan educational interventions that help residents understand the price that everyone pays for homophobia and heterosexism.

3. Residence life departments must understand that gay, lesbian, and bisexual students have some special needs for privacy. If there were no homophobia in the world, this would not be necessary. But homophobia is very much alive, and institutions need to be mindful of it as they look at issues related to roommates and room assignments.

4. Institutions and departments need to develop and promote statements of diversity that include sexual orientation.

5. Institutions need to develop mechanisms to respond effectively to incidents of harassment. This means that staff are trained and willing to confront such incidents, and that there is a panel or group that investigates the incidents and recommends appropriate responses.

6. Issues related to sexual orientation need to be considered when recruiting, hiring, and training staff. This may mean some significant changes in all three areas, but the payoffs are enormous for everyone.

Creating new awareness and encouraging new behaviors are never easy. It takes time, perseverance, and courage. But staff owe it to themselves and their students to recognize and celebrate the spectrum of sexual orientation. To fail in this endeavor means that all students have been denied an opportunity to learn the skills necccessary to live and work in diverse communities.

REFERENCES

Bendet, P. (1986, August–September). Hostile eyes: A report on homophobia on American campuses. *Campus Voice*, pp. 30–37.

Body, J. (1986, March). *The healthy community.* Workshop presented at the Northeast Lesbian and Gay Student Union Conference, Brown University, RI.

Bourassa, D. M., & Cullen, M. (1988, May). Programming: Bringing gay, lesbian, and bisexual issues to the forefront. *National Association for Campus Activities Profile Newsletter*, pp. 1–5.

Bowles, J. K. (1981). Dealing with homosexuality: A survey of staff training needs. *Journal of College Student Personnel, 22,* 276–277.

D'Augelli, A. R. (1989a). Homophobia in a university community: Views of prospective resident assistants. *Journal of College Student Development, 30,* 546–552.

D'Augelli, A. R. (1989b). Lesbians' and gay men's experiences of discrimination and harassment in a university community. *American Journal of Community Psychology, 17,* 317–321.

Diffloth, N. (1987). *Workshops on homophobia and homosexuality for college campuses.* New York: National Lesbian and Gay Resource Center.

The fight over gay rights. (1984, May). *Newsweek on Campus,* pp. 4–10.

Goodwin, M., & Roscoe, B. (1988). AIDS: Student knowledge and attitudes at a midwestern university. *Journal of American College Health, 36,* 214–222.

Hughes, M. S. (1987). Black students' participation in higher education. *Journal of College Student Personnel, 28,* 532–545.

National Lesbian and Gay Task Force. (1988). *Antigay violence, victimization, and defamation in 1988.* Unpublished manuscript.

National Lesbian and Gay Task Force. (1984). *Student organization packet.* Washington, DC: National Lesbian and Gay Clearinghouse.

Nyberg, K., & Alston, J. (1977). Homosexual labeling by university youth. *Adolescence, 12*, 541–546.

Yuh, M. (1987, Spring). Res Ed urges gays to be RAs. *The Stanford Daily* [Stanford University, CA].

Chapter 6

ADDRESSING GAY, LESBIAN, AND BISEXUAL ISSUES IN FRATERNITIES AND SORORITIES

Michael J. Hughes
California State University—Northridge

Social fraternities (both men's and women's) claim as one of the benefits of membership intimate interpersonal relationships within the chapter. In most instances on today's campuses, these relationships develop in single-sex organizations. The social fraternity is one of the few remaining opportunities for gender-specific group identification on the campus outside of participation on an athletic team. Fraternities, as mutually selective student organizations, provide opportunities for both nonmembers and members to become acquainted and to evaluate each other in terms of "mutual attractiveness" as a basis for establishing a long-term commitment to the desired intimate relationships.

This process, known as rush, bears a striking resemblance to our cultural concept of dating. Nonmembers are "courted" to come to parties and other events at which the members set up elaborate ways to display their best image. Nonmembers similarly act in ways that they hope will make themselves appear attractive and likable to the members. Fraternity members evaluate the rushees and invite those whom they like back for another look. Rushees likewise make the same judgments in deciding whether or not to accept an offer for a second encounter. This process continues until a "bid" or offer of membership is made by the fraternity and accepted by the nonmember. At this point, it might be said that the two parties are "going steady." This process involves the students in many interesting and complex issues.

The issues in seeking out desirable single-sex groups become even more complex and confusing when the process interweaves with the personal dynamics of young lesbian, gay, or bisexual students in the early stages of sexual identity exploration, especially in terms of same-sex attractiveness. This chapter focuses on the special issues affecting students who choose to participate in the Greek-letter community. Gay, lesbian, or bisexual students in this community may experience not only the cohesiveness and intimacy of fraternal organizations but also increased alienation and frustration in their attempts to manage perceived conflicts between personal and group values.

ISSUES FACED BY THE INDIVIDUAL

Although there are many personal challenges and obstacles that must be faced by all gay, lesbian, and bisexual students, those who choose to join a fraternity may be exposed to additional pressures. For most students, participation in rush and membership education processes in fraternities takes place early in their collegiate career, with most joining these groups during their freshman year. At this point in their personal development, according to at least one theorist, the students are working to achieve competence, manage emotions, and become autonomous (Chickering, 1969). These three developmental vectors are all precursors to the ability of the student to establish identity, including sexual identity. Kohlberg (1981) stated that most entering college students are at the Conventional Level of cognitive/moral development, that is, at the stage in which adhering to mutual interpersonal expectations and conforming are preeminent. Doing the right thing is defined in terms of playing a "nice role" and following rules to maintain the group and the group system. Given these developmental constructs, one can hypothesize that the majority of students entering into the Greek-letter system are doing so because of the close interpersonal relationships and bonding that are offered.

For the student who is also beginning to explore feelings and thoughts of sexual identity, especially in terms of same-sex relationships, the task of conforming to the norms for the good of the group can be both confusing and threatening. As the student explores a sexual orientation that is not considered the norm within the campus environment, the student may feel like a renegade, may feel quite isolated. In a study of psychological adjustment, Miranda and Storms (1989) determined that positive lesbian and gay identification is related to effective self-labeling and self-disclosure. At Cass' (1979) second stage of homosexual identity development, Identity Comparison, the student is involved in the process of acknowledging and accepting the social alienation that arises because of feeling different and separated from the peer group. For the lesbian, gay, or bisexual student in a Greek-letter organization, this perceived alienation may be intensified because the student has expended much time and energy to become a member of the fraternity. In labeling or disclosing his or her feelings, the gay, lesbian, or bisexual student is breaking the rules of the common order. The student thereby suppresses this personal development with more energy than might normally be exerted.

In working with fraternities and sororities, the author has noted that many chapter activities, especially social events and the informal discussions that are part of the "bonds" of fraternity membership, are distinctly heterosexual. These activities put a great deal of pressure on the gay, lesbian, or bisexual member to deny personal experience and conform to the group norm. Discussions become a continuing arena for deception rather than an opportunity for exploring diversity. Additionally, when alternative lifestyles are brought up, it is usually in a negative and hurtful manner. This may further alienate the member from the fraternal group. In fact, many students report that they feel a need to compensate and express an overtly heterosexual orientation in order to feel secure within the chapter.

Regular fraternity-sorority social events generally focus on meeting someone of the opposite gender for a continued dating relationship. This focus is obviously inappropriate for the gay, lesbian, or bisexual member. Chapter programming, therefore, does not meet the needs of all chapter members and again positions the gay or lesbian member into a role of deceit and deception. Rather than teaching appropriate skills and coping methods for dealing with a multifaceted world, these situations encourage students to withdraw further into themselves and to repress personal values, traits, and characteristics.

Fraternity housing may also prove to be limiting for the gay, lesbian, or bisexual member. Although it may be acceptable for a member to have an opposite-gender boyfriend or girlfriend spend the night in the chapter house, this practice is not normally acceptable within a same-gender relationship. This differentiation sends a strong signal to the member that his or her relationship is not valued and is likely to be condemned within the chapter. Further, this prohibition blocks the opportunity for the member to experience and practice relationship behaviors that are an important part of the process of developing mature interpersonal relationships.

ISSUES FACED BY THE CHAPTER

The issues that are faced by the individual gay, lesbian, or bisexual student within a fraternity may also prove to be troublesome for the entire fraternal organization. For many chapters, the concern comes down to a matter of group survival in the competitive arena of attracting new members. Is it possible to uphold the oath to "be my brother's/sister's keeper" and let the needs of the individual come before the needs of the group? After all, fraternity is based on close interpersonal relationships, and most chapter functions operate on the basis of increasing the level of intimacy within these relationships. On the one hand rituals speak of valuing others, of high ideals, and of respect for one's fellow human beings. On the other hand, there is the reality that others on campus have not undertaken these oaths of commitment to the group and individuals within the group. The prejudice and intolerance that is normally expressed toward the individual lesbian, gay, or bisexual student may be transferred to the group. Hurtful stereotypes and labels may also be applied to the fraternity, often just to gain a competitive edge for acquiring new members or status within the Greek-letter community. The fraternity may lose its ability to function effectively. For example, at a large western campus false rumors about being a "gay house" recently caused a fraternity's membership to drop from 60 to 3 in 4 years ("Fraternities lose," 1990). The decision for the fraternity members comes down to supporting the individual or supporting their fraternity's self-survival.

Other scenarios may take place within the chapter that can be equally troublesome for the members and for the ongoing survival of the chapter. For example, in a recent incident at a large eastern university, a fraternity man discussed his homosexuality with officers of the chapter. When the officers brought this issue before the full chapter, they received mixed reactions. Many members of the chapter said "Hey, this is great! We are becoming more diversified and our brotherhood is strong enough that someone trusted us enough to reveal this very personal part of his life." Other chapter members, however, were appalled and declared that they could not "relate to this person anymore at all. He should not be considered a brother" (A. M. Herman, personal communication, April 12, 1989).

The strong emotional reactions in such incidents cause great stress within an organization and create situations that student leaders are often not trained to handle. Additionally, alumni sentiments often reflect the diversity of opinions in the undergraduate chapter. Such internal conflicts harm the chapter as factions form, as communication patterns within the chapter change, and as members decide that they can no longer support or belong to an organization that takes a stand that is strongly opposed to their own on such a highly controversial and emotional issue. Conversely, such internal conflicts can be used to ensure a healthy environment within the chapter when the undergraduate students become engaged with the issues, participate in an insightful developmental process, and resolve their concerns. It is up to fraternal affairs professionals and the (inter)national fraternity to seize upon this kind of opportunity for an educational intervention.

In some cases, the chapter opens itself to the same type of harassment that many individuals experience once they come out of the closet. The fraternity chapter with an openly gay, lesbian, or bisexual member is often subject to vandalism: pink triangles or hurtful graffiti painted on the house or other property is not uncommon. Individual fraternity members who are supportive of a gay, lesbian, or bisexual brother or sister may be subjected to harassment and physical and psychological violence. Other Greek chapters often cease programming and interacting with the fraternity in order to avoid "guilt by association." Individual fraternity members may lose friends and acquaintances and experience an isolation similar to that so often experienced by the gay, lesbian, and bisexual student. All of this pressures the undergraduate fraternity members to avoid the conflicts, produced by campus intolerance and ignorance, that may result from their fraternity having an openly gay, lesbian, or bisexual member.

Although there is no substantial evidence to indicate cause and effect, it may be that it is this fear of being labeled a gay chapter that may prompt fraternity chapters to participate readily in homophobic acts. Numerous national reports describe fraternity groups harassing gay student organizations, ridiculing gay programming taking place on campus, and openly threatening gay students. Two incidents at a large eastern university clearly illustrate this point: In the first, two gay men who were to speak at a fraternity observed a car outside the house with the words "Kill Queers" painted on the fender. In the second, a bus outside a fraternity house was painted with the slogan "Drink Beer, Kill Queers" ("In the news," 1988). There is rarely a formal relationship between governing organizations (Interfraternity Council, Panhellenic Council, Black Greek Council) and groups that represent gay, lesbian, and bisexual students, although the Greek groups are likely to have formal relationships with other campus centers for issues of diversity. Coprogramming with the Gay Student Union may generally be limited to instances that are mandated through a judicial process.

PROBLEMS OF MULTIPLE COMMUNITY MEMBERSHIP

For some gay, lesbian, and bisexual students the decision to join a fraternal organization is complicated further by their membership in other communities on the college or university campus, whether these be ethnic student communities, disabled student communities, or other communities based upon socioeconomic status, age, or religiosity. Within each of these communities, there is a series of protocols for interpersonal relationships that a student must accept and conform to in order to be successful within that community. For the student who chooses to belong to several different communities, there are many additional pressures to change and conform to the norms of those communities. Developmentally, this situation is difficult and potentially harmful for the younger student who may feel that he or she must wear many masks rather than be accepted as one consistent and integrated person. This may be especially painful for gay, lesbian, and bisexual students who are struggling to remove their sexual orientation masks and come out of the closet.

Further, in many African-American, Latino, and other ethnic communities, religious and other influences continue to play an important role in condemning homosexuality. Some historically ethnic fraternal organizations (as well as many historically Caucasian groups) place a greater emphasis on heterosexuality in member recruitment and retention programs, chapter activities, and interaction with the larger community. Students may feel intimidated and afraid of being isolated from both their ethnic and fraternal communities.

These students also are hindered by the lack of role models within their communities who share their joint memberships. They may have a role model within each separate community but have difficulty finding support for facing the type of combined racist and homophobic ostracism and prejudice that they may be perceiving and experiencing. In fact, a role model in one community may even be involved in defamation of the student's other community. This situation puts the student in a position of hiding community membership, normally his or her sexual orientation and/or fraternal affiliation. This is unhealthy for the positive development of the student. Additionally, this problem eliminates the element of trust and honesty that should be the cornerstone of any and every mentoring and role modeling relationship.

EXTERNAL PRESSURES

Fraternities are unique student organizations in that there are many external constituent groups that have a strong interest in, and often a strong influence on, the undergraduate chapter. Key among these groups are the alumni. These older members of the chapter frequently help to maintain traditions and history. Further, alumni generally act as leadership role models for chapter officers and assist in problem resolution. Although this involvement is generally viewed as positive, there are instances in which alumni involvement can be troublesome.

For many alumni, such contemporary issues as diversity and tolerance were not part of their undergraduate experience. For these alumni, their first opportunity to work with an openly gay, lesbian, or bisexual person may be in response to a student in the undergraduate chapter, either through an openly gay, lesbian, or bisexual student participating in rush or when an officer or member reveals his or her sexual identity. The alumni is put in the position of responding to his or her own personal biases and prejudices concerning homosexuality for the first time, in a very public forum, in front of the fraternity. This is not the best way to learn about and challenge one's own beliefs; thus the resolution is often awkward and at times may be hostile.

Additionally, many fraternity houses are owned or controlled by alumni housing corporations. If alumni have not been educated about current social issues, practices and policies may be put in place that do not reflect tolerance and sensitivity. Some alumni housing board members may respond to an openly gay, lesbian, or bisexual fraternity member by suggesting that a housing contract be revoked or not issued because of their concerns about that member living in close proximity to other students. This action may not be in accordance with local or school regulations and laws, but it may be implemented within the rules of the private housing corporation anyway because of the ignorance and fear associated with homophobia.

In the same manner, parents may raise concerns about an openly gay, lesbian, or bisexual fraternity member, especially in the case of a housed organization. Issues may be raised before the fraternity, both locally and nationally; before the school administration; and sometimes before the community in which the fraternity is located. Thus because of some parents' homophobic prejudices and intolerance, the individual student involved in the situation, the fraternity as an organization, and possibly the host campus may be harmed. This effect may be greater at religiously affiliated colleges and universities, both in terms of parent pressure and pressure from the institution.

It should be noted that this type of attention brought upon a fraternity by an outside constituency may also provide the impetus for that outside agency and others to become engaged in a review of policies and practices related to gay, lesbian, and bisexual persons. Local and campus housing ordinances and rules may be changed to ban discrimination based upon sexual orientation or to accommodate same-sex partners, as was implemented by Stanford University in the fall of 1990. Campus policies ought to be reviewed and amended to include sexual orientation as a form of discrimination. Local media attention may provide youth with accurate information (and potential role models) about positive and healthy gay, lesbian, and bisexual persons and lifestyles. Members of the local community may be challenged to face their own bigotry concerning sexual orientation so that personal growth and tolerance is heightened.

INTERNATIONAL FRATERNITIES AND SORORITIES[1]

In the winter of 1990, a Survey of Responses to Homophobic Issues in Fraternities, a questionnaire designed by the author, was sent to all National Interfraternity Conference, National Pan Hellenic Council, and National Panhellenic Conference fraternity executive directors and a randomized sample of respective (inter)national presidents to "describe more accurately the current situations and interventions that exist regarding our gay/lesbian/bisexual fraternity members." The response rate was particularly low (16%). Researchers have come to expect approximately a 33% response rate to the single administration of a questionnaire (Campbell & Stanley, 1963). The response rate was far lower for this survey, but those officers

---

[1]The research survey and focus-group interviews described in this section were conducted through the assistance of Stanford University, where the author served as fraternal affairs adviser.

who responded provided some insightful information for consideration.

Very few fraternities responded to the question in which they were asked to report any "situations in which you have been asked for guidance or asked to intervene." Some groups reported that guidance had been sought from a chapter officer or undergraduate student once a member decided to come out of the closet. In some cases the guidance requested was "Can we expel this member?" Generally the assistance sought was in terms of continuing to support the individual while at the same time protecting the reputation of the fraternity. In these cases, the contact with the general fraternity was usually a result of a previously existing personal contact with a staff member or officer of the general fraternity and an undergraduate student.

Many officers reported that they had not been involved with the general fraternity and that they had perceived hesitancy on the part of the undergraduates to involve the general fraternity. One executive director stated that there is "a fear that the national fraternity will close the chapter because it could have a reputation for being a gay fraternity. [There is] a definite reluctance to do anything except handle the issue internally." Another officer reiterated this point: "I am also a realist and do believe that collegiate members have the ability to keep what they perceive as controversial quiet." Others felt that there is often a lack of understanding and communication between the undergraduates and the general fraternity. In this case, the students just do not consider the fraternity, which is at a distant location, to be a resource for this type of issue.

Several officers spoke about the membership selection and education process of fraternal organizations and attributed the lack of incidents within their organizations to these factors. As one president reflected, "We market the team approach in rush, which indirectly benefits all individuals in a very positive way but clearly implies that sometimes the desires and needs of each individual must be subjugated for the good of the group." In a campus or community environment that has not addressed the issues of homophobia in a positive manner, "the good of the group" may indicate secrecy about sexual orientation by either the individual or the group.

When asked to "describe the issues and concerns that are important factors for your general fraternity when involved in a situation like this," the respondents overwhelmingly prioritized "the rights of the individual paramount to any other consideration," and that "the individual is treated with dignity and fairness." There was general agreement that the student's sexual orientation is not the issue but rather the extent to which the student's behaviors become disruptive to or constitute violations of chapter standards. Further, it was felt that the individual student needs to accept some responsibility for being sensitive to the controversial nature of sexual orientation and "to respect others' lifestyles just as she (he) would expect the same in return." There was a strong sentiment that it is important to ensure that the student continue to feel comfortable within the organization.

The interests of the chapter, especially in terms of image and campus reputation, were often also cited as important considerations. Officers believed that this goal is best accomplished by "assurance that the best professional processing of the information be made to the chapter members," and by "all concerned being processed into a position of measuring the situation against the chapter's perception of the meaning of brotherhood." Other respondents felt that this can be achieved through "educational support and resources for the chapter's acceptance of diversity" and "avoid[ing] stereotypes." Interestingly, no one considered addressing issues external to the group. Rather, there was a feeling of empowering the student members to accept and appreciate the diversity within the chapter.

During the 1989 Association of Fraternity Advisers/National Interfraternity Conference Annual Meeting in Dearborn, MI, the author conducted a focus group discussion with several (inter)national fraternity presidents, professional fraternity staff members, and Greek advisers. Group members reported, with regret, that the response of the fraternity is usually to act to "save the chapter" once the fraternity is contacted for intervention. As it was described, the general fraternity is often contacted only after the campus situation has gone to the point of the chapter being stigmatized because of a gay member. In most instances, chapter members respond in a relatively positive and supportive manner to the member's revelation of sexual orientation. The campus community, however, responds in a manner that harasses, isolates, and traumatizes the chapter, to a point where it has difficulty in operating. Because of the resources that the general fraternity has invested in the chapter, including history on the campus and alumni involvement, the fraternity normally responds in a way that will protect the ongoing interest of the organization, sometimes at the expense of an individual member. Although regret in taking this position was expressed, members of the group felt that this is the prudent immediate decision for the fraternity. Concern was expressed that it is necessary for both the (inter)national fraternity and the local chapter to take the time and effort to attempt to address the individuals in these situations, but that the business needs of the organization are the first priority.

As previously mentioned, undergraduate chapters rarely contact the general fraternity concerning issues of homophobia. The members of the focus group reiterated this point, explaining further that contact is usually initiated only at the point when there is a crisis on the campus. There was a sincere desire on the part of these leaders to be able to intervene with the chapter before the chapter is being adversely affected. They believed that if notification of the incident occurs during the early stages of the conflict, the general fraternity can respond, along with the campus administration, and provide educational resources in a manner that serves the developmental needs of the chapter members and of the fraternal community. This was their preferred resolution.

Although no one has developed programs or interventions to deal specifically with the issues of sexual orientation within the Greek-letter community, several fraternities cited examples of programs to deal with diversity and tolerance and of programs to deal with gender and personal self-esteem issues. There was strong agreement that these issues need to be addressed more fully in the future, and there was a definite desire for programs that do so.

It is important to remind the reader that the number of responses to the questionnaire was very low. The author appreciated the candid feedback and responses received from a number of fraternities. No follow-up was conducted to increase the return rate from the survey or to determine reasons for noncompliance with the survey administration. It may be assumed that fraternity executives and officers (who are generally alumni volunteers) are already overwhelmed with paperwork and surveys concerning their organizations and practices. It may also be assumed that nonrespondents have not been asked to address these issues within their organizations so therefore felt they have no basis for answering the questions. However, the high level of no responses may also indicate a prevailing level of homophobia within some (inter)national fraternal organizations. Some leaders may still see avoidance as the best policy for dealing with these threatening issues. More research will prove insightful as all student organizations begin to deal further with issues of gay, lesbian, and bisexual members and alumni.

EXERCISES TO EXPLORE ISSUES OF HOMOSEXUALITY

This section contains three examples of the types of structured group exercises that may be utilized with fraternal groups in exploring the issues of diversity and homosexuality. The author has used these exercises with great success in both small, single organization programs as well as in larger mixed-group and mixed-gender settings. Additionally, these exercises have been presented to other fraternal affairs advisers who have reported utilizing them with success, especially in small group settings.

RUSH RECOMMENDATIONS

The exercise "Rush Recommendations," a rank order exercise that can be utilized with younger students or those students who are just beginning to explore issues of diversity and differences, allows each student to examine his or her value system as it relates to personal differences. In coming together with the larger group, the student is afforded the opportunity to hear and examine various points of view. In this manner, personal schemas are challenged and openness to diversity is initiated. Group discussions in smaller, more personal and intimate settings are likely to follow this exercise. This exercise introduces the subject, establishes a forum for discussion, illustrates divergent thoughts and feelings, and sets up a milieu that makes it safe for students to continue to explore these issues on a personal basis.

Exercise 1: Rush Recommendations

Goals

1. To allow students the opportunity to examine issues of diversity and experience how one's own biases affect decision making
2. To allow students to experience divergent thoughts and values related to issues of diversity
3. To challenge value systems and beliefs.

Group Size: Unlimited. Individual groups should be no larger than 8 to 10 participants.

Time Required: Approximately 1 hour and 15 minutes.

Materials:

1. One copy of the Rush Recommendations Questionnaire for each participant.
2. Pen or pencil for each participant.

Physical Setting: Room large enough for comfort of participants formed in small groups.

Process:

1. Without prior discussion, the facilitator asks participants to fill out the Rush Recommendations Questionnaire on an individual basis.
2. Once all participants have completed the questionnaire, groups are instructed to select five rushees, by consensus, that should receive bids from the fraternity.
3. After all groups have completed the task, or after 45 minutes, the facilitator stops the exercise. Each group should be asked to report to the larger group which rushees were going to be offered bids.

Process Questions:

1. Why were certain rushees selected by all groups or by a majority of groups?
2. Were there any rushees that were quickly eliminated from consideration? Why?
3. Who were the most controversial rushees? Why? What does this say about the way that we judge people?
4. What issues came out in your group decision making that were controversial? Where was there a strong disagreement of opinion? What happened when this disagreement occurred?

Variations:

1. Sorority rushees may be used instead of fraternity rushees for predominantly women's groups.

Rush Recommendations Questionnaire

You have been elected to the Chapter Rush Committee. One of the responsibilities of the committee is to make recommendations to the chapter regarding men that should receive bids. The IFC on campus has established a rush quota so that each chapter can have an equitable rush. The committee can therefore only recommend five (5) rushees.

Individually rank the men that you would like to see receive a bid, with "1" being your highest preference. Then, as a group, prepare your rush report by rank ordering the rushees from highest to lowest in preference.

Your Ranking	Group Ranking	
_____	_____	Mark—Sophomore Pre-Med major. 3.7 GPA. Has been involved in the Gay Student Union and states, when confronted, that he is homosexual. Strong leader, well respected, very outgoing.
_____	_____	Steve—Freshman Business major. 2.9 GPA. Seems to be a nice guy but is very shy and quiet. Appears to be very interested in the chapter.

———— ————   Dave—Freshman Engineering major. 3.2 GPA. Very dynamic and energetic. Worried about the financial commitment as he is from a single-parent lower income home and is going to school on a full scholarship.

———— ————   Tony—Sophomore Public Administration major. 3.0 GPA. Is very interested in the chapter. Worked for 4 years before returning to college. Has been married.

———— ————   Lance—Freshman Psychology major. 3.0 GPA. Is the only Black (or Latino, Chicano, Asian) rushee that has rushed your chapter. Has made several friends and seems likable.

———— ————   Eric—Junior Pre-Law major. 3.7 GPA. Has been active in several campus organizations including Student Government, Intramurals Council, and the Fellowship of Christian Athletes. A real "politician."

———— ————   Tim—Freshman Performing Arts major. 3.3 GPA. A very likable man. Appears effeminate in his actions. Wants to be very involved with the chapter.

———— ————   Joel—Freshman Accounting Major. 2.5 GPA. Has been to every rush party. Only seems to be interested in the fraternity as a place to party and socialize. Talks a lot about drinking and has shown up at two rush functions slightly intoxicated. A legacy.

———— ————   Doug—Sophomore Political Science major. 3.4 GPA. Very humorous, outgoing, and fun. Was in a car accident several years ago and is now a parapalegic confined to a wheelchair.

———— ————   Gary—Junior Phys. Ed. major. 2.6 GPA. A "BMOC." Definite "looks man," seems to know everyone on campus including "all the pretty· 'girls'," cheerleading captain. Seems to be fairly interested in the chapter. Has a "major attitude" about being a "BMOC."

DESENSITIZATION

"Desensitization" is an exercise that helps students look at the ways that labels and/or stereotypes are used to repress others, especially lesbian, gay, and bisexual students. In brainstorming the many stereotypes, terms, and images that are commonly associated with lesbian, gay, and bisexuals, students may more fully realize the limited nature of their perceptions of these issues as well as the ways that oppression is expressed on the campus. Once this awareness has been created, students have the opportunity to accept personal responsibility for challenging the larger community, and each other, on these labels.

Exercise 2: Desensitization

Goals:

1. To build commonality, trust, risk-taking, openness
2. To learn to be nonjudgmental
3. To examine the way stereotypes and labels limit our potential for interaction with others.

Group Size: Unlimited.

Time Required: Approximately 45 minutes

Materials: Newsprint to record responses.

Physical Setting: Room large enough for comfort of participants. Circle or theatre seating.

Process:

1. Participants are asked to brainstorm as many stereotypes, terms, or images as possible about homosexuality and gay, lesbian, and bisexual students. These are recorded on the newsprint.
2. After no more responses can be solicited, the facilitator processes the list with the participants.

Process Questions:

1. Are all or a majority of the stereotypes typically associated with gay men rather than including lesbians? Bisexuals? Why?
2. Are all of the images negative/hateful images rather than including items like long-term lovers, oppressed, living in fear, isolation? Why?
3. Are all of the images of White persons rather than of other ethnic backgrounds? Why? What new images come to mind when you think of ethnicity or religiosity?
4. How do you allow these images to limit your interactions or openness to others? How might this awareness be used to improve yourself? Or support friends and colleagues?

WITHIN THE CHAPTER

The exercise "Within the Chapter" can be used within a leaders' meeting or within a chapter setting with more mature members of the group to discuss the particular issues and parameters of homophobia. In asking the group members to reach a consensus about group action, each member is encouraged to explore his or her own value system, relate these values to those of the other members of the group, put all of these convergent influences into the dynamics of an organization and a larger societal and cultural norm, and then commit to some appropriate response. Members are not only engaged in self-reflection but are also forced to look at the interconnectedness of interpersonal and intergroup mores.

Exercise 3: Within the Chapter

Goals:

1. To allow students to examine the issues of homophobia as they are related to chapter operations and interpersonal relationships
2. To allow students to examine the interconnectedness of interpersonal and intergroup mores.

Group Size: The exercise works well with small, intimate groups, usually no larger than 30 persons.

Time Required: Approximately 1 hour.

Materials: A copy of the story "Within the Chapter" for the facilitator.

Physical Setting: Comfortable setting with seats for each participant. Circle seating or relaxed "living-room" environment works best.

Process:

1. The facilitator explains to the group that they are going to be presented with a chapter management concern. They are to listen to the story and focus on their own response and values.
2. The facilitator reads the story "Within the Chapter" aloud to the group.
3. Following the story and a short pause for the participants to think about their response, the facilitator processes the exercise.

Discussion Questions:

1. How should the chapter respond to this incident? What are the real issues? What are the chapter concerns? What are the different constituencies that are involved that complicate this issue? What is the

role of each person in handling this incident? What do you want to see happen?
2. What are the internal versus external issues? Are they different or the same? What are the differences?
3. What differences exist for you between the physical and the emotional relationships in this situation? Is sexual identity limited to sexual behavior or are there other dimensions to be considered?
4. What resources are available to assist you with this situation—the institution, your advisers, the national fraternity?
5. How does this situation make you feel? What are your personal issues/values in dealing with this situation? What can you do to address these concerns?
6. Does the situation change if Chuck and/or Jeff are younger brothers in the chapter? Not officers? Not well known? Associates/pledges? What if a brother had walked into this situation instead of the sorority dates?
7. Does the situation change if the scenario involves two sorority sisters? In what ways? Why?

Within the Chapter: The Story

The chapter is holding its annual spring formal. As is tradition, the chapter has gone away for the weekend festivities and each brother has rented a hotel room. Soon after the banquet on Saturday evening, the chapter vice president and his best friend in the chapter excuse themselves from their dates explaining that they want to run back to the room, go to the bathroom, have a couple of "brotherly shots," and just generally freshen up. Both dates have sorority sisters who they want to talk to and also know almost everyone in the chapter so they feel very comfortable remaining at the dance while the men are away "for a couple of minutes."

Chuck, the chapter vice president, is a senior and has been voted Outstanding Brother by the chapter. He is friendly, outgoing, considerate, really works hard to help build the chapter, always takes time to talk to brothers or help them out with problems, always volunteers to work on special committees or projects, and plays on almost every IM team. He is well respected within the Greek system, is the current IFC president, and is well liked by several administrators and faculty members. Chuck is a "looks man" and is considered a real "catch" by a lot of women.

Jeff, the other brother, is a junior and has been following in Chuck's footsteps. Everyone is expecting him to be elected into a high position, either in the chapter or in IFC, during spring elections. He is very personable and outgoing, warm and considerate, and a real comedian.

Chuck and Jeff go to Chuck's room and are gone for quite some time. Their dates become impatient and want to dance so they decide to go to the room to break up the party that they know is going on upstairs.

Chuck's date has a key to the room, and upon entering, the two women find Chuck and Jeff lying on the bed, having oral sex. When confronted by the women, Chuck and Jeff admit that they have had a relationship with each other for "some time."

RESOURCES

Several professional associations provide additional resources concerning these issues. Although no organization has formalized a relationship between gay, lesbian, and bisexual issues and fraternities, the following associations have sections that respond to issues within each of these constituencies. As a general rule these organizations are quite willing to share information and assistance.

- The *American College Personnel Association* has a Greek Affairs Task Force located within the the jurisdiction of Commission IV: Students, Their Activities, and Their Communities. Additionally, the Standing Committee on Gay, Lesbian, and Bisexual Concerns can address particular issues and trends within that community. ACPA publishes the *Journal of College Student Development*, a research journal that periodically addresses issues of fraternity membership or sexual orientation. ACPA can be contacted through the American Association of Counseling and Development, 5999 Stevenson Avenue, Alexandria, VA 22304. Telephone: 703-823-9800. The AACD also publishes a counseling journal, the *Journal of Counseling and Development*, which occasionally addresses issues of sexual orientation and identity.
- The *Association of Fraternity Advisers (AFA)* addresses issues of student development within the fraternal co-curriculum. Various resources are available including consultation, program suggestions, reports and monographs from committees, and the Association's journal, *The Fraternity Newsletter*. The April 1990 issue specifically addressed issues of homophobia in the Greek and campus community. The Association of Fraternity Advisers can be contacted at PO Box 68506, Indianapolis, IN 46268.
- The *National Association of Student Personnel Administrators* has a Fraternity and Sorority Network that is composed of regional representatives. The network addresses issues of importance relevant to Greek systems and may be contacted at 1700 18th Street, Washington, DC 20009-2508. Telephone: 202-265-7500. NASPA produces the *NASPA Journal*, which provides reports that may be relevant to fraternal organizations.

The interfraternity organizations that represent the three major clusters of social fraternal organizations may also be contacted for additional assistance or resources:

- The *National Interfraternity Conference* can be contacted at 3901 West 86th Street, Suite 390, Indianapolis, IN 46268. Telephone: 317-872-1112.
- The *National Pan Hellenic Council* can be contacted through any member fraternal organization.
- The *National Panhellenic Conference* can be reached at 3901 West 86th Street, Suite 380, Indianapolis, IN 46268. Telephone: 317-872-3185.

There are currently two fraternal organizations that were formed with the interests of the lesbian, gay, and bisexual student as paramount:

- *Lambda Delta Lambda* is a sorority in which women can be open about their sexual orientation. The group can be contacted at 118 MG-405 Hillgard, UCLA, Los Angeles, CA 90024-1376. Telephone: 213-825-6322.
- *Delta Lambda Phi* is a fraternity "to provide dignified and purposeful social and recreational activities for progressive men, to lead in determining the role of individual men in society, and to improve the image of sexual minorities." Delta Lambda Phi can be contacted % Vernon L. Strickland III, Esq., Box 57184, Washington, DC 20037. Telephone: 202-857-8026. There are currently eight chapters of Delta Lambda Phi nationally.

CONCLUSION

Fraternities are viewed by many persons as insulated communities in which oppressive attitudes and behaviors are allowed, and even encouraged. These perceptions are reinforced on a regular basis through highly publicized incidences and acts of homophobia involving fraternity members. Conversely, fraternities can be utilized by educators as extremely powerful student communities in which educational initiatives can be undertaken. Because of the strong interpersonal relationships that denote these student organizations and because of the single-sex nature of most groups, candid and frank discussions about issues of sexually (heterosexuality, bisexuality, and homosexuality) can take place that will challenge the individual to work toward a campus climate of tolerance and acceptance of all persons.

By combining the resources of the campus, the (inter)national organization, and the alumni, students can be presented with many perspectives on the issues. As educators and as fraternity members, we need only to commmit ourselves to addressing these issues and confronting intolerance within our chapters. Given a challenge, fraternities have proven that they can tackle difficult issues and accept responsibility for building on proud traditions for a more perfect future.

REFERENCES

Campbell, D. T., & Stanley, J. C.(1963). *Experimental and quasi-experimental designs for research.* Chicago: Rand McNally.

Cass, V. C. (1979). Homosexuality identity formation: A theoretical model. *Journal of Homosexuality, 4,* 219–235.

Chickering, A. W. (1969). *Education and identity.* San Francisco: Jossey-Bass.

Fraternities lose national support. (1990, February 19). *National On-Campus Report,* p. 5.

In the news. (1988, June 12). *Gay Community News,* p. 4.

Kohlberg, L. (1981). *The philosophy of moral development.* San Francisco: Harper & Row.

Miranda, J., & Storms, M. (1989). Psychological adjustment of lesbian and gay men. *Journal of Counseling and Development, 68,* 41–45.

Chapter 7

WORKING WITH GAY AND LESBIAN STUDENT ORGANIZATIONS

Dick Scott
California State University—Northridge

Gay and lesbian students at colleges and universities, like other students with common concerns, have formed organizations through which to pursue their interests, advocate change, and provide support for themselves and others. At a number of universities, for example, Columbia, Rutgers, and Oregon, the organizations were formed in the year following the June 1969 Stonewall riots in New York City. Throughout the ensuing 20 years, students at campuses across the country have started new organizations. In 1987 the National Gay Task Force's mailing list contained 300 student groups (Berrill, 1989).

There is little consistency between gay and lesbian student groups at the various campuses. Although most have between 10 and 50 members, they range in size from 4 members to 400 with no correlation between the group's size and the institution's enrollment. Most campuses have one gay and lesbian group; however, multiple groups, up to five in number, are not uncommon (Berrill, 1989). When there is more than one group, the difference between groups may be based on gender, on political philosophy, or on function.

Most student organizations use the words *gay* and *lesbian* in their names. The names are often abbreviated to form an acronym such as GALA (Gay and Lesbian Association) or LAGA. On some campuses a name without such reference is used to help enable the group to meet without harassment. Some student groups also use the term *bisexual* in their name; however, this is not a standard practice. In this chapter, the term *gay and lesbian student organization* is used to refer to the entire spectrum of such groups. Regardless of the group's name, student organizations are usually open to all students and often to faculty and staff members as well.

This chapter is divided into five sections, each of which focuses on a different aspect of gay and lesbian student organizations. The first section addresses the basic purposes such groups serve on campuses. The section on institutional relationships reviews the legal basis upon which gay and lesbian organizations are recognized and receive university privileges. The third section delineates the structures of student organizations and the categories used to group them. This is followed by a primer on forming a student organization and a fifth section on the variety of programs and services that gay and lesbian student groups offer. At the end of the chapter is a short list of resources that will be helpful to those forming a student group.

THE ROLE OF GAY AND LESBIAN STUDENT ORGANIZATIONS

Gay and lesbian student organizations, like student organizations in general, perform a variety of functions on college and university campuses. They organize social activities, act as political action groups, provide emotional support, run services, and organize educational programs. Such activities may be provided for their members, for gay and lesbian students in general (and those who have not yet come out), or for the campus community as a whole. In addition, student organizations provide a place where students can develop interpersonal, organizational, and leadership skills. Openly gay or lesbian students may find that other student groups deny them the opportunity to participate actively; thus gay and lesbian student organizations may offer them the only opportunity for such development. Often, particularly where there is only one gay and lesbian student group, the organization serves more than one, or all, of these functions.

SOCIAL ROLES

Gay and lesbian student organizations can provide activities (and consequently, places) at which students can meet, interact, and develop friendships while being open about their sexual orientation. Functions such as dances, parties, banquets, receptions, trips, or other organized activities serve these purposes. As a student organization, the group has access to university facilities in which such activities can be held and may have access to funds and financial procedures that enable the facilities and needed services to be secured. In many communities, this may be the only public space where gay and lesbian students can meet. Even in communities with gay and lesbian bars, these facilities may not be available to students under age 21. For students who are just coming out or who are new to the community, organizational social activities may be the only way in which they establish contact with other gay and lesbian students.

POLITICAL ROLES

Student organizations can serve as political action groups both on and off campus. Within the campus structure, they may provide a means to influence campus policies and procedures that affect gay and lesbian students. The student group can develop and gather support for statements on nondiscrimination on the basis of sexual orientation and on harassment based upon sexual orientation. They may also be effective in making various campus services (health center, residence halls, library, student union) more responsive to the needs and concerns of gay and lesbian students. Such organizations can also play a role in the larger political community by providing a means for gay and lesbian students to become involved with and influence political candidate election campaigns, ballot initiatives, and legislative actions. A major part of such a role is providing informed comment on how potential legislation or candidates' platforms may affect gay men and lesbians.

SUPPORT ROLES

Gay and lesbian organizations serve as a support mechanism for students who are coming out or who are having problems with family, friends, faculty and staff, or other students because of their sexual orientation. In one-on-one and group discussions, students can talk about their feelings and problems, hear from others who have had similar problems, and explore potential solutions. Very often simply having a sympathetic listener can help a student deal with a problem or work through the coming out process. The student organization provides students with a means of finding peers who are sympathetic.

SERVICE ROLES

Student organizations can provide a variety of services to gay and lesbian students that are not provided by the institution or the community. These can include hot lines (anonymous telephone lines for information, discussion, and referrals), peer counseling, newsletters and pamphlet distribution, testing for sexually transmitted diseases, referrals for health and counseling services, discussion groups, library and resource centers, housing and job boards, speakers bureaus, and information on activities and organizations in the community and at other colleges and universities.

EDUCATIONAL ROLES

A major role of student organizations is educating gay and lesbian students as well as the larger campus community on a variety of gay and lesbian topics. Speakers, films, panel discussions, workshops, and theme weeks all can be part of a program designed to inform the campus community about sexual orientation, homophobia, the problems gay and lesbian students encounter as the result of discrimination, and other such issues.

DEVELOPMENTAL ROLES

Student organizations and group involvement serve an important role in the development of students. Students who participate in organizations learn how to work with others, how to organize and manage groups of people, and how to develop and work within procedures and policies. Special skills such as public speaking, financial management, and publicity and promotion techniques can also be learned. Although these opportunities are available in most student organizations, gay and lesbian students may choose not to be involved in them for fear of rejection or harassment or may find the opportunity blocked by homophobia and discrimination. Gay and lesbian student groups may be the only opportunity open to such students for their development. Leadership in these groups may also open the way for leadership in the larger campus community by providing a means by which students can demonstrate their abilities to the campus leadership.

INSTITUTIONAL RELATIONSHIPS

Relationships between institutions of higher education and organized student groups generally revolve around several basic issues: recognition, funding, college or university privileges, and subjection to college or university policies and procedures. As student organizations, gay and lesbian groups should be subject to the same policies and procedures and receive the same benefits as other student organizations. However, some such groups have had to secure these benefits through a series of legal challenges that have resulted in one set of standards for public institutions and another set of standards for private institutions.

RECOGNITION

The right to association and recognition by the institution has generally been established at public colleges and universities. Key to this determination was the 1972 U.S. Supreme Court ruling in *Healy v. James*. Seven universities, plus the city of Anchorage, Alaska, and the state of Florida, have attempted to deny gay and lesbian students the right to associate using the same basic legal arguments. These arguments have been rejected by the courts on the basis of *Healy v. James*.

> To the argument that homosexuality is illegal, the courts have responded that advocacy is different from action and that a group could not be denied recognition until it was actually found breaking the law. To the argument that homosexuality is abhorrent, courts have applied the *Healy* opinion that that is not a valid reason to restrict association. As for the argument that these groups' activities would harm students, the Supreme Court has responded that "undifferentiated fear or apprehension ... is not enough to overcome the right to freedom of expression" (*Tinker v. Des Moines Independent School District*, 1969, at 508). Finally, the courts have consistently stated that the granting of recognition by an institution does not imply support, agree-

ment, or approval of the organization's purpose. (Maloney, 1988, p. 286)

This line of reasoning may not apply to private institutions, however. In *Gay Rights Coalition v. Georgetown University* (1988), it was ruled that the District of Columbia Human Rights Act could not compel the university to express religious approval or neutrality toward any group or individual. Because university recognition included a religiously guided institutional approval of the student groups, the university could deny recognition to the organization. However, the court differentiated between recognition and the provision of facilities and services and ruled that the Act required nondiscrimination in the granting of benefits to student organizations regardless of university endorsement.

FUNDING AND COLLEGE OR UNIVERSITY PRIVILEGES

Once a gay organization has received college or university recognition, it should expect to receive the same benefits as other student organizations and should follow the same procedures to obtain them. "Opinions rendered by the Supreme Court and the federal appeals courts are consistent in their message: schools may enforce reasonable regulations of time, place, and manner that apply equally to all groups, regardless of the group's message" (Maloney, 1988, p. 289). These rulings apply to the variety of college or university privileges such as access to campus facilities for meetings and functions, posting of materials, distribution of literature, and fund raising. The privileges and procedures are generally published and available through the student activities office, the office of the dean of students, or a similar campus office.

Funding may be provided through a delineated procedure. However, funding is not guaranteed to student organizations, only the right to apply for funding (*Gay and Lesbian Students Association v. Gohn*, 1988). Where distribution of funds is handled through a student committee, gay student organizations may wish to request that the members of the committee be counseled on unbiased decision making in regard to funding. Although the institution should not attempt to influence the students' decision, students can be counseled to overlook personal bias in the decision making. In a recent case the U.S. Court of Appeals for the Eighth Circuit ruled that the gay and lesbian students association's rights were violated when the student senate denied the group's request for funding on the basis of content of ideas that the association wished to express (*Gay and Lesbian Students Association v. Gohn* 1988).

SUBJECTION TO COLLEGE OR UNIVERSITY POLICIES AND PROCEDURES

Once a student organization is recognized by the institution, it is subject to established policies and procedures that are available from the student activities department or another campus office. These policies and procedures may include statements that make them inclusive of applicable federal, state, and local laws and ordinances. It is also not uncommon for an organization to be expected to exercise some control over the behavior of its members, and guests, at group functions or, in some cases, at unofficial gatherings of members.

Failure to follow established campus policies and procedures can result in disciplinary measures being taken against the organization. Such measures may include temporary suspension of recognition or withdrawal of recognition with a stated period of time before the organization can reapply for recognition. Generally there are established procedures, including opportunities for hearings and appeal, that the institution follows when disciplining an organization.

For a gay and lesbian student organization, following the campus regulations may be particularly important. Although recognition at a public institution cannot be withheld because of the nature of the organization or the content of its programs, violations of campus policy or applicable laws can become a reason for withdrawal of recognition. Likewise, violation of campus regulations or applicable laws by a number of members at an official or unofficial organizational activity can become a reason for disciplinary action. In instances where individual members violate campus regulations or applicable laws, the organization may aid in its own defense by taking disciplinary actions, including suspension or expulsion if warranted, against the members involved. Campus precedent and advice of the campus student activity officer can be used as a guide in such cases.

STUDENT ORGANIZATION ADVISER

Some institutions require or strongly encourage student organizations to have an on-campus faculty or staff adviser. The official role of the adviser varies from campus to campus, but common responsibilities include informing the organization's leaders and members about campus policies and procedures, signing a variety of official documents including financial transactions and facility reservation contracts, serving as a liaison between the organization and the student activities officer, advising about organizational processes and activity planning, and advising the leaders on their responsibilities and leadership techniques.

It should be noted that an adviser need not be a gay man or a lesbian to be an effective adviser. The adviser's major role is to assist in the organization's operations: operating within campus rules, groups dynamics, leadership, and activity planning. An adviser who becomes involved in content may not be an effective adviser, and he or she may foster a personal agenda rather than assisting the organization's members to develop their own.

TYPES OF STUDENT ORGANIZATIONS

Student organizations are usually classified by institutions into functional categories such as academic, fraternities and sororities, governing groups, honor societies, international, political, religious, service, special interest, and sports. Most often, gay and lesbian student organizations are classified as special interest or political organizations; however, on campuses with more than one such organization, differentiation among organizational purposes suggests that other classifications are appropriate. Thus, a gay peer counseling group may be a service organization, a group of students interested in gay studies may be an academic organization, and a campus chapter of Dignity, an organization of Catholic gay men and lesbians, may be classified as religious. When such groups are not properly classified, it needs to be noted to the student activities officer for correction because different benefits may be obtained for certain categories of organizations.

Student organizations may also be classified by type of structure. They may be coalitions, committees, simple organizations, or complex organizations. The type of organizational structure chosen needs to be based upon the purpose, the number of members, and the type of participation expected of the members.

On campuses where the gay and lesbian organization's membership becomes large, it is not uncommon for it to split into two or more organizations. These organizations usually differentiate among themselves on the basis of function, philosophy, or other logical division. Although some view this division as counterproductive to the furtherance of gay and lesbian issues, it is usually beneficial.

Multiple organizations generally allow more students to become involved both because of the existence of more leadership positions and because of the better chance for an individual to identify with a more specific purpose rather than the broad, general purposes that a sole organization tends to have. In such instances, one organization may be very prominent and visible, attracting those students who are out and comfortable in being open about their sexual orientation. Such an organization may be involved in social or political action activities. Another organization may have a low profile and accommodate those students who are coming out. Its primary activities may be discussion groups and social gatherings for its members.

DEVELOPING A GAY AND LESBIAN STUDENT ORGANIZATION

The logistics of forming a gay and lesbian student organization are much the same as those for starting any student organization. The three basic steps are:

- finding other interested students
- developing a statement of purpose and operating procedures
- meeting institutional requirements.

The National Gay and Lesbian Task Force Campus Project has developed a *Student Organization Packet* that provides advice to individuals interested in starting a gay and lesbian student organization. It also publishes a newsletter *Organizing for Equality*.

The first step for any individual interested in starting a student organization is to go to the campus student activities office or similar department. An inquiry needs to be made as to whether an organization already exists. Gay and lesbian student organizations exist under various names that do not always readily identify the purpose to a campus newcomer. Office staff can provide information on how to contact an existing organization. It may also be that an organization exists on the institution's records but is inactive. If this is the situation, it may be possible to "take over" the existing organization rather than start a new one. A defunct organization can also be revived, usually with less work than starting a new organization from scratch because existing purpose statements and operating procedures can be adopted rather than created. In some circumstances, there may be funds held in trust that will be available to a new group that meets certain criteria. These possibilities and the appropriate procedures can be discussed with student activities staff.

Copies of the institutional policies and procedures concerning student organizations and any required forms need to be obtained, read, and understood. Advisers in the student activities office can answer questions and provide assistance. Inquiries need to be made regarding deadlines for filing for recognition and funding. Finally, the student activities office staff may also provide assistance in finding an adviser, arranging meeting rooms, and publicizing initial meetings. If the assistance is not offered, ask for it. It may have been not offered simply because no other organization asked for it in the past.

Generally, recognition of a new organization is contingent upon the registering of a minimum of members (or officers), an adviser, and the filing of a statement of purpose and operating procedures (constitution and bylaws). Sample documents (or recommended documents) and forms may be part of the materials obtained from the student activities office. Deadlines and procedures for filing these documents need to be adhered to as there may be only one or two periods each semester for obtaining recognition. The process may also involve a hearing before a student committee or a meeting with a member of the institution's staff.

An initial meeting of interested students needs to be arranged and publicized. The location needs to be at a convenient location with proper room accommodations. The student center (student union) usually provides such facilities. If the policy of the student center is to provide rooms to recognized groups only, ask the staff how to get assistance in setting up an initial organizing meeting. If a potential adviser has been identified, that person should be invited to the meeting as should a member of the student activities staff. These people can explain the process and procedures for starting an organization and offer suggestions on how to get started. In addition, their presence may mitigate harassment of the group or may assist in getting appropriate institutional reaction to the harassment.

The initial meeting should consist of allowing potential members to get to know each other, discussing the need for and potential purposes of the organization, explaining the policies and procedures related to student organizations, and securing agreement for a second meeting (it may help to have the date and place arranged previously). Names, addresses, and phone numbers of potential members can be collected, but no one should be forced or intimidated into signing up. This list can be used to remind potential members of the second meeting. The meeting can be followed by an informal social activity.

The second and additional meetings need to take on more structure, with time devoted to introducing new potential members and discussion of organizational purposes and activities. Once agreement on these is reached, a simple structure can be developed and temporary leaders elected. Assignments can be made to each member to enable the group to meet recognition requirements and, as an indirect effect, to keep all members involved.

SERVICES AND PROGRAMS

As indicated above, gay and lesbian student organizations serve a variety of purposes on the college or university campus. It is unlikely that any two organizations provide the same array of services in a given year because each organization's program needs to be developed to meet the needs of its members and its campus community. Services and programs offered by such groups include the following:

SERVICES

Speakers bureau. Students are identified and trained to speak on a variety of topics to classes and other student groups. Sometimes the services are made available to off-campus groups.

Discussion groups. These groups primarily serve organizational members and other gay and lesbian students. A discussion facilitator is in charge of the group. For some topics, it may be advisable to work with the campus counseling center in securing a trained and experienced counselor to lead the discussion. Topics include coming out, relationships with parents and friends, self-worth, masculinity, and feminity. Discussion groups are ongoing over a series of sessions.

Workshops. These organized and structured sessions on various topics are usually completed in one session.

Resource library. Collections of gay-themed or related books, newspapers, pamphlets, and other materials in an office or other location for members to read and use are particularly valuable where the campus library does not carry such materials or where such materials are difficult to access.

Referral services. Providing referrals to counselors, lawyers, and doctors is important when there are issues of confidentiality related to sensitivity to sexual orientation.

Hot lines. Individuals can call these telephone numbers to ask questions and discuss personal issues. Telephones are usually staffed by trained volunteers during publicized hours. Referrals are made, as appropriate, to other volunteers or professionals.

Disease testing.   Sensitivity to sexual orientation is important in testing for sexually transmitted diseases and other conditions. Usually such a service is staffed by volunteer doctors and nurses.

Peer counseling.   This service covers a variety of approaches, including simply having other students available to listen to those with problems as well as providing trained volunteer counselors to assist students with personal problems. Such a service can often be a first contact for a student just coming out; thus issues of sensitivity and confidentiality are important.

Housing/job boards.   These provide listings of available housing, roommates, jobs, and other services offered to gay men and lesbians by others who are gay or lesbian or by nongay individuals who do not discriminate on the basis of sexual orientation.

PROGRAMS

Most programs are offered either for organizational members at the meetings of gay and lesbian student organizations or as programs open to the entire campus community. They may be developed and produced in conjunction with the campus program board.

Film series.   Movies with gay themes or with major gay characters are screened for members or for the campus community.

Lecture series.   Speakers on gay issues are hosted.

Social events.   Receptions, dances, banquets, parties, and other activities are organized, with the primary purpose of allowing gay and lesbian students to relax, meet each other, and enjoy the company of others. Very often these activities provide the only gay-oriented social life for those under the legal age for entry to bars.

Awareness weeks.   These multiday events include a variety of gay and lesbian theme programs. Such programs might include a major speaker, workshops on a number of topics, a noontime performance by a gay or lesbian musical group, and a dance or concert.

Homophobia workshops.   These are programs designed to acquaint nongay members of the campus community with issues related to discrimination toward gay men and lesbians.

AIDS awareness education.   Programs include trained speakers available to classes and student groups as well as pamphlets, banners, condom give-away programs, and newspaper ads.

Newsletters.   These publications, usually for members but often generally distributed, provide information on upcoming events and gay and lesbian issues and happenings.

Trips.   These organized social activities held off campus may include roller and ice skating as well as theatre and concert going.

Conferences. Some campus organizations host students from other area campuses for annual conferences of workshops, speakers, and social activities.

Alumni groups. A number of campuses have developed gay alumni groups. In some cases these have received official recognition by the alumni association of the institution. Such groups can provide speakers, contacts for jobs, and other assistance.

OTHER ACTIVITIES

Advocacy. Student organizations can advocate change in various campus policies and procedures that negatively affect gay and lesbian students. They can bring issues to the attention of the administration and campus leadership while allowing affected students anonymity. Among policies addressed are library book and magazine collections, residence hall policies, counseling center services, and health center activities.

Sexual orientation discrimination statements. Many campus organizations have successfully conducted drives to include sexual orientation in the institution's statement of nondiscrimination.

Harassment policies. Student groups have developed and had implemented policies dealing with harassment on the basis of sexual orientation in the institution's student conduct code.

CONCLUSION

In the last two decades, gay and lesbian student organizations have formed on many campuses across the country. In some cases, court action has been required to secure for them the recognition and privileges granted other student organizations. These organizations play a variety of social, political, support, service, educational, and developmental roles on the college campus. Student affairs professionals can, by working with these organizations, provide a variety of activities and services for the campus community and an important resource for gay and lesbian students.

REFERENCES

Berrill, K. (1989). Report of the Campus Project of the National Gay and Lesbian Task Force. Unpublished report. Washington, DC: National Gay and Lesbian Task Force.

Gay and Lesbian Students Association v. Gohn, 850 F.2nd 361 (Ark. Cir. 1988).

Gay Rights Coalition v. Georgetown University, 536 A. 2d (1 D.C. App. 1988).

Maloney, G. W. (1988). Student organizations and student activities. In M. J. Barr & Associates, *Student services and the law* (pp. 284–295). San Francisco: Jossey-Bass.

RESOURCES

Resources particularly useful for gay and lesbian student organizations include the following organizations and publications:

Boston Intercollegiate Lesbian & Gay Association
  c/o GAMIT, 50-306 Walker Memorial, MIT, Cambridge, MA 02139
National Gay and Lesbian Task Force Campus Project
  1517 U Street NW, Washington, DC 20009; (202) 332-6483
  The task force has two publications that may be of value. These are the *Student Organization Packet* (1984), which explains how to organize a student group, and the newsletter, *Organizing for Equality*.
Western States Lesbian/Gay Students United
  500 Landfair Avenue, Los Angeles, CA 90024

Bourassa, D., & Cullen, M. (1988). Programming: Bringing gay, lesbian, and bisexual issues to the forefront. *Profile*. Columbia, SC: National Association for Campus Activities.

Keeling, R. (Ed.). (1986). *AIDS on the college campus*. Rockville, MD: American College Health Association.

Palmer, B. C., & Palmer, K. R. (1983). *The successful meeting master guide for business and professional people*. Englewood Cliffs, NJ: Prentice-Hall.

Russo, V. (1980). *The celluloid closet: Lesbians and gay men in American film*. New York: Harper & Row.

Wolfers, E. E., & Evansen, V. B. (1980). *Organizations, clubs, and action groups: How to start them, how to run them*. New York: St. Martin's.

Chapter 8

LIFE PLANNING AND CAREER COUNSELING WITH GAY AND LESBIAN STUDENTS

Cheryl Hetherington
Hetherington & Associates, Iowa City, Iowa

According to Freud the basic requirements of human existence are meaningful love and work. For gay men and lesbian women, there exist special issues in career and life planning that do not concern heterosexuals. The coming out process and career exploration both involve various stages, none of which follow a specific timetable for duration or age appropriateness (Hetherington & Orzek, 1989). As gay men and lesbian women proceed through the career decision-making process, they may be influenced by environmental, social, and intrapsychic factors that are different from those that influence heterosexual individuals. This chapter addresses these factors as they relate to gender issues, stages of sexual identity development, career counseling concerns, and, finally, implications for career counselors.

Although the general public holds stereotypes concerning vocational choices of gay men and lesbian women, few empirical studies have focused on their career decision-making process (Hetherington, Hillerbrand, & Etringer, 1989). As early as 1954, Lambert stated that for gay men, "vocational guidance is the most constructive therapeutic approach that could be made in helping homosexual clients to improve their social adjustment" (p. 524). Blair (1972) asserted that the vocational issues of gay men largely have been ignored, and Canon (1973) suggested that until the early 1970s most career counselors did not have to contend with their clients' homosexual orientation, possibly because of the clients' reluctance to disclose this important piece of information. Neuhring, Fein, and Tyler (1974) proposed that prejudicial attitudes and stereotypes of career counselors inhibit effective career counseling.

LESBIAN WOMEN'S ISSUES

Gender may be more significant than sexual orientation in explaining differences in career choice and life planning. According to Harren, Kass, Tinsley, and Moreland (1979), the "most influential predictor of gender-dominated choices is gender" (p. 232). Yet lesbian women may be affected differently than heterosexual women by the gender-role attitudes that have been found to be a powerful decision-making influence in the career arena. Gender-role differences have been suggested between lesbian and heterosexual women (i.e., more lesbian women than heterosexual women endorse gender roles typical of men) (Palmer, 1981). These findings suggest possible differences in career decision-making processes and factors between lesbian and heterosexual women.

In one recent study, Etringer, Hetherington, and Hillerbrand (1990) surveyed lesbian women, gay men, and heterosexual college students on career decision making. Lesbian women showed the least amount of uncertainty, and lesbian women and heterosexual men were the most satisfied with their career choices. This is consistent with Sang's (1977) findings that women who identify themselves as lesbians in adulthood assume that they will be self-supporting from an early age. As a result, they may choose male-dominated careers in order to be more self-supportive.

Female psychology and information about socialization help in better understanding these differences. Gilligan (1982) identified differences in psychological development between men and women. She argued that for women self-image is reflected through interpersonal processes during conflict resolution. Women are taught to be nonassertive, other oriented, and caretaking. They are caught in a conflict between behaving in gender-appropriate ways or being gender inappropriate (i.e., assertive, unemotional, competitive) in the interest of forming a positive self-image (Ballou & Gabalac, 1985; Bernard, 1975; Foxley, 1979; Gilligan, 1982). The bind, therefore, is that to be gender appropriate women must behave in ways identified with a one-down status; accepting that status makes the development of a positive self-image difficult, if not impossible.

Lesbian women do not escape the female socialization process that trains them to be passive, dependent, and other oriented (Bell & Martin, 1978), but the gender inappropriateness of their sexual orientation forces them to consider additional issues when resolving this conflict. For lesbian women, positive self-image cannot come only from gender appropriateness; instead, the development of a positive self-image may need to involve a positive valuing of gender inappropriateness if they are to value their lesbianism (Wolfe & Stanley, 1980). In the process of incorporating lesbianism into self-image, lesbian women may suffer from gender confusion and isolation because of their awareness of being different from other women in some fundamental way (Vargo, 1987).

Lesbian women come to terms with internalized and externally encountered homophobia in the process of creating a positive self-image as well as of resolving the double bind that all women face: being female and being perceived as less psychologically healthy than men (Broverman, Broverman, Clarkson, Rosenkrantz, & Vogel, 1970). There is much to be learned about the effect of lesbianism on the development of self-esteem. Peplau, Cochran, Rook, and Padesky (1978) suggested that lesbians construct self-images differently than heterosexual women. It is possible that the interplay between lesbianism and the development of self-esteem can affect the ease or difficulty with which a positive self-image can be achieved.

GAY MEN'S ISSUES

Men are socialized to be primary breadwinners, to be strong, unemotional, and expert, and to always know the right thing to do. Yet, according to Etringer, Hetherington, and Hillerbrand (1990), gay men report the highest uncertainty about their career choices and more dissatisfaction with their career choices than lesbian women and heterosexual men.

Jones (1978), for example, used a number of case histories to illustrate the unique problems and difficulties that gay men face in the career decision process. He noted the impact of discrimination in the military services, of the long-held fears concerning gay men teaching children, and of the fears concerning gay men working in social service occupations, in business, and in numerous other professions. In an attempt to guide counselors who deal with gay men, he noted possible career opportunities in such areas as decorative arts, fashion design, the fine arts, and entertainment. However, Jones' suggestions themselves perpetuate stereotypes and instill limiting and potentially harmful ideas in career counselors about appropriate careers for gay men.

In a similar vein, Brown (1975) gave an autobiographical account detailing how his sexual orientation influenced his choice of vocation and the location in which he chose to live. He chronicled a number of personal and professional sacrifices he had to make in concession to privacy. Brown's experience suggests that for gay men it is necessary to consider sexual orientation during all stages of the career development process.

Blair (1972) noted value systems, self-esteem, and discrimination as crucial variables in understanding the vocational decision-making process of gay men. Researchers and theorists need to address for gay clients such issues as social and economic pressures, discrimination, occupational information that is relevant to gay male students, AIDS-related fears in the work environment, and self-image as well as the issues of "less than free choice" and self-esteem. At present, these issues are ignored (Hetherington, Hillerbrand, & Etringer, 1989).

STAGES OF GAY OR LESBIAN IDENTITY AND CAREER CONCERNS

Understanding where a student falls on the gay identity development continuum has important implications for the career counseling process. As discussed in chapter 1, several models of gay identity development have been proposed, and these models can help counselors interpret and clarify the experience of gay and lesbian students facing career decisions. Within each stage of development, the career exploration process can be very different. The four stages proposed by Levine and Evans in Chapter 1 include (1) First Awareness, (2) Self-Labeling, (3) Community Involvement and Disclosure, and (4) Identity Integration.

In the First Awareness stage people feel alienated but are silent about their alienation. It is a stage of "not knowing," of uncertainty. Later in this stage, people begin to think of themselves as being gay or lesbian, and the process of first coming out may interfere with career decisions (Botkin & Daly, 1987). This time in a gay or lesbian person's life is full of emotional confusion, and an attempt to make career decisions during the First Awareness or Self-Labeling stages is difficult. The student may be anxious, scared, and unwilling to self-disclose. Understandably, such a person is reluctant to disclose to a counselor. At this same time, students may face social pressures (i.e., college graduation) that force them to make career decisions despite the personal confusion they are experiencing.

During the early stages, a bottleneck effect may disallow career exploration. In the coming out process, other parts of a person's life are often "on hold." Grades may fall, and students may be shifting their social activities and friends. During such stress-producing changes, career exploration may be difficult. The career counselor can help by not taking any anger expressed by the student personally and by providing support during this process.

During the Self-Labeling stage, attention to coming out and career decision making can lead to the integration of both processes. Gay and lesbian students may have misconceptions about careers open to them; they have grown up with mainstream stereotypes and may feel limited by them. They may also have little information about the gay or lesbian culture, or the information they do have may be limited. Access to positive gay and lesbian role models working in the community is especially helpful at this time.

During the Community Involvement and Disclosure stage, students may be difficult to work with during career counseling. They may only be interested in gay or lesbian activities and friends and be unwilling to consider working with heterosexuals or on career decisions. They go through a grieving process, and they may primarily be concerned with unresolved conflicts about the social unacceptability of being gay or lesbian.

At the Identity Integration stage, students are considerably more ready to work on integration of lifestyle and career. They may have many questions about occupations and the acceptance of gay and lesbian people in the working world. Information that is both general and specific to gay and lesbian career choices is helpful at this stage.

The amount of time that it takes students to arrive at the Identity Integration stage varies. The stage of gay or lesbian identity development at which any student may be, at any point in time along this continuum, is unpredictable. What is generally true is that the process of developing a gay or lesbian identity is long and arduous. Also generally true is that the process occurs during the formative years of one's adult and professional life.

According to the *APA Monitor* (Riddle & Morin, 1977), a typical gay man or lesbian woman becomes aware of homosexual feelings when he or she is approximately 13 years old. Yet the average age by which a gay male or lesbian women develops a positive gay identity is approximately 31. This 18-year span is filled with difficulties related to coming out in addition to other developmental experiences typical of young adults.

CAREER COUNSELING CONCERNS

Although few research and conceptual studies have been conducted in the area of career issues for gay and lesbian clients, several specific issues can be discerned. Each of these issues affects the career and life planning process.

MINORITY GROUP STATUS

It may be helpful to conceive of gay and lesbian students as a nonethnic minority. Minority group status for gays seems appropriate for both practical and theoretical reasons (Hetherington, Hillerbrand, & Etringer, 1989). With minority group status, the problems are redefined. Many problems reside with the predominant culture or society, not with gay and lesbian students. Thus, the prejudicial attitudes and stereotypes become objects of scrutiny, and assumptions that the minority group must change its inherent identity are no longer assumed. Most universities and states have statutes concerning discrimination against people by gender, race, and creed. Many also have statutes that include standards regarding sexual orientation in their statements on nondiscrimination. Counselors can educate themselves and their students regarding these statements.

NEGATIVE STEREOTYPES

Special groups are often the victims of negative or disparaging stereotypes that are frequently an impediment to the career choices and advancements of the involved groups. One survey (Newton, 1978) found that 50% of the respondents thought gay males were a high security risk for government jobs. This finding is consistent with the prevailing myth that gay males are in some way psychologically disturbed (Morin & Garfinkle, 1978). In this study, 56% of the people sampled thought that gay men should have equal rights in terms of job opportunities but that these rights should be denied in certain so-called sensitive occupations, such as school teacher, clergy, physician, and armed forces member.

Stereotypic attitudes were demonstrated when Botkin and Daly (1987) asked a general population of 120 college students to indicate what jobs were most interesting to gay males, lesbians, and heterosexual men and women. The top three stereotypical gay male professions were photographer, interior decorator, and nurse. The top three predicted choices for heterosexual men were doctor, photographer, and engineer. The top three stereotyped lesbian professions were auto mechanic, plumber, and truck driver, whereas the top three occupations listed for heterosexual women were interior decorator, nurse, and dietitian. It is interesting that the occupations listed for lesbian women do not require a college degree. Lesbian women may therefore experience double negative stereotypes due to their gender and their sexual orientation.

ACQUIRED IMMUNE DEFICIENCY SYNDROME (AIDS)

With the increasing prevalence of AIDS and the fact that gay men are reported as a high-risk group for this disease, those who are uncomfortable with gay men have more reasons to rationalize and defend their homophobia and discrimination. People may justify their antigay attitudes or behavior on the fear of getting AIDS; some even blame gay men for causing AIDS. Counselors, placement recruiters, and students may have concerns and fears related to this frightening disease. It is the responsibility of all university officials, including career counselors, to know the facts about AIDS. Education of all staff is important so that staff members can, in turn, educate students. The American College Health Association states that "the primary response of colleges and universities to the AIDS epidemic must be education" (Keeling, 1986, p. 1).

Beyond issues of fears of AIDS and its contagiousness, of increasing anxiety, and of further entrenchment of homophobia, there are a host of intrapersonal, interpersonal, and possibly legal issues to consider. Career counselors, after educating their clients about occupations and career opportunities, must deal with the social issues related to the work environment. There are decisions about whether and when to disclose one's lifestyle to employers and fellow employees and considerations of the potential impact of this knowledge on the work climate and on career stability and advancement. Although the author knows of no studies about these issues, clinical observations and common sense indicate that these are vital to the career concerns of gay men and lesbian women.

Similarly, legal issues in this arena are only beginning to be defined and addressed. Mandatory human immunodeficiency virus (HIV) testing, restriction of job duties and responsibilities, and covert or overt discrimination toward gay men are all concerns that can influence career choice and advancement.

LIMITED ROLE MODELS

Exposure to diverse and competent role models is limited for many minority groups. Among its many effects, the lack of exposure restricts awareness and choice of occupational possibilities. Hetherington and Barcelo (1985) discuss mentoring as important for women of color and the concerns for support for younger members of a minority group, and this applies to gay men and lesbian women. In many cases, gay men and lesbian women in the work world are literally an invisible minority (Pope, Ehlen, & Mueller, 1985). They are invisible not only to heterosexuals but also to other gay and lesbian people. Thus they often make career decisions without awareness of how other gay and lesbian people employed in the occupations under consideration made their decisions and how choices were implemented. According to Schneider and Tremble (1986):

> Developmental tasks such as building self-esteem, a sense of identity, and social skills are especially complex for gay or lesbian adolescents. The ubiquitous homosexual stereotypes, the inaccessibility of appropriate and visible gay and lesbian role models, and the absence of gay and lesbian peers delay some aspects of maturation and have important consequences as the homosexual adolescent approaches adulthood. (p. 99)

One duty of career counselors is to provide access to a diverse collection of role models, including gay and lesbian professionals. As indicated earlier, it is necessary to be aware of prevailing norms and the presence of appropriate support and resource groups for referrals. Making resources and role models available to gay and lesbian students can serve many useful purposes.

THE TRANSITION FROM SCHOOL TO WORK

For gay and lesbian clients, occupational choice is only half the battle. Many need to plan strategies to ease the transition into an occupation. The college or university community provides a more or less insular world, which is unlike the work world. The college or university gay and lesbian community also may be a more comfortable and sensitive environment in which initial gay and lesbian identity issues can be explored. The gay and lesbian student may need to be prepared to live without what may be a relatively tolerant or supportive college or university milieu.

Also worthy of note are geographical considerations. Certain areas of the country have substantially larger gay or lesbian populations than others (Hillerbrand, Hetherington, & Etringer, 1986). This relationship between geography and gay and lesbian community size may assume greater importance for gay and lesbian students than for heterosexual students. Other issues that may emerge in moving from school to work include decisions about partner relocation, social interaction issues on and off the job, and establishment of new support systems.

ISSUES FOR GAY AND LESBIAN COUPLES

Career decisions for gay and lesbian couples are especially difficult. In a survey (Winkelpleck & Westfeld, 1982), gay and lesbian couples cited employment discrimination as one of the major issues facing them. Those in gay or lesbian relationships have numerous issues besides career choice to consider, including (a) how to present the relationship, (b) how to introduce their partner, (c) whether to acknowledge the lover relationship openly, and (d) how to deal with social events. When a gay or lesbian person is interviewing for a new position in a different location, he or she struggles with how open to be with a potential employer when asking for help in finding work for a partner. The interviewee risks rejection and judgment based on his or her sexual orientation in addition to qualifications for the job. Another dilemma occurs regarding professional social events, where employees are encouraged to bring their spouses or partners. For gay or lesbian employees, there are professional risks in bringing their partners and personal risks when partners are not invited into their work world. When the relationship is necessarily separate from the person's work life, feelings of loneliness and rejection are common. Another practical matter that needs attention is the lack of access to job benefits provided to heterosexual spouses (i.e., health insurance, social security payments). However, to date there is little information regarding this issue that suggests changes from the status quo.

IMPLICATIONS FOR CAREER COUNSELORS

Review of the conceptual work in career counseling and gay and lesbian issues suggests several areas that career counselors can address.

SELF-ASSESSMENT

Each counselor and agency needs to engage in a self-assessment process regarding traditional career counselor roles, techniques, and values in order to offer effective services to the gay and lesbian community. This examination ideally takes place whenever counselors find themselves working with clients of any minority group, who, because of their minority status, may have special needs or place special demands on counseling professionals. It is advantageous for agencies to invite gay and lesbian professionals to provide training for the staff. For example, in late fall a lesbian staff member in a counseling center compiled a list of special issues that gay and lesbian students face during the holidays. She distributed this to all staff members to help them better understand and serve their gay and lesbian students. A topic for staff development and training each year can include "career counseling with gay and lesbian students" (and other minority students). The extent to which this training is a publicly known process influences the number of minority group students who are willing to avail themselves of the agency's services.

PROVISION OF SPECIALIZED PROGRAMMING

Provision of special programs is the ideal, but political and administrative realities often act to thwart the best of intentions. Blair (1972) cited a survey of directors of counseling centers and deans of students who acknowledged that gay and lesbian students have distinct problems in finding employment, but who also acknowledged that they did not have resources or services for this population.

Even if special programming is offered, does it make a difference? In a career program on "Being Gay or Lesbian in the Work Place" conducted by the author, it was difficult to assure the necessary anonymity of attendees. Although advertised university-wide and sponsored by the counseling center, it was not endorsed or sponsored by a gay and lesbian student group. As a result, attendance was severely limited. Meetings with gay and lesbian campus organizations can better deal with such issues as networking with other gay and lesbian students who have the same or related occupational interests, coping with discrimination, legal rights, and resume writing. See chapter 7 on gay student organizations for additional suggestions.

Resumes may pose particular problems for some gay and lesbian students. Often, gay and lesbian students active in campus gay and lesbian organizations have considerable organizational, leadership, and administrative experience. How this information is discussed in interviews or stated on a resume has profound implications for the student. Career counselors can help gay and lesbian students

decide if, how, or when to discuss their sexual orientation with interviewers.

LIFESTYLE COUNSELING

Gay and lesbian students may be confused or concerned about the
kind of lifestyle they wish to maintain once employed. Because of
their susceptibility to discrimination and prejudice, gay and lesbian
students need to pay close attention to their public lifestyle. The
extent to which their public lifestyle reveals their sexual orientation
is dependent on a number of factors. In one gay men's counseling
group that dealt with special issues related to being gay in a straight
society, major concerns included how and when to tell parents, sib-
lings, and friends about their gay lifestyle; job security; gay marriage; adoption of children; alcoholism; and sexually transmitted
diseases (Boyum, 1978). The counselor can help isolate and clarify
some of these factors.

Some have asserted that career counselors are unlikely to be involved in the decision to come out. This is not necessarily the case.
It is highly likely that this decision may be examined at several
points, including (1) during the initial career decision, (2) during
the decision about when and how to acknowledge sexual orientation,
and (3) while dealing with the reactions of employers, co-workers,
supervisors, family, and friends to sexual orientation disclosure
(Milburn, Eldridge, & Hetherington, 1988). Understanding the gay
identity development models is helpful in assisting gay and lesbian
clients at these crucial points.

In what may be a major difference from other minority groups,
gay men and lesbian women must decide whether, when, and to
what degree to disclose their minority status. The process of coming
out involves daily decisions. For example, a gay or lesbian employee
can speak in terms of "we" (self and partner) or "I" when talking
with colleagues about weekend activities. The counselor can help
the student deal with these kind of decisions that create conflicts
between private lifestyle and public lifestyle. The decision to remain
completely private means that there may be chronic stress with fear
of being discovered. The counselor can help the student who has
made such a decision decide how to manage stress, how to feel more
comfortable with his or her sexual orientation, and how to maintain
a manageable or comfortable identity on the job. Chapter 9 provides
more information on helping students with identity concerns.

Gay and lesbian students may need and desire information that
can be difficult to find. Chapter 13 provides a list of professional

associations and other resources for gay men, lesbian women, and bisexual people.

EMPLOYMENT DISCRIMINATION

Hedgpeth (1979–1980) examined employment discrimination law and the rights of gays and lesbians. She noted that until recently no protection was given to those discriminated against because of their affectional orientation. Legal protection has been extended in some recent cases, although Hedgpeth (1979–1980) noted that this is a less-than-perfect state of affairs. For example, in many cases gay and lesbian people maintain a publicly gay or lesbian lifestyle; and if they are active in gay and lesbian rights politics, they are in danger of being fired because of "unfitness" criteria. Federal, state, administrative, and judicial protection of the gay and lesbian person's employment is sporadic and unreliable. Counselors need to be familiar with information regarding employment practices in federal, state, and local agencies and organizations as well as in businesses.

One visible demonstration of an agency's or a counselor's commitment to provide special services to gay and lesbian clients is the creation of an antidiscrimination policy that includes sexual orientation. A career counseling and placement agency can publicize its own policy prohibiting employment discrimination against gay and lesbian students. For more information regarding statements on services for gay and lesbian people, see chapter 4.

UTILIZATION OF ROLE MODELS

In many cases the role models that are available to heterosexual clients are not useful for gay clients. Counselors can tap into the existing gay community and also explore the possibility of utilizing institutional resources (e.g., externships and internships). Externships or cooperative education placements may not be available for clients who wish to explore businesses or organizations owned or operated by members of the gay and lesbian community. Career counselors and counseling agencies need to support and encourage gay and lesbian professionals who might consider serving as role models for students.

CONCLUSION

The career planning process and the coming-out process both entail various stages, none of which follow a precise timetable for duration or age appropriateness. Understanding the career development and career decision-making process for gay and lesbian students is an important step in providing appropriate career services for this special population. Several issues are of concern to the career counselor. These include models of gay and lesbian identity development, negative stereotypes, AIDS, minority group status, employment discrimination and limited role models, transition from school to work, and attention to gay and lesbian couples. Career counselors can begin to improve career services for gay and lesbian students by providing self-assessments, provisions for specialized programming, lifestyle counseling, information on employment discrimination, and positive gay and lesbian role models as well as job search information.

REFERENCES

Ballou, M., & Gabalac, N. W. (1985). *A feminist position on mental health.* Springfield, IL: Thomas.

Bell, A. P., & Martin, S. (1978). *Homosexualities: A study of diversity among men and women.* New York: Simon and Schuster.

Bernard, J. (1975). *Women, wives, and mothers.* Chicago: Aldine.

Blair, R. (1972). *Vocational guidance and gay liberation.* The Otherwise Monograph Services, No. 19. Washington, DC: National Task Force on Student Personnel Services and Homosexuality.

Botkin, M., & Daly, J. (1987, March). *Occupational development of lesbians and gays.* Paper presented at the annual meeting of the American College Personnel Association, Chicago.

Broverman, I. K., Broverman, D. M., Clarkson, R. E., Rosenkrantz, P. A., & Vogel, S. R. (1970). Sex-role stereotypes and clinical judgments of mental health. *Journal of Consulting and Clinical Psychology, 34,* 1–7.

Brown, D. A. (1975). Career counseling for the homosexual. In R. D. Burack & R. C. Reardon (Eds.), *Facilitating career development.* (pp. 234–237). Springfield, IL: Thomas.

Boyum, R. (1978). Gay counseling group. *Journal of College Student Personnel, 19,* 75.

Canon, H. J. (1973). Gay students. *Vocational Guidance Quarterly, 21,* 181–185.

Etringer, B. D., Hetherington, C., & Hillerbrand E. (1990). The influence on sexual orientation of career decision making: An initial investigation. *Journal of Homosexuality, 19*(4), 103–111.

Foxley, C. (1979). *Nonsexist counseling*. Dubuque, IA: Kendall-Hunt.

Gilligan, C. (1982). *In a different voice*. Cambridge, MA: Harvard University Press.

Harren, V. A., Kass, R. A., Tinsley, H. E. A., & Moreland, J. R. (1979). Influence of gender, sex-role attitudes, and cognitive complexity on gender-dominant career choices. *Journal of Counseling Psychology, 26*, 227–234.

Hedgpeth, J. M. (1979–1980). Employment discrimination law and the rights of gay persons. *Journal of Homosexuality, 5*(1/2), 67–78.

Hetherington, C., & Barcelo N. B. (1985). Womentorship: A cross-cultural perspective. *Journal of National Association for Women Deans, Administrators, and Counselors, 49*(1) 12–15.

Hetherington, C., Hillerbrand, E., & Etringer, B. D. (1989). Career counseling with gay men: Issues and recommendations for research. *Journal of Counseling and Development, 67*, 452–454.

Hetherington C., & Orzek, A. (1989). Career and life planning with lesbian women. *Journal of Counseling and Development, 68*, 52–57.

Hillerbrand, E., Hetherington, C., & Etringer, B. D. (1986, March). *Career counseling with gay and lesbian students*. Paper presented at the annual meeting of the American College Personnel Association, New Orleans.

Jones, G. P. (1978). Counseling gay adolescents. *Counselor Education and Supervision 18*, 144–152.

Keeling, R. P. (1986). *AIDS on the college campus*. Rockville, MD: American College Health Association.

Lambert, C. (1954). Homosexuals. *Medical Press, 2*(32), 523–526.

Milburn, L., Eldridge, N. S., & Hetherington, C. (1988, March). *Relationship, career, and self-concept. The lesbian perspective*. Paper presented at the annual meeting of the American College Personnel Association, Miami, FL.

Morin, S. F., & Garfinkle, E. M. (1978). Male homophobia. *Journal of Social Issues, 34*, 29–47.

Neuhring, E. M., Fein, S. B., & Tyler, M. (1974). The gay college student: Perspectives for mental health professionals. *The Counseling Psychologist, 4*, 64–72.

Newton, D. E. (1978). Homosexual behavior and child molestation: A review of the evidence. *Adolescence, 8*(49), 29–34.

Palmer, S. (1981). *Role stress*. New York: Prentice-Hall.

Peplau, L. A., Cochran, S., Rook, K., & Padesky, C. (1978). Loving women: Attachment and autonomy in lesbian relationships. *Journal of Social Issues, 34*, 7–27.

Pope, R., Ehlen, K. J., & Mueller, J. A. (March, 1985). *The hidden minority*. Paper presented at the annual meeting of the American College Personnel Association, Baltimore.

Riddle, D., & Morin, S. (1977, November). Removing the stigma: Data from individuals. *APA Monitor*, p. 26.

Sang, B. E. (1977). Psychotherapy with lesbians: Some observations and tentative generalizations. In E. I. Rawlings & D. K. Carter (Eds.), *Psychotherapy with women: Treatment toward equality*. Springfield, IL: Thomas.

Schneider, M. S., & Tremble, J. B. (1986). Training service providers to work with gay or lesbian adolescents: A workshop. *Journal of Counseling and Development, 65*, 98–99.

Vargo, S. (1987). The effects of women's socialization on lesbian couples. In Boston Lesbian Psychologies Collective (Eds.), *Lesbian psychologies: Explorations and challenges* (pp. 161–173). Urbana, IL: University of Illinois Press.

Winkelpleck, J., & Westfeld, J. S. (1982). Counseling considerations with gay couples. *Personnel and Guidance Journal, 60*, 294–296.

Wolfe, S. J., & Stanley, J. P. (1980). *The coming out stories*. Watertown, MA: Penelope.

Chapter 9

COUNSELING GAY AND LESBIAN STUDENTS

Natalie S. Eldridge
Boston University

David C. Barnett
University of Illinois at Chicago

This chapter takes a historical look at therapeutic approaches to gay and lesbian clients and examines current theoretical perspectives. Although mental health professionals have moved away from illness models for understanding homosexuality, little training is provided to practitioners about alternative conceptualizations of gay or lesbian lifestyles. Campus counseling professionals are likely to have extensive training in psychology, social work, medicine, student development, or pastoral counseling. Yet they are unlikely to have received formal training to work with lesbian or gay clients. For example, in one study, graduate counseling students admitted to feeling inadequately trained to deal with lesbian and gay clients (Thompson & Fishburn, 1977).

Few clinicians disagree that successful therapy, regardless of the theoretical approach of the therapist, is based on foundations of empathy, understanding, and respect for clients. Understanding the unique perspective of a client requires careful listening skills. The flexibility to identify, in some way, with the pain of a client stems from empathy and respect in therapeutic relationships. A therapist working with an international student faces challenges to understand the meaning of the student's presenting concern in light of the student's cultural context. This process generally leads the therapist to a heightened awareness of his or her own cultural context and its inherent assumptions that might conflict with assumptions of the client. In a similar way, therapists working with gay, lesbian, or bisexual students must challenge their own assumptions about sexual/affectional orientations when trying to understand and empathize with these clients. This is true regardless of a therapist's sexual/affectional orientation because we have all been raised in a culture biased toward heterosexuality. Due to the culturally enforced invisibility of this minority group and the powerful heterosexual assumptions in our culture, unique barriers to the development of understanding, empathy, and respect exist for therapists working with gay, lesbian, and bisexual clients.

This chapter begins with a historical perspective of religious and clinical views of homosexuality and an examination of the reasons why lesbian and gay students seek psychotherapy. Next, a focus on the various barriers to treatment, for both clients and therapists, provides a context for consciousness raising. Finally, some guidelines for therapists and counseling centers are outlined to assist in counseling students who are exploring their identities and working through related developmental issues.

HISTORICAL PERSPECTIVES

Most college and university students are uneducated about issues of sexual orientation. When instructors teach their students about the many contributions of gay men and lesbians throughout history, they typically fail to make known the contributor's sexual orientation. This renders gay men and lesbians invisible in fields such as history, mathematics and science, politics, literature, and the arts. Even if gay men and lesbians are included, most public and private school educations in this country present only negative images of homosexuality. One can argue this is a result of a taboo on open discussion of homosexuality that tends to foster homophobia and sanctions against lesbian, gay, and bisexual people (Human Rights Foundation, 1984). Thus, students arrive on campus with an inheritance of culturally induced and supported homophobia and a lack of knowledge with which to combat it.

Contemporary attitudes toward gay men, lesbians, and bisexual people are grounded in acts of persecution, denigration, and rejection spanning hundreds of years. Awareness of this history helps one comprehend what sets the stage for understanding homosexuality in clinical arenas today.

As noted in the introduction to this book, discussions about homosexuality are culture specific, with standards of a given period dictating the viewpoints. This section examines the impact of Christianity's views of homosexuality as sin, the shifts in perspective to medical models construing homosexuality as pathological, the research suggesting homosexuality is a normal variation, and, finally, the advent and impact of the gay and lesbian liberation movements.

HOMOSEXUALITY AS SIN

The early Catholic Church promulgated views that homosexuality was a sin attributable to depravity. The state concurred and imposed extreme penalties for men and women who made love to individuals of the same gender. According to Boswell (1980), in 13th-century Spain, homosexuality carried a penalty of castration or of execution by stoning. The French civil code of 1270 also punished homosexual acts with castration for men and clitorectomies for women. Those brave enough to risk repetitions of their "crime" risked having limbs severed or even execution.

The earliest civil law in England to deal specifically with homosexuality was enacted in 1533. It made homosexuality a felony punishable by death. Not until the 1860s was the death penalty tempered to imprisonment for "gross indecency." Imprisonment continued to be sanctioned until 1967.

A hundred years ago in most of the Western world, homosexuality was viewed as a vice attributable to depravity, a perspective shared by most Christian religions of the time. These religious views, codified into law, defined homosexuals as criminals. The "cure" was often public censure and private penance. Contemporary Americans may seem more enlightened yet still display these old attitudes via laws in 22 states punishing acts of "sodomy" by two persons of the same gender.

HOMOSEXUALITY AS PATHOLOGY

The late 19th century saw the birth of modern psychiatry and psychology. For the first time, the medical community viewed homosexuality as a clinical condition. Legal sanctions continued, and homosexuals were seen as degenerates and objects of pity. Jean Charcot, the French hypnotist, made early "cure" attempts, but failures led him to decide homosexuality was hereditary.

Sigmund Freud, however, rejected moral labels for homosexuality. He cited injustices of cultural standards demanding the same behavior in sexual life from everyone. Freud (1951) frequently detailed contributions of gay men, such as Leonardo da Vinci, and noted the persistent presence of homosexuality in all cultures. He criticized writings that assumed gender confusion led to a homosexual object-choice (an object is defined as a person with whom one falls in love and desires erotically).

Freud suggested that a goal of psychoanalytic treatment is to identify determinants of object-choice rather than view homosexuality itself as a problem. Colleagues and disciples of Freud did not always make this distinction. Instead, they worked to discover sources of this "psychological neurosis." This began a shift by the medical/psychiatric profession toward labeling homosexuality as a mental aberration that warranted treatment instead of condemning it as sinful. For example, Helene Deutsch (1945) explained lesbianism as having two "causes"—one biologic and one psychogenic. The latter cause reflected difficulties due to narcissism and "arrested development." She believed sources of lesbianism resided in a girl's relationship with her mother. The daughter, realizing she cannot have her mother as a love object, does not transfer affections to her father but rather to other women. Deutsch promoted the notion that psychogenic aspects overwhelm a biologic demand for heterosexuality. In the early 1920s, Carl Jung (1964) wrote, "The more homosexual a man is, the more prone he is to disloyalty and to the seduction of boys" (p. 107). Other psychoanalytic writers posited fixation, narcissism, castration complex, or castration anxiety as suggested sources of homosexuality. None offered a pathology-based explanation of heterosexuality and all assumed homosexuality was unnatural. Views of pathological homosexuality led clinicians to attempt to cure it and to allow "natural predispositions" to heterosexuality to surface.

Research by psychiatrist Irving Bieber (1962) and colleagues sought to demonstrate origins of male homosexuality—a disease seen as a hidden, incapacitating fear of women. Bieber felt homosexuality served as a way to get love and acceptance from other men that one could not get from one's father. Significant bias in these studies stems from multiple roles played by these researchers. These roles created numerous confounds in the design, execution, analysis, and interpretation of their work. Despite attempts to establish the effectiveness of various approaches to treatment of the "disease," most of their predominantly homosexual patients showed little or no change. One of Kinsey's collaborators, Wardell Pomeroy, maintained a standing offer to administer the Kinsey research instruments to any of Bieber's purported "cures." Bieber acknowledged that of the 20 cures from 106 attempts, only one case would qualify, but Bieber was on such bad terms with that patient that he could not call on him (Isay, 1989).

In addition, clinicians tended to identify and write only about gay men and lesbians who sought psychotherapy. It is not surprising they found support for notions of pathology in clients' depression, failed relationships, loneliness, and isolation. If one based descriptions of characteristics of heterosexuals only on those who entered psychotherapy, one would have the same wealth of examples to conclude heterosexuality is pathological.

The medical model set the stage for clinicians to view their task as "curing homosexuality." Until ethical considerations intruded, clinicians in the 1960s conducted aversion therapy by administering electric shocks to men to extinguish their erotic response to other men (Feldman & MacCulloch, 1965). Although this extreme practice has been stopped, there is, nonetheless, considerable anecdotal evidence that many therapists still try to "convert" gay men and lesbians to a heterosexual orientation. Silverstein (1977) argued it is impossible for clients to volunteer for sexual orientation change as societal pressures do not allow free choice in the matter. Rather, he viewed such clients as suffering from low self-esteem and guilt. Thus, a therapist who agrees to try to help such clients change is actually serving to humiliate and to punish these clients for violating rules of our society.

Masters and Johnson (1979) claimed they successfully reverted or converted individuals with homosexual orientations to heterosexual orientations in a few weeks. They worked with 33 men married to women or living in long-term heterosexual relationships and 21 men with casual female partners. Masters and Johnson accepted only 13 women (7 married or in a long-term committed relationship with a man) for such treatment. For various reasons, they denied treatment to 16 other men and three women. The predominant reason expressed by these individuals for seeking change was social pressure to be heterosexual (e.g., job security, maintenance of a marriage). Masters and Johnson's attempts at follow-up after treatment were difficult. They lost contact with 16 men and three women. Yet they published "failure" rates for treatment of 20 to 23% based on the total sample size over 1 to 5 years. By excluding missing data, this figure climbs to over 29%. Criticism leveled at this research identifies three major flaws. First, they used varying lengths of follow-up to determine success. Second, the researchers paid little attention at follow-up to the participants' incentive to misrepresent their involvement in heterosexual relationships and to hide their desire for or participation in homosexual behaviors. Finally, Masters and Johnson elected to treat a very restricted sample—very motivated bisexuals.

One can find examples of homophobic attitudes by writers describing counseling theories that, in themselves, do not advocate that homosexuality is pathological. In 1972, Eric Berne stated a male homosexual does not want to leave a "script world which is populated by women who are dangerous and hateful schemers, or else innocent and occasionally amiable weirdos. All he wants to do is live more comfortably in that world, and only rarely does he wish to see women as real people" (p. 351). Berne's theory of Transactional Analysis offers no basis for these comments on homosexuality.

Another example of such attitudes is Ellis and Harper's (1979) description of Ellis' work with a "compulsive or obligatory" male homosexual to enable him to overcome his fear and act on hetero-sexual impulses. Presumably, this man's fear and resentment blocked these impulses. In their view, "literally tens of thousands of males get addicted to it [compulsive homosexuality] each year because it originally seems an easy way out for them—considering how diffi-cult we often make it for the young male to fulfill himself sexually with the young female" (p. 189). It seems highly unlikely, however, that gay men would face great difficulties simply for "easier" access to sexual gratification. Such difficulties include discrimination in employment, housing, and insurance; rejection by families; antigay violence; and other manifestations of homophobia. Nothing in Ellis' theory on the establishment of irrational thinking suggests any one sexual orientation is preferable to any other.

HOMOSEXUALITY AS A NORMAL VARIATION

The pioneering research of Alfred Kinsey and his colleagues (Kin-sey, Pomeroy, & Martin, 1948; Kinsey, Pomeroy, Martin, & Geb-hard, 1953) documented the frequency and prevalence of homosexual behavior among men and women in this country. They found a larger percentage than expected of men and women who were sexually active with same-sex partners throughout adolescence and adult-hood. For some, these experiences were sporadic, but often to the exclusion of heterosexual experiences. This research quashed public notions that homosexuality was primarily experimentation by trou-bled adolescents or characteristic of only a tiny number of adults. Kinsey refused to equate homosexuality with psychopathology and advocated repeal of repressive laws used to punish people for what he viewed as well within the normal range of adult behavior. Kin-sey's Institute for Sex Research continues to carry on his work and research ideas.

Not all was negative in writings or research by clinicians. Evelyn Hooker's pioneering research first documented the lack of difference between gay and nongay peoples on most psychological variables. She found similar psychological adjustment in nonclinical populations for these two groups. Previous writings had almost always looked at gay men and lesbians engaged in psychotherapy and generalized to nonclinical populations. Hooker's (1957) research on nonclinical samples using the Rorschach found it impossible to distinguish between gay and heterosexual men. Gonsiorek (1977) offered a review of research that noted results of psychological testing on homosexual and heterosexual populations failed to support the belief that homosexuality per se was a psychiatric illness.

THE IMPACT OF GAY LIBERATION

The gay liberation movement and gay political groups began to develop in the late 1960s and early 1970s. Their agendas included opposition to diagnosing homosexuality as a form of illness. In tandem with empirical research documenting the lack of differences in psychological adjustment among gay men, lesbians, and heterosexuals, these efforts bore fruit. December 1973 marked deletion by the American Psychiatric Association (APA) of homosexuality from its nomenclature of mental disorders. A committee of the APA had studied homosexuality thoroughly and reported its findings and recommendations for review and approval. When adopted, the APA declared homosexuality "by itself" does not necessarily constitute a psychiatric disorder and deplored discrimination against lesbian and gay peoples. A group of those dissatisfied with the outcome of the traditional process made the rare step of calling for a referendum of the membership to overturn the APA Board of Trustees' decision. The membership, however, voted to affirm the board's position (Bayer, 1981).

In place of homosexuality, however, a new diagnostic category appeared in the next edition of the diagnostic manual (*DSM-III*), namely Ego-dystonic Homosexuality (APA, 1980). This category was for those who stated they were not comfortable with and were unable to "adjust to" their homosexuality. Considering the prevalence of homophobia in our society, it is unlikely very many gay, lesbian, or bisexual individuals escape discomfort, uncertainty about, and difficulties with their sexual orientations. There was no listing of Ego-dystonic Heterosexuality in the manual. In 1987, the APA deleted Ego-dystonic Homosexuality from the *DSM-III-Revised*. Despite this declaration, many psychiatrists and psychologists continue to treat homosexuality as a mental illness, with efforts to "cure" someone of same-sex attractions.

In 1977, the American Psychological Association's Division 9, the Society for the Psychological Study of Social Issues, formed a task force at Harvard University to study the nature of sexual orientation and relevant concerns. Their report detailed ignorance and misinformation about gay men and lesbians among both lay and professional people (Paul, Weinrich, Gonsiorek, & Hotvedt, 1982).

Other social pressures, such as feminism, are also working to change the climate in which society views gay men and lesbians. Researchers began looking at women's issues and addressed male bias in human development theories. Their data questioned the fundamental superiority of male development and challenged notions that women follow the same developmental pathways as men. This attention promoted reexamination of conceptual frameworks that assumed heterosexuality as the only natural outcome for human development processes.

The advent of recognized lesbian and gay student groups also has had an impact on the atmosphere of the college or university campus. As these organizations developed, many lobbied campus counseling centers to facilitate support groups for lesbian and gay students. Staff of counseling centers often served a consultative role with these student organizations. More recently, many of these groups began to invite bisexual students to join. For some, this meant changing the name of their organizations to be more inclusive. For others, it included efforts to sensitize the campus to the needs of bisexual people—including sensitizing counseling center staff. On a few campuses, gay and lesbian faculty and staff are now forming organized groups of their own. These groups offer mutual support and may lobby for adoption of affirmative action policies that include sexual orientation as a protected class. Some groups also advocate for recognition of domestic partnerships and offering of appropriate benefits by the college or university. Despite such gains, the National Gay and Lesbian Task Force still finds it necessary to collect statistics on the number of violent acts directed at gay men and lesbians on American campuses.

REASONS WHY LESBIAN AND GAY STUDENTS SEEK PSYCHOTHERAPY

Gay and lesbian students come to college and university counseling centers for many of the same reasons any student seeks counseling—choosing a major; test anxiety; conflicts with roommates, friends, or family; problems in a romantic relationship; or an emotional upset. The primary reasons for seeking help are to seek assistance with various developmental issues (Coleman & Remafedi,

1989). Sexual orientation may be neither a presenting concern nor an underlying basis for a student's request for counseling. The general societal climate about sexual orientation, however, may influence how students view their problems or may limit options students consider in handling these problems.

An example of a typical concern is a lesbian student seeking counseling to help her decide between a career as an English teacher or as a journalist. Her primary problem is her career identity. Her fear that she may eventually experience discrimination against lesbian teachers complicates her concerns. Family issues may also compound the situation (e.g., her parents want her to be a business major to assure she will be economically self-sufficient).

Following are some themes that may be overlooked in working with lesbian or gay clients. They are mentioned here to alert the clinician to explore these areas. Certainly all of them are not applicable to all clients. For example, intolerance and isolation are influenced by the strength and breadth of the student's current support system. Cross-cultural conflicts may play a greater role for some than for others. Each theme, however, merits some consideration with any client. It is important to note these themes do not necessarily reflect pathology on the part of these students—any more than it certifies pathology when heterosexual students seek help. The severity of these problems, however, can be heightened by heavy repression and stigmatization of gay and lesbian people in this country (Dworkin & Gutierrez, 1989).

INTOLERANCE AND ISOLATION

The external impact of homophobia on gay and lesbian people can be quite traumatic. People known or believed not to be heterosexual may be rejected by their families, fired from their jobs, lose custody of their children, or find themselves targets for violence. College and university students are not exempt from the negative effects of discrimination and rejection. For example, campus programming tends to target heterosexual students. Students rarely find films or speakers discussing lesbian or gay issues. Often, only a lesbian and gay student organization sponsors programs on these issues. Campus social events are geared to heterosexual couples. A lesbian or gay couple brave enough to attend a dance on campus may find their choice quite a challenging act to some other students. In addition, a campus typically offers few role models of openly gay or lesbian faculty or staff. Thus, college students can readily feel alone with gay or lesbian feelings and quite isolated from their peers.

Intolerance from other students may make campuses hostile environments. Typical campus graffiti intimidates many lesbian and gay students. Imagine the impact of entering a classroom, glancing at a bulletin board, and seeing "DIE FAG" scrawled on a flyer announcing an AIDS education program. Flyers trying to inform lesbian and gay students about upcoming events face destruction or defacement—at times within minutes after posting. Faculty may provide forums, sometimes inadvertently, for homophobic students to condemn lesbian, gay, and bisexual people during class. Such behavior perpetuates the invisibility of lesbian and gay people in academia. Students suspected or known to be gay or lesbian in residence halls may face conflicts with roommates and others on their floor or section. A resident may demand a homosexual roommate be moved out. Other residents may harass lesbian and gay students and attempt to make the environment so uncomfortable that students make their own requests to move. Closeted residents often face pressure to date heterosexually.

When one considers the toll of isolation, discrimination, and harassment endured by lesbian and gay students, it is not surprising that some of these individuals approach counseling centers for advice or support. For example, students preparing to come out to their parents may come to the counseling center for help in deciding when and how to approach this task. Some students may come to the center for help and support after coming out if they receive an unexpected negative reaction from their family. A student experiencing conflicts with a roommate may ask for help from the center to determine if the housing staff are "safe" people to approach concerning these problems.

CROSS-CULTURAL CONFLICTS

Students of color at predominantly Anglo campuses often seek support and validation from peers who are members of their group. There is often the belief (and at times, the reality) that disclosing one's gayness or lesbianism endangers that support or acceptance.

African-American students, at times, feel they have to choose between being African-American or being gay or lesbian (Cornwell, 1978). Social messages given, especially to men, are that marriage and family always come first (Loiacano, 1989). Encounters with other men may occur only in bars or other secretive areas. The few open role models for gay or lesbian couples in the community provide little support for long-term, same-sex romances. Without the support and nurturance found useful in the coming out process in the White community, these gay and lesbian students turn to the African-

American community but find extensive homophobia—particularly in Black churches (Clayborne, 1978). For example, one can readily find those who believe there are no gay or lesbian African Americans. Homosexuality is often viewed as a White phenomenon. Little empirical research exists on African-American views about homosexuality (Mays & Cochran, 1988).

Most Latin-American cultures strongly emphasize primacy of the family as a basic societal unit. Involvement of extended family and close friends makes it difficult to maintain a sense of privacy. For gay or lesbian people, this may result in intense awkwardness when relatives inquire about marriage prospects. Many of these cultures train children to show respect by answering family members' questions. An individual may respond with a half-truth that the right person has not come along to marry. This may result, however, in arranged introductions with "eligible" people by these concerned family members. Such encounters may serve to further the sense of deception and distance from the family that many of these students experience.

In many Latino societies, a male may use the culturally accepted notion that his sexuality is a difficult force to control. His quest to satisfy himself in whatever way possible may include sex with another man. Keep in mind sexual behavior with other men may not equal being homosexual or bisexual for these men (Carrier, 1989). Latino males who have sex with other men may not identify with gay men and may actively reject information targeted to gay or bisexual students as irrelevant to them. Societal pressure of "¿qué dirán?" (what will people say?) is a powerful force (Caraballo-Diéguez, 1989). It may keep Latino/Latina students from attending meetings of campus gay, lesbian, and bisexual student organizations for fear of being seen and having to justify their attendance to others. The widespread influence of conservative Catholicism may increase the level of guilt of Hispanic men and limit them to furtive sex contacts rather than connecting with the gay communities (Malyon, 1982). When seeking counseling, these students may be reluctant to work with professionals who are not bilingual and conversant with their home culture. For many, an additional barrier is a cultural norm to keep personal problems within the confines of the family unit. Revealing deeply personal information to a counselor, even when one is reluctant to tell one's family, may feel like an additional violation of the privacy of the family.

African-American and Latin students are not the only gay and lesbian people of color to endure isolation. There is often little support in the home community to be gay or lesbian for any student of non-Caucasian heritage. When they attempt to seek support from student lesbian and gay organizations, typically they find programs and structures most comfortable for Caucasian students. Therefore, for such minorities within a minority, existing support networks may fail to offer conducive environments for exploring feelings, examining behaviors, and working to develop a positive identity as a gay or lesbian person of color.

International students may face additional obstacles. First, these students must confront their internalization of their home culture's values about homosexuality. For many, a return to their native country may mean returning to a place where they can be disowned, imprisoned, or even killed for their sexual behavior. Some clients do not have the option of permanent residence in the United States. Their counselors face the dilemma that helping clients become more comfortable with their sexual orientations in our culture may increase their discomfort and isolation in their home countries. In addition, the U.S. Immigration and Naturalization Service is still legally authorized to refuse homosexuals entry into the United States. Thus, a family visit may entail serious consequences upon return if Immigration determines or even suspects one is gay or lesbian. Students with this awareness may also be reluctant to engage in therapy and reveal information that they perceive puts their visa status in jeopardy.

CONSEQUENCES OF INTERNALIZED HOMOPHOBIA

There is ample research that shows no difference in the emotional adjustment and amount of mental illness in homosexuals as compared to heterosexuals (Reiss, 1980). It is important to keep these data in mind to refute the tradition of viewing lesbian and gay people as pathological by nature. If pathology exists, it more often finds its origins in society's hatred and bigotry rather than as a by-product of one's sexual orientation.

When an individual internalizes society's antigay, antilesbian attitudes, the results can be devastating. In a study of people in the San Francisco area, Bell and Weinberg (1978) detailed a wide range of these negative consequences. Gay men reported they were more lonely, worried, depressed, and tense than were their heterosexual counterparts. Far more gay men and lesbians considered suicide an option than did heterosexuals. In one study, 30% of gay men and 35% of lesbians were dependent on alcohol or reported drinking excessively (Saghir, Robins, Walbran, & Gentry, 1970a, 1970b). In another study, Weinberg and Williams (1974) found 29.4% of a gay male sample reported drinking more than they should (i.e., all the time). A more recent work (Ziebold & Mongeon, 1982), again reported up to 30% of the homosexual population, versus 10% of the heterosexual population, are alcoholic.

If one views a homosexual identity as pathological, there are temptations to interpret such statistics as support for that view and to ignore studies that report no differences in emotional adjustment between heterosexual and homosexual populations. Alternatively, more enlightened clinicians adhere to the stance of the American Psychological Association that "homosexuality per se implies no impairment in judgment, reliability, or general social and vocational capabilities" (Conger, 1975). From this perspective, the influence of oppression and homophobia is viewed as the treatment target. A recent report from the Task Force on Bias in Psychotherapy with Lesbians and Gay Men (Committee on Lesbian and Gay Concerns, 1990) provided evidence that many clinicians practice from a biased perspective, leading to inappropriate care for lesbian and gay male clients. The report also offered illustrations of practitioners who provide unbiased and helpful treatment with this population.

AIDS AND HIV INFECTION

College students are a microcosm of society and, hence, are vulnerable to the ills one finds in society at large. Some students seeking counseling may present anxiety over AIDS. Indeed, according to Platt (1987), college students comprise a large portion of the population for which the potential transmission of HIV (human immunodeficiency virus) is high. Official preliminary results of a Centers for Disease Control (CDC) study indicated a HIV-seropositive rate for college students in their sample (N = 17,000) of 2 students per 1,000 (CDC, 1989). Yet evidence indicates many college students have incomplete or misleading understandings of safer sexual practices (Halstead, Vitous, & Derbort, 1990). This may be a result of the young adult's developmental stage, which includes sexual experimentation, establishing relationships, and learning to negotiate intimacy. Many college students, at the peak of their youth, feel "invincible" and invulnerable to invisible killers such as AIDS (Gray & Saracino, 1989). This feeling of invulnerability acts as a barrier for learning how to avoid HIV infection because such a student has a sense that "it won't happen to me."

It is critical for counselors to be informed about AIDS when working with all college students, but especially when working with gay and bisexual male clients. Some students may continue high-risk sexual practices that place their partners and themselves at risk for contracting HIV. Counselors must be aware of risks of infection and be able to discuss explicitly various methods of risk reduction as well as barriers to practicing these methods (Martin, 1989). Some students will seek help to deal with their fear of infection, despite their rigid adherence to safer sex guidelines. They may have difficulties getting involved in relationships or expressing their sexuality due to their anxiety.

Other students contemplating being tested to learn if they are seropostive to HIV-antibodies may seek counseling to consider several factors: How will they emotionally react to the information? What resources/plans do they have should the results be positive? What are their plans should the results be negative? What impact will these results have on their relationships with others? Are the results going to be anonymous and confidential? Once tested, seropositive as well as seronegative students may need support. Those who are seronegative may experience mixtures of relief and of guilt that they are uninfected when friends and lovers may be infected (Martin, 1989). Counselors can offer support to practice safer sex behaviors and should confront high-risk behaviors with these individuals.

Clients who are seropositive show varied responses (Martin, 1989). Some view the information as a death sentence and react with extreme anxiety and despair. Others experience a loss of sex drive (Gold, Seymour, & Sahl, 1986) and feel guilt and shame as well as anger at themselves, at the world, at the government, and, especially, at the medical community. In counseling, one can help clients develop healthier lifestyle habits and learn stress reduction techniques. Consultation with medical staff is quite appropriate. In addition, clients face decisions concerning when to reveal their antibody status as well as concerning employment, insurance, will and estate planning, and relationships. Students in a couple in which one is seronegative and the other is positive may face difficult times. The negative partner may feel threatened or overwhelmed by HIV. When both are seropositive, there may be blame if one believes the other infected him. If a coupled relationship ends, it is often useful to explore what the relationship was like before knowledge of HIV infection was present (Carl, 1990).

Finally, for all gay men and lesbians, seropositive or not, illness, dying, death, and grief now play a major role in their community.

This reality may be depressing or frightening. Despite the mutual support for the grieving process in the lesbian and gay community, at times individual counseling is appropriate. College and university students may have experienced the loss of friends or of mentors in the community. Counselors should be alert for signs of the stress of grief—depression, anxiety, unusual lethargy or free-floating anger. Martin (1989) suggests post-traumatic stress disorder (PTSD) is a possibility for those who have lost many friends and have others remaining who are ill. The symptoms of PTSD—such as recurrent and intrusive recollections or dreams of the event(s), persistent avoidance of activities that arouse recollection of the event(s), diminished interest in significant activities, feeling detached from others, constricted affect, sleep disturbance, memory impairment, survivor guilt, or hyperalertness—can be viewed as the normal reactions one has to a catastrophic situation instead of as a pathological response to normal difficulties one faces in life.

COMPULSIVE SEXUAL BEHAVIOR

Some gay and bisexual male clients may present themselves for help with a "sex addiction." These men typically are engaging in anonymous sexual contacts with other men, often in semipublic areas such as rest rooms. Their description of this drive to seek sexual contacts has a compulsive quality to it. Rather than a celebration of their sexuality, these men describe their encounters as somewhat furtive and guilt ridden and often at the expense of other activities and values. Keep in mind that this behavior has parallels in heterosexual singles bars on weekend nights as men and women seek partners for overnight casual encounters. Some writers argue that the label *sexual addiction* in this Age of AIDS places gay men in danger of being designated societal criminals and may threaten their civil liberties (Kyle, 1988; Levine & Troiden, 1988). It can be argued that if this behavior interferes with a client's ability to concentrate energies on academics or work, label or not, the behavior may deserve the respectful attention of a counselor. Sexually compulsive behavior may also inhibit the formation of positive, intimate relationships. Finally, some clients may feel threatened by loss of control over this behavior and seek help to avoid threats to careers, relationships, and lives (Pincu, 1989). Difficulties in accepting a primarily homosexual orientation and feelings that same-sex intimacy is not an acceptable option, as well as low self-esteem, often play a key role in maintaining this pattern of behavior. Treatment must address issues of loneliness, intimacy, and honesty (Carnes, 1983, 1989).

DOMESTIC VIOLENCE IN LESBIAN AND GAY RELATIONSHIPS

The lesbian and gay communities have paid little attention to battering in same-sex relationships. Thus, this violence has been mostly invisible. Individuals being battered often report feeling lonely and isolated by this wall of silence (Hart, 1986). As in heterosexual relationships, battering serves as a vehicle to control the thoughts, beliefs, or conduct of one's intimate partner or to punish resistance to such control. Most information on battering comes from the domestic violence movement (based on heterosexual relationships), undocumented personal testimonies by battered lesbians, studies currently in progress, and anecdotal and clinical experience (Morrow & Hawxhurst, 1989). A survey of books written for lay audiences on gay and lesbian relationships failed to identify any that discuss battering.

Walber (1988) described the various forms of domestic violence reported by gay men and lesbians as including both physical and nonphysical abuse as a manifestation of sexism and socialization around power and control issues. She stated there is an assumption that physical abuse in same-sex relationships is not really dangerous or harmful because the partners are assumed to be of similar size and strength. She countered that assumption with statements of survivors who report quite severe patterns of abuse.

Some lesbian students may offer concerns about being in a battering relationship. Until recently, the issue of violence in lesbian relationships was invisible. Now, a variety of articles and a book have addressed this issue (Leeder, 1988; Lobel, 1986; Morrow & Hawxhurst, 1989). It is critical that therapists not simply translate concepts based from research and understanding of heterosexual battering relationships to these women. Instead, therapists need to be guided by the lesbian survivors of battering themselves. Attention needs to focus on safety for the woman being battered, empowerment of the survivor, and assistance in helping the survivor heal. Counseling for the batterer is also important, and a different therapist is usually required.

Violence in gay male relationships remains very hidden. Little about this concern has appeared in the popular press (Califa, 1986). Only one scholarly book focuses on domestic violence in gay male relationships (Island & Letellier, 1991). It is also likely such violence is underreported. The stigma against men reporting rape is quite high. When attempting such a report, a man is likely to face disbelief or outright hostility from the police (Anderson, 1982). Reports of domestic violence in a gay relationship seem likely to elicit similar reactions from police. Walber (1988) stated that because men have been traditionally socialized to use violence and power to control others, it becomes difficult to identify domestic violence in their lives. Men, supposedly in control of their lives, should thus be immune from victimization, especially within the context of a relationship. When reality differs from this socialized ideal, a man may feel shame and fear others' reactions to this information. Unfortunately, there also seems little written about gay batterers (Walber, 1988). The literature focuses almost exclusively on male batterers in heterosexual relationships.

INTEGRATION OF ISSUES

The problems described above are not the reasons gay male and lesbian students most frequently seek counseling. More than sexual orientation, one's age and student status may dictate the sort of issues for which one requires outside help. The developmental issues students face are not unique to one's sexual orientation. For example, dating and forming intimate relationships comprise a primary developmental activity for most college students. For the student with a nonheterosexual orientation, counseling may provide the only safe place the student has to discuss his or her feelings and experiences in negotiating this developmental task. It is important that the counselor not only focuses on the "problems" that the client brings concerning his or her relationships but also provides the client with a broader context from which to view these relationships (De Cecco, 1988; Eldridge, 1990). Bibliotherapy is often a useful technique (see the listings of resources in chapter 13).

BARRIERS TO TREATMENT

Social stigmas may hinder a person's ability to seek therapy to discuss feelings about same-sex sexual attractions or behaviors. Counseling trainees with minimal exposure to homosexually oriented individuals tend to have fairly high levels of homophobia (McDermott & Stadler, 1988). Such attitudes can pose a problem because many clients do not have a strong preference for a gay or lesbian therapist. A recent study (McDermott, Tyndall, & Lichtenberg, 1989) of Midwestern gay and lesbian university students found that whereas 49% preferred a gay or lesbian therapist, 39% reported they thought a counselor's sexual orientation did not make a difference. If such a student encounters a homophobic therapist, he or she may find the experience damaging or at least unhelpful, may terminate counseling, and may not seek help with another therapist. Those students preferring an openly gay or lesbian therapist often find such options are simply unavailable on their campus. This points to the need for all university counselors to learn how to deal affirmatively, knowledgeably, and effectively with gay and lesbian students and their issues.

As noted earlier, several studies found nearly a third of gay men and lesbians in their samples to be dependent on or abusive of alcohol or other drugs. Alcohol treatment centers, however, tend to identify or report very few gay or lesbian clients (Finnegan & McNally, 1987). The invisibility of nonheterosexual individuals in these settings may impede dramatically the progress a client makes in recovery. Gay or lesbian students may use alcohol, the current drug of choice for college students, in an effort to medicate away anxiety or depression arising from external and internal homophobia (Kus, 1990).

BARRIERS TO THERAPISTS WORKING WITH GAY AND LESBIAN CLIENTS[1]

Morin and Charles described bias in understanding lesbians and gay men as "an insidious ingression into the microcosm of psychological theory, practice, and therapeutic intervention" (1983, p. 310). This chapter assumes such bias is common, to some degree, in the work of most therapists, whether they are straight, bisexual, lesbian, or gay. Awareness of inherent barriers is assumed to be the best method to combat potential bias. Two barriers that may impede a therapist's work with lesbian and gay clients are the therapist's own stereotypes and the therapist's heterosexual bias. In working with couples, an additional barrier is a tendency to overemphasize gender roles in the conceptualization of intimate relationships.

---

[1]Part of this section is from "Gender issues in counseling same-sex couples" by N. S. Eldridge, 1987, *Professional Psychology*, 18, pp. 567–569. Copyright 1987 by the American Psychological Association. Adapted by permission of the publisher.

STEREOTYPING

Gender stereotypes can act as barriers to effective work with gay and lesbian populations by dictating assumptions about a client's sexual orientation. These assumptions can be automatic and unconscious; the concept of heterosexuality is embedded in and related to a whole set of assumptions derived from gender stereotypes. Although initial impressions or assumptions can be adjusted as more information is gathered, sexual orientation, sex role, gender identity, and behavioral characteristics are often erroneously linked together.

A therapist might, for example, assume a new female client has a female gender identity, has an affectional and sexual orientation toward men, and possesses a set of psychological and behavioral characteristics generally associated with being female in this culture. However, upon learning this new client is a lesbian, the therapist may quickly replace the original assumptions with a new set of assumptions. Her behaviors may be viewed as revealing a more "masculine" gender identity, assumptions about the set of psychological characteristics she possesses may be changed, and different sex-role attitudes and behaviors may now be expected, all based on the limited information about her sexual orientation.

This tendency to link gender identity, psychological attributes, and gender-role behavior to sexual orientation is faulty reasoning, however, as each of these aspects of an individual varies independently from the others (Spence, Deaux, & Helmreich, 1985). This linking tendency in stereotyping behavior suggests a likelihood to take in information about someone that fits internal stereotypes while dismissing information that does not fit. In fact, research has indicated people are more tolerant and accepting of gay men who fit stereotypes than of those who do not (Herek, 1984). For example, the gay theater major is more tolerated than the gay football player.

Another influence upon stereotyping of lesbians and gay men is the "hidden" nature of these populations; they are present but generally not visible. A primary function of stereotypes is to fill in the gaps where information is missing. Preconceptions and attitudes about others are generally based on experience. The less direct the experience is, the greater the reliance on cultural stereotypes gathered secondhand. Unlike a person's race or sex, an individual's sexual orientation cannot generally be determined based on physical cues; thus, it is difficult to identify lesbians, gay men, or bisexuals in order to gather information about these groups to replace the stereotypes. Instead, individuals who fit physical or behavioral stereotypes are assumed to be gay or lesbian, whereas anyone else is assumed to be heterosexual. This, of course, acts to strengthen the stereotypes while giving the appearance of providing additional information about the population itself. Therapists who rely on these sorts of cues with their clients run the risk of making erroneous assumptions of heterosexuality that can cause clients considerable anxiety and often influence whether, or what, a client discloses. A good way to avoid this situation is to develop a habit of using gender-neutral language when exploring the relationships of *any* client, until the client clearly specifies the sex of the particular partner referred to. In working with bisexual students, the importance of avoiding assumptions of gender are particularly important.

Another aspect of stereotyping that can be problematic for therapists, especially when dealing with a hidden population, is the tendency to gather information and draw conclusions about that population solely from one's own clinical experiences. Moreover, the research available on gay men and lesbians is predominantly based on clinical samples. Broader, descriptive data on lesbian and gay populations have only recently begun to reach mainstream journals in our field.

Finally, another function stereotyping serves is to create a clear distinction between an individual and the stereotyped group. For example, heterosexist individuals, threatened by the possibility that gay men and lesbians are more similar to heterosexuals than different, are likely to retain stereotypes about lesbians and gay men. Because of the negative valuation of homosexuality in the larger culture, considerable pressure exists to distinguish oneself from this label. The failure to recognize and understand one's own homophobic reactions, then, can be a significant barrier to a therapist's work with lesbians and gay men.

HETEROSEXUAL BIAS

The stereotyping discussed thus far is compounded when working with students having relationship concerns, or with same-sex couples. Yet concerns about intimate relationships are quite often presenting concerns for all college and university students seeking counseling services. Views of how individuals in couples relate to one another are largely influenced by what has been labeled in the literature as *heterosexual bias*. Morin (1977) has defined heterosexual bias as "a belief system that values heterosexuality as superior to and/or more 'natural' than homosexuality" (p. 629). For most, an understanding of intimate relationships is based on heterosexual models. Although the range of types of heterosexual models is beginning to increase, there exists a tendency to judge relationships against some internalized ideal model that includes marriage and children.

For the therapist working with a same-sex relationship, heterosexual bias can be a significant barrier, particularly if it is unrecognized. If the therapist has heterosexual bias, he or she tends to measure the health of a same-sex relationship by how similar it is to an ideal heterosexual union. For example, a high level of intimacy in a lesbian relationship might be seen as "psychological fusion" or "an inability to differentiate," based on an observation that expressed intimacy level falls on the high end of the norms the therapist has gathered from observation of and work with heterosexual couples. Or perhaps a long-term relationship between two men may be considered dysfunctional because they engage in sexual behavior outside the relationship, which is often viewed as a sign of trouble or dissatisfaction in heterosexual marriages. This tendency to measure same-sex relationships by "deviance" from heterosexual norms biases both the assessment of the problem and the outcome goals of any therapeutic intervention with a same-sex couple.

Another way in which heterosexual bias may affect the therapeutic situation involves how a therapist relates to the partners in couple therapy. Several questions suggest some of the potential influences of heterosexual bias in working with couples: Do we tend to have different ways of bonding or interacting with the member of the couple who is our sex than with the member who is the other sex? If so, what does that tell us about our response to gender in our work with couples? What happens when we work with same-sex couples? Do we relate to both members of the couple according to our stereotypes about their gender, or do we treat one as the "more masculine" and one as the "more feminine" based on subtle differences we observe between the partners? How will these potential choices affect our therapy? These are all critical questions for therapists working with same-sex couples.

GENDER-ROLE EMPHASIS IN VIEWING INTIMATE RELATIONSHIPS

Another factor that affects how an intimate relationship is viewed is the salience of gender roles in the observer's understanding of how a couple functions. This emphasis on gender roles has been encouraged by the research on intimate relationships. Rarely do social scientists have a variable so truly dichotomous as "sex." Individuals are either male or female. Because of this clear distinction, data suggest differences between the sexes are often given uncritical, sometimes unjustified credence. In addition, research that does not demonstrate gender differences has been less likely to be published than research that does (Wallston, 1981).

Members of most dyads generally take on particular roles in relation to one another. However, because the study of intimate relationships has focused on heterosexual pairs, the gender roles and differences typical of such couples have become standards for evaluating the behavior and interaction in intimate relationships. Some researchers are trying to break away from this approach in studying relationships by deemphasizing the gender differences and assessing the far wider band of gender overlap (McHugh, Koeske, & Frieze, 1981; Wallston, 1981). Yet thinking tends to be organized along gender lines: Women are more relationship oriented, men are more instrumental; women are more expressive, men are more achievement motivated. Such generalizations may provide clues for understanding heterosexual couples but pose a dilemma when applied to same-sex couples. One common, but erroneous, way this dilemma is often handled is to assign gender roles to the partners as a way to understand their interaction. Therapists may struggle with this dilemma to the point that, uncertain of how to assign roles, they ask clients point blank who tends to play the "male" role and who plays the "female" role in the relationship. Reports of such occurrences indicate that clients generally respond in disbelief, followed by a sinking awareness that the therapist neither sees nor accepts their relationship for what it is.

GUIDELINES FOR THERAPISTS AND EDUCATORS[2]

A survey of therapists' attitudes, knowledge, and concerns about counseling lesbians and gay men revealed a strong need for therapist training (Graham, Rawlings, Halpern, & Hermes, 1984). Prior to 1975, when the American Psychological Association removed homosexuality from its list of mental disorders, the common therapeutic strategy for dealing with lesbian and gay male clients included diagnosis, some explanation of the causative factors, and an attempt

---

[2]Part of this section is from "Gender issues in counseling same-sex couples" by N. S. Eldridge, 1987, *Professional Psychology, 18*, pp. 570–571. Copyright 1987 by the American Psychological Association. Adapted by permission of the publisher.

to change the client's sexual orientation. This approach is still being used today (Committee on Lesbian and Gay Concerns, 1990). Newer strategies, however, have been developed that involve assisting clients to integrate lesbian and gay identities into a fulfilling lifestyle. Although training needed to put this new perspective into practice is beginning to be offered by professional organizations and at conferences, it is still mostly unavailable in graduate programs and is not required for licensure (Graham et al., 1984). It is not the purpose of this chapter to outline specific counseling techniques or approaches. It is assumed those doing therapy or counseling on a college or university campus have been trained to do this work. Rather, we focus here on inherent barriers that face many student affairs staff who find themselves assisting lesbian or gay students. Issues raised in the preceding section suggest a few basic guidelines for therapists working with lesbian or gay students, and for individuals responsible for training mental health professionals.

Be mindful of heterosexual bias. This bias can be subtle and insidious in nature. Am I making assumptions about a client's sexual orientation? What cues am I using to make these assumptions? Am I accurate, or am I stereotyping? Am I imposing a heterosexual pattern on a relationship by assigning a "male" and a "female" role to the partners? Discussing these questions with colleagues and, where appropriate, with clients may also be useful.

Use gender-free language. Developing the habit of using gender-free language when exploring relationships with *any* client can be useful in several ways. It provides a message to all clients that the therapist is aware intimacies can exist between members of the same sex and, furthermore, that the therapist is open to receive information about these relationships or feelings. It may provide a subtle educational tool for some clients who have given little consideration to same-sex relationships; for others, it may be a stimulus for them to look at their own feelings toward members of their sex and to explore those feelings in therapy. Finally, consistent use of gender-free language can be a consciousness-raising experience by helping to keep the issues of heterosexual bias and gender stereotyping in the foreground of the therapist's awareness.

Become familiar with models of lesbian and gay identity formation. These models address the process by which an individual comes to develop a positive, integrative lesbian or gay identity, an essential foundation for affirmative work with lesbians and gay men. Theories of lesbian and gay development have emerged in the literature only within the last 13 years (Berzon, 1979; Cass, 1979; Clark, 1977; Kimmel, 1978; Morin & Schultz, 1978). (See chapters 1 and 2 in this book for more extensive discussions of identity development and developmental issues for lesbian and gay male students.)

Identify and use a consultant.   A consultant can be a colleague with more experience with gay or lesbian clients, or a friend who is familiar with the gay or lesbian communities. Many professional associations now have formal or informal groups of members interested in lesbian and gay concerns. Such groups can provide a variety of resources useful in counseling students or for training purposes. These groups also serve as networks to identify consultants in a particular speciality area or geographical region. For example, both the American College Personnel Association and the National Association for Student Personnel Administrators have recognized committees or task forces for lesbian, gay, and bisexual issues. Many campuses have a lesbian and gay student organization. These groups may be excellent vehicles to understand the climate for lesbian, gay, and bisexual students on your campus.

Learn about local support networks.   Networks for lesbians may be totally different from those for gay men, with bisexual networks different still. Are lesbians welcome at certain gay events? Where can bisexuals feel safe to be out about their orientation? Therapists who are knowledgeable about differences among various resources can encourage clients to become involved in appropriate support networks. Finding positive lesbian or gay role models can be a powerful tool for building self-esteem and allaying fears and stereotypes based on misinformation or lack of information.

Explore the cultural context of each student.   Therapists need to understand the specific cultural context of the student regarding attitudes toward sexuality. This might include exploration of the student's family context, cultural and/or religious affiliations, and the peer groups on campus with whom the student currently identifies.

Appreciate differences between lesbians, gay males, and bisexuals. Individuals with little information about these populations often tend to lump them together. Yet a familiarity with women's development can be much more useful in understanding lesbian experiences than is a familiarity with theory on gay lifestyles derived from research on men. At this time, bisexuality is relatively invisible, even within lesbian and gay circles. There is often discrimination against those who identify themselves as bisexual both by heterosexuals and gay and lesbian communities.

Become aware of specific boundary issues and ethical concerns in working with these populations.   Bisexual, gay, and lesbian therapists particularly need to note that gay and lesbian populations form quite small communities. Boundary issues need to be explored and considered carefully in the light of professional ethics and personal lifestyles (Brown, 1988; Gonsiorek, 1987). In a small college town, the campus gay, lesbian, and bisexual organization may form the major source of social activities and political action for gays in the broader community. Do you want to run into several clients at all community events you may attend? Are your friends also likely to be friends with your clients? Consultation on boundary and ethical concerns is highly recommended.

Use bibliotherapy.   You do not need to be the sole source of information for clients, even if they are very closeted about their sexual orientation. Excellent books and pamphlets are available, in both fiction and nonfiction forms, to help one learn about the variety of experiences for lesbian, gay, and bisexual individuals. The final chapter of this book provides one means to locate these resources.

Consider referral when appropriate.   The authors believe all therapists who sensitize themselves to concerns of gay, lesbian, and bisexual people can do effective work with these clients. Yet there are times when referring clients to others is an appropriate choice. Perhaps a client is at a stage in the development of his or her identify where working with a gay or lesbian therapist would be optimal. Perhaps you have worked so well with other lesbian, bisexual, or gay clients that your caseload is becoming too homogeneous. If you work with a lot of people with AIDS or with many clients who have lost lovers and friends to HIV-related illness, you may feel too drained to accept new clients with these concerns for a while. In such cases, referral to other professionals seems ethical and wise. Before making such referrals, one needs to assess if a counseling service is affirmative in its work with gay, lesbian, and bisexual clients.

GUIDELINES TO ASSESS IF A COUNSELING CENTER IS GAY AND LESBIAN AFFIRMATIVE

Students with other than heterosexual concerns have good reason to approach therapy with caution and skepticism. Some avoid counseling services at their institutions for fear of repercussions in other aspects of their educational experience. Others turn to campus counseling services because their needs are pressing and they are unsure of alternatives. The decision on where to seek counseling depends on the student and on the environment in which the college or university is housed.

This section provides guidelines lesbian, bisexual, and gay students can use to assess the climate of counseling services available on their campuses. At the same time, these guidelines can be applied by college or university staff to ascertain appropriateness of outside services as referral sources for gay, lesbian, and bisexual students. Finally, additional guidelines are included that can help counseling center staff members do a thorough self-assessment of their own services to lesbian, gay, and bisexual populations.

Positive written acknowledgement of lesbian, gay, and bisexual students:

- If the center uses a form to collect personal data from new clients, can a person completing the form validate a significant relationship, or does the form simply offer check-off boxes for married, divorced, and single? If the form asks for family data, is there a place to record information about a lover or domestic partner, or is the only space available labeled spouse?
- If the center has new clients complete a problem checklist, does it include gay and lesbian issues? If so, does the language include, for example, *problems with homosexuality, confusion over sexual preference*, or *lesbian and gay concerns*? Consider the implications of such language in terms of how these students are viewed by the agency: Is their sexual orientation a "problem," something to "adjust to," or an important and valuable aspect of a person seeking help?
- Does the center offer groups for gay men and lesbians? If so, are they publicized outside of the counseling center or only to clients already in the system?

Verbal recognition of gay, bisexual, and lesbian concerns:

- If a new client requests to see a gay or lesbian counselor for intake, does the reception desk staff attempt to honor the request if possible (as they probably try to honor a request to see a female counselor)? How do staff deal with requests to be assigned to a gay or lesbian counselor for treatment?
- If a client asks a staff therapist about his or her sexual orientation, does he or she seem comfortable discussing the subject (regardless of whether the therapist declines to share the information immediately)?

Visible resources for lesbian, gay, and bisexual students:

- If the center subscribes to magazines and newspapers for a waiting area, are any of these gay or lesbian publications? If booklets on various topics are offered, are any of special interest to lesbians or gay men (e.g., coming out, dealing with antigay and antilesbian harassment, safer sex, AIDS)?

- Do all staff have information about local resources for gay, lesbian, and bisexual people that may complement, supplement, or replace campus services?

Outreach to lesbian, gay, and bisexual students:

- Do staff of the center provide a liaison function with any gay, lesbian, and bisexual student or staff organizations on campus?
- When providing outreach programs, when appropriate, do counselors use examples of gay and lesbian situations or use neutral language so gay, lesbian, and bisexual participants can apply concepts to themselves without having to translate pronouns or labels to fit?
- Is there heterosexist language in handouts that are distributed by the center?

Advocacy:

- Does the center take an active stance against heterosexism and oppression on campus? Such activities may include staff representation on committees that deal with discrimination, HIV infection, women's issues, or other areas where issues of oppression are considered.
- If the center publishes its own nondiscrimination statement, does it include sexual orientation?
- When the center adds or replaces staff, does it advertise in publications likely to be read by gay or lesbian candidates (e.g., *Out On Campus*, newsletter of the Standing Committee for Lesbian, Gay, and Bisexual Awareness of ACPA)? Is there a commitment to seek gay, lesbian, and bisexual staff members in order to serve gay, lesbian, and bisexual populations effectively? Are job announcements mailed to lesbian and gay agencies, organizations, and media?
- When candidates are interviewed for jobs, does the center attempt to identify and to screen out people who hold heterosexist attitudes or who do not have a commitment to ending discrimination against all oppressed groups?

SUMMARY

In this chapter, a historical overview provided a context in which to understand current practice in counseling gay, lesbian, and bisexual students. Although these students come to counseling with many of the same concerns as their heterosexual peers, issues found to be especially pertinent to these groups, or issues likely to be overlooked, have been highlighted. Much of the chapter is devoted to various counselor attributes or conditions that can be barriers to the effective treatment of these special student populations. Finally, specific guidelines were suggested to help counselors, university staff, and students themselves promote more appropriate and affirmative treatment of gay, lesbian, and bisexual students on campus.

REFERENCES

American Psychiatric Association. (1980). *Diagnostic and statistical manual of mental disorders* (3rd ed.). Washington, DC: Author.

Anderson, C. L. (1982). Males as sexual assault victims: Multiple levels of trauma. In J. C. Gonsiorek (Ed.), *Homosexuality and psychotherapy: A practitioner's handbook of affirmative models* (pp. 145–162). Binghamton, NY: Haworth.

Bayer, R. (1981). *Homosexuality and American psychiatry.* New York: Basic Books.

Bell, A. P., & Weinberg, M. S. (1978). *Homosexualities: A study of diversity among men and women.* New York: Touchstone.

Berne, E. (1972). *What do you say after you say hello?* New York: Bantam.

Berzon, B. (1979). Developing a positive gay identity. In B. Berzon & R. Leighton (Eds.), *Positively gay* (pp. 1–14). Millbrae, CA: Celestial Arts.

Bieber, I. (1962). *Homosexuality: A psychoanalytic study.* New York: Basic Books.

Boswell, J. (1980). *Christianity, social tolerance, and homosexuality: Gay people in Western Europe from the beginning of the Christian era to the 14th century.* Chicago: University of Chicago Press.

Brown, L. S. (1988). From perplexity to complexity: Thinking about ethics in the lesbian therapy community. *Women in Therapy, 8,* 13–26.

Califa, P. (1986, March 4). Battered lovers: The hidden problem of gay domestic violence. *The Advocate,* pp. 42–46.

Caraballo-Diéguez, A. (1989). Hispanic culture, gay male culture, and AIDS: Counseling implications. *Journal of Counseling and Development, 68,* 26–30.

Carl, D. (1990). *Counseling same-sex couples.* New York: Norton.

Carnes, P. (1983). *Out of the shadows: Understanding sexual addiction.* Minneapolis: CompCare.

Carnes, P. (1989). *Contrary to love: Helping the sexual addict.* Minneapolis: CompCare.

Carrier, J. M. (1989). Gay liberation and coming out in Mexico. In G. Herdt (Ed.), *Gay and lesbian youth* (pp. 225–252). Binghamton, NY: Harrington Park.

Cass, V. C. (1979). Homosexual identity formation: A theoretical model. *Journal of Homosexuality, 4*, 219–253.

Centers for Disease Control. (1989, May 12). *AIDS and HIV infection in the United States: Update. 38* (5), (4th printing).

Clark, D. (1977). *Loving someone gay.* Millbrae, CA: Celestial Arts.

Clayborne, J. L. (1978). Blacks and gay liberation. In K. Jay and A. Young (Eds.), *Lavender culture* (pp. 458–465). New York: Jove/HBJ.

Coleman, E., & Remafedi, G. (1989). Gay, lesbian, and bisexual adolescents: A critical challenge to counselors. *Journal of Counseling and Development, 68*, 36–40.

Committee on Lesbian and Gay Concerns, American Psychological Association. (1990). *Final report of the Task Force on Bias in Psychotherapy with Lesbians and Gay Men.* Washington, DC: Author.

Conger, J. (1975). Proceedings of the American Psychological Association for the year 1974: Minutes of the annual council of representatives. *American Psychologist, 30*, 620–651.

Cornwell, A. (1978). Three for the price of one: Notes from a gay Black feminist. In K. Jay and A. Young (Eds.), *Lavender culture* (pp. 466–476). New York: Jove/HBJ.

De Cecco, J. P. (Ed.). (1988). *Gay relationships.* Binghamton, NY: Haworth.

Deutsch, H. (1945). *Psychology of women.* New York: Grune and Stratton.

Dworkin, S. H., & Gutierrez, F. (1989). Counselors be aware: Clients come in every size, shape, color, and sexual orientation. *Journal of Counseling and Development, 68*, 6–8.

Eldridge, N. S. (1990). Relationship satisfaction in lesbian couples. *Psychology of Women Quarterly, 14*, 43–62.

Ellis, A., & Harper, R. A. (1979). *A new guide to rational living.* North Hollywood, CA: Wilshire.

Feldman, M. P., & MacCulloch, M. J. (1965). The application of anticipatory avoidance learning to the treatment of homosexuality: I. Theory, technique, and preliminary results. *Behavior Research and Therapy, 2*, 165–183.

Finnegan, D. G., & McNally, E. B. (1987). *Dual identities: Counseling chemically dependent gay men and lesbians.* Center City, MN: Hazelden.

Freud, S. (1951). *Civilization and its discontents* (James Strachey, Trans.). New York: Norton.

Gold, M., Seymour, N., & Sahl, J. (1986). Counseling HIV seropositives. In L. McKusick (Ed.), *What to do about AIDS: Physicians and mental health professionals discuss the issues* (pp.103–110). Berkeley: University of California Press.

Gonsiorek, J. (1977). Psychological adjustment and homosexuality. *JSAS Catalog of Selected Documents in Psychology, 7*, 45. (Ms. No. 1478).

Gonsiorek, J. (1987, August). Ethical issues for gay male therapists. In L. Garnets (chair), *Ethical and boundary issues for lesbian and gay therapists.* Symposium conducted at the meeting of the American Psychological Association, New York.

Graham, D. L., Rawlings, E. I., Halpern, H. S., & Hermes, J. (1984). Therapists' needs for training in counseling lesbians and gay men. *Professional Psychology: Research and Practice, 15,* 482–496.

Gray, L. A., & Saracino, M. (1989). AIDS on campus: A preliminary study of college students' knowledge and behaviors. *Journal of Counseling and Development, 68,* 199–202.

Halstead, R. W., Vitous, W. P., & Derbort, J. J. (1990, August). *College student knowledge, attitudes, and risk tolerance toward safe and unsafe sexual behaviors.* Paper presented at the meeting of the American Psychological Association, Boston, MA.

Hart, B. (1986). Preface. In K. Lobel, *Naming the violence: Speaking out about lesbian battering* (pp. 9–16). Seattle: Seal.

Herek, G. M. (1984). Beyond "homophobia": A social psychological perspective on attitudes towards lesbians and gay men. In J.P. De Cecco (Ed.), *Homophobia: An overview* (pp. 1–21). Binghamton, NY: Haworth.

Hooker, E. A. (1957). The adjustment of the overt male homosexual. *Journal of Projective Techniques. 21,* 17–31.

Human Rights Foundation Inc. (1984). *Demystifying homosexuality: A teaching guide about lesbians and gay men.* New York: Irvington.

Isay, R. A. (1989). *Being homosexual: Gay men and their development.* New York: Avon.

Island, D., & Letellier, P. (1991). *Men who beat the men who love them: Battered gay men and domestic violence.* Binghamton, NY: Haworth.

Jung, C. G. (1964). *The collected works of C.G. Jung* (Vol. 10). New York: Vintage Books.

Kimmel, D. C. (1978). Adult development and aging: A gay perspective. *Journal of Social Issues, 34,* 113–130.

Kinsey, A. C., Pomeroy, W. B., & Martin, C. E. (1948). *Sexual behavior in the human male.* Philadelphia: Saunders.

Kinsey, A. C., Pomeroy, W. B., Martin, C. E., & Gebhard, P. H. (1953). *Sexual behavior in the human female.* Philadelphia: Saunders.

Kus, R. J. (1990). Alcoholism in gay and lesbian communities. In R. J. Kus (Ed.), *Keys to caring: Assisting your gay and lesbian clients* (pp. 66–81). Boston: Alyson.

Kyle, G. R. (1988, October 5–19). Sexual fascism comes to town. *Frontiers,* pp. 19–20.

Leeder, E. (1988). Enmeshed in pain: Counseling the lesbian battering couple. *Women and Therapy, 7,* 81–99.

Levine, M. P., & Troiden, R. R. (1988). The myth of sexual compulsion and addiction. *Journal of Sex Research, 25,* 347–363.

Lobel, K. (1986). *Naming the violence: Speaking out about lesbian battering.* Seattle: Seal.

Loiacano, D. K. (1989). Gay identity issues among Black Americans: Racism, homophobia, and the need for validation. *Journal of Counseling and Development, 68,* 21–25.

Malyon, A. (1982). Psychotherapeutic implications of internalized homophobia in gay men. *Journal of Homosexuality, 7,* 59–69.

Martin, D. J. (1989). Human immunodeficiency virus infection and the gay community: Counseling and clinical issues. *Journal of Counseling and Development, 68,* 67–72.

Masters, W. H., & Johnson, V. E. (1979). *Homosexuality in perspective.* New York: Little, Brown.

Mays, V. M., & Cochran, S. D. (1988). The Black women's relationships project: A national survey of Black lesbians. In M. Shernoff & W. A. Scott (Eds.), *The sourcebook on lesbian/gay health care* (2nd ed.) (pp. 54–62). Washington, DC: National Lesbian and Gay Health Foundation.

McDermott, D., & Stadler, H. A. (1988). Attitudes of counseling students in the United States toward minority clients. *International Journal for the Advancement of Counseling, 11,* 61–69.

McDermott, D., Tyndall, L., & Lichtenberg, J. W. (1989). Factors related to counselor preference among gays and lesbians. *Journal of Counseling and Development, 68,* 31–35.

McHugh, M. C., Koeske, R. D., & Frieze, I. H. (1981). *Guidelines for non-sexist research.* Unpublished manuscript. (Available from I. H. Frieze, Department of Psychology, University of Pittsburgh.)

Morin, S. F. (1977). Heterosexual bias in psychological research on lesbianism and male homosexuality. *American Psychologist, 32,* 629–637.

Morin, S. F., & Charles, K. A. (1983). Heterosexual bias in psychotherapy. In J. Murray & P. R. Abramson (Eds.), *Bias in psychotherapy* (pp. 309–338). New York: Praeger.

Morin, S. F., & Schultz, S. J. (1978). The gay movement and the rights of children. *Journal of Social Issues, 34,* 137–148.

Morrow, S. L., & Hawxhurst, D. M. (1989). Lesbian partner abuse: Implications for therapists. *Journal of Counseling and Development, 68,* 58–62.

Paul, W., Weinrich, F. D., Gonsiorek, J. C., & Hotvedt, M. E. (Eds.). (1982). *Homosexuality: Social, psychological, and biological issues.* Final report of the SPSSI Task Force on Sexual Orientation. Beverly Hills, CA: Sage.

Pincu, L. (1989). Sexual compulsivity in gay men: Controversy and treatment. *Journal of Counseling and Development, 68,* 63–66.

Platt, J. (1987). The future of AIDS. *The Futurist, 21,* 10–16.

Reiss, B. F. (1980). Psychological tests in homosexuality. In J. Marmor (Ed.), *Homosexual behavior* (pp. 269–311). New York: Basic Books.

Saghir, M. T., Robins, E., Walbran, B., & Gentry, K. E. (1970a). Homosexuality: III. Psychiatric disorders and disability in the male homosexual. *American Journal of Psychiatry, 126,* 1079–1086.

Saghir, M. T., Robins, E., Walbran, B., & Gentry, K. E. (1970b). Homosexuality: III. Psychiatric disorders and disability in the female homosexual. *American Journal of Psychiatry, 127,* 147–154.

Silverstein, C. (1977). Homosexuality and the ethics of behavioral interventions: Paper 2. *Journal of Homosexuality, 2,* 205–211.

Spence, J. T., Deaux, K., & Helmreich, R. L. (1985). Sex roles in contemporary American society. In G. Lindzey & E. Aronson (Eds.), *Handbook of social psychology* (pp. 149–178). Reading, MA: Addison-Wesley.

Thompson, G. H., & Fishburn, W. R. (1977). Attitudes toward homosexuality among graduate counseling students. *Counselor Education and Supervision, 17,* 121–130.

Walber, E. (1988). Behind closed doors: Battering and abuse in the lesbian and gay community. In M. Shernoff & W. A. Scott (Eds.), *The sourcebook on lesbian/gay health care* (2nd ed.) (pp. 250–256). Washington, DC: National Lesbian and Gay Health Foundation.

Wallston, B. S. (1981). What are the questions in the psychology of women? A feminist approach to research. *Psychology of Women Quarterly, 5,* 597–617.

Weinberg, M. S., & Williams, C. J. (1974). *Male homosexuals: Their problems and adaptations.* New York: Oxford University Press.

Ziebold, T. O., & Mongeon, J. E. (Eds.). (1982). Alcoholism and homosexuality [Special issue]. *Journal of Homosexuality, 7.*

Chapter 10

Issues of Gay, Lesbian, and Bisexual Student Affairs Professionals

Maura Cullen
University of Massachusetts at Amherst

Jim Smart
University of Miami

How do gay, lesbian, and bisexual people integrate their sexuality into their professional life? There are two answers. One is the way porcupines make love—very carefully. The other is the way prize fighters maneuver a bout—with courage, determination, and a lot of fancy footwork. Either way, it's worth the effort (Rochlin, 1979).

For gay, lesbian, and bisexual professionals, the work place generates a host of concerns. The topic of homosexuality is one that is laden with myths and stereotypes. "Of all the professions, education is probably the most discriminatory against homosexual individuals. By its very nature, education requires the establishment of relationships with colleagues, students, and parents. Furthermore, each of these groups often holds its own set of stereotypes" (Olson, 1987, p. 73). According to a survey conducted by the National Institutes of Mental Health (Olson, 1987), 75% of these people would deny a homosexual's right to choose teaching as a career. The presence of gays, lesbians, and bisexuals in the field of education appears to be a higher threat than in most other careers.

This chapter focuses on gay, lesbian, and bisexual student affairs professionals and the unique concerns that they confront daily on our college and university campuses. What are the motivations, complications, and consequences of coming out or not coming out at work? How do gay, lesbian, and bisexual professionals maintain personal relationships, and what roles do these relationships have in the work environment? What are the legal implications and employment concerns for the gay, lesbian, or bisexual professional caught in a cycle of widespread discrimination? These concerns are reviewed in an attempt to gain a better understanding of the work climate for gay, lesbian, and bisexual professionals.

For a professional, there is an expectation of professionalism, which can be defined as "professional status, methods, character, or standards" (*American Heritage Dictionary*, 1975). Homophobia has a severe impact on the perceived character of gay, lesbian, and bisexual professionals. Their sexual orientations are often viewed as causing deterioration of the standards set by the profession. Though this view is contradictory to the principles of education, its effects are profound not only for the individual but also for the system itself. In an age when higher education is thought to be "embracing" diversity, it is clear that this diversity either does not include gays, lesbians, and bisexuals or places conditions on their inclusion.

COMING OUT

"To be known or not to be known?" This is a question that all gay, lesbian, and bisexual professionals encounter at some point. Though individuals cannot choose their sexual orientation, gay, lesbian, or bisexual persons must decide how open they want to be with their sexual identity. The question evolves to "Do I acknowledge who I am and come out or do I continue to live a dual identity and remain in the closet?" This decision is a difficult one, one that has implications for gay, lesbian, and bisexual individuals perhaps for the rest of their lives. But before discussing the implications of coming out, it is important to understand the reasons and implications for *not* coming out.

Bell and Weinberg's study (cited in Levine & Leonard, 1984) found that the most commonly used coping strategy for lesbian employees was to hide their sexual identity. Two-thirds of these lesbians concealed their identity from their employers and nearly half concealed it from their co-workers. It is not unusual for gay, lesbian, and bisexual professionals to maintain a dual identity: the professional self and the personal self. When conversations arise involving the personal self, the gay, lesbian, or bisexual individual either refrains from participating or creates stories in an effort to belong to the majority group. One major factor that keeps gays, lesbians, and bisexuals in the closet is fear. Three-fifths of the participants in a

study conducted by Levine and Leonard (1984) expected discrimination if their sexual orientation was discovered. Many gays, lesbians, and bisexuals fear they will be fired, demoted, overlooked for
promotions, or ostracized and harassed by colleagues.

This dual existence can be very costly to the gay, lesbian, and
bisexual person. Feelings of isolation and fear drain energy, which
in turn limits the productivity of gay, lesbian, and bisexual employees. These employees, in an effort to keep their sexual orientation hidden, opt out of certain committee assignments or decline
from facilitating training programs associated with gay, lesbian, or
bisexual issues. Though these professionals might be able to offer
valuable insight to such committees or programs, the risk of participation is seen as too high. This not only lowers the productivity
of the gay, lesbian, or bisexual professional, but it also may result
in lower social interaction. One lesbian described this lack of integration in this way:

> There is pressure to act straight. . . . I do not feel free to
> share certain aspects—most really—of my life away from
> the job with my co-workers. This results in my feeling de-
> tached and alienated from the people with whom I work; I
> hate hiding. (Levine & Leonard, 1984, p. 194)

Because the pressure of being in the closet is so great, some professionals choose to change career paths to better fit their gay, lesbian,
or bisexual lifestyle. Many create their own businesses and organizations to avoid the homophobia typical of most organizations
(Levine & Leonard, 1984). No one is certain just how many student
affairs professionals have left higher education for this reason.

Why would anyone choose to share his or her sexual orientation
in the work place? Perhaps a better question is how could anybody
not share it? One's sexuality, whether gay, lesbian, bisexual, or
heterosexual, is part of a person's identity. It influences friends,
social life, and choice of careers. It underlies values, spiritual growth,
and emotional development. In both subtle and not so subtle ways,
sexuality is a defining influence, a primary part of how we perceive
the world in which we live.

For most people, it is common to discuss children and spouses,
anniversaries and weddings, in offices and informal work relationships. These conversations often render gay, lesbian, and bisexual
professionals invisible and isolated. But closeted gay, lesbian, and
bisexual professionals often feel they have no choice except to remain
closeted. To choose otherwise would be too great a risk. Unfortunately, these fears are not without foundations.

One obvious consequence that the gay, lesbian, and bisexual professional may experience in coming out at work is discrimination. Stoddard's study (cited in Poverny & Finch, 1988), which included lesbians and gay men, found that 21% of the participants had encountered discrimination on the job because of their sexual orientation. Yet in Friberg's study (cited in Poverny & Finch, 1988), employers were increasingly sophisticated in their prejudicial hiring practices, often making it difficult to prove antigay discrimination when it occurred. Many higher education administrators admit off the record that they will not hire an openly gay, lesbian, or bisexual person. The irony is that at some level they probably have hired gay, lesbian, and bisexual professionals without knowing it.

Discrimination can take two forms: formal and informal. Formal discrimination includes the use of institutionalized procedures to restrict such things as job promotions and salary increases as well as firings and increased or decreased job responsibilities (Levine & Leonard, 1984). Exemplifying this type of discrimination are institutions that do not have nondiscrimination clauses covering sexual orientation, that do not provide equal status and rights to gay and lesbian couples who want to take a live-in position, and that deny spousal rights to gay and lesbian couples.

Informal discrimination consists of noninstitutionalized policies that permit harassment and other related unofficial actions by supervisors or colleagues (Levine & Leonard, 1984). Such discrimination includes, but is not limited to, verbal and physical harassment, damage to personal belongings, serving as the focus of jokes and gossip, and ostracism.

A significant challenge facing the gay, lesbian, or bisexual professional is deciding whether or not to come out to her or his supervisor. Having the support of the person who is the supervisor and evaluator affects performance. It contributes to how valued one feels. Given the ethical standards of the student personnel profession and the nature of people attracted to this work, the risks today are far less than they were a decade or two ago. Still, the gay, lesbian, or bisexual professional needs to be cautious when revealing such information. Work relationships have been enhanced by sharing such information, but they have also been destroyed. It is not unheard of for people in supervisory positions to sanction a gay, lesbian, or bisexual subordinate. Consequences range from firings or demotions to more subtle and frequent forms of discrimination such as giving poor evaluations to the subordinate, withholding information, passing the person over for promotions, not taking the person seriously, and not validating ideas or suggestions.

Some individuals may not have the luxury of choice on when to come out. Often there are rumors concerning a person's sexual identity, which the individual may or may not have to face, depending upon their intensity and impact. Occasionally, others report the orientation of the gay, lesbian, or bisexual professional without her or his consent. Such an action can result in feelings of betrayal and isolation for the gay, lesbian, or bisexual person. It is also a violation of confidence that can lead to shattered relationships and continued misperceptions that heterosexuals cannot be trusted. It is vital that colleagues understand the necessity of allowing gay, lesbian, or bisexual individuals to control and determine if and how they will come out.

Parents and students may show concern regarding the employment of a gay, lesbian, or bisexual staff member. Employers should concern themselves with bona fide occupational qualifications and performance. Gay, lesbian, and bisexual persons need to be considered a protected class of people just like people of color, women, and people with disabilities. Affirmative action and nondiscrimination clauses name and therefore protect these groups. Nondiscriminatory hiring policies offer an unusual opportunity not only to educate the parents but also to make it clear that the college or university will not succumb to homophobia. For many administrators such encounters stretch their own levels of homophobia. But as Sydney Smith once said, "It is the greatest of all mistakes to do nothing because you can only do a little. Do what you can" (Olson, 1987, p. 81). Student affairs professionals must continue to strive beyond their own individual limits in hopes of achieving the true mission of our institutions, namely, education.

For gay, lesbian, or bisexual professionals who have come out, there is no turning back. Despite the constant homophobia that exists around them, they must continue to hold true to who they are and what they believe. By coming out, gay, lesbian, and bisexual professionals gain back some of what was taken from their self-esteem and self-image. They can begin to feel more comfortable about who they are. They are able to become better employees, supervisors, and colleagues. One "out" professional stated it this way: "I feel as though I am an integrated part of a bigger reality, and I enjoy it. I don't have to worry about being found out or losing my job; I expend no energy by having to hide" (Levine & Leonard, 1984, p. 194).

For colleagues, support staff, and students this new information regarding sexual orientation may affect their perceptions of the gay, lesbian, or bisexual professional and his or her abilities and insight.

Those with positive attitudes toward the gay, lesbian, or bisexual professional will view this as a situation with more possibilities. This person can now provide insight, visibility, and support on issues that society encourages to stay underground. Those with negative feelings may be threatened and may want to avoid any future interactions with the gay, lesbian, or bisexual professional.

As described in previous chapters, gay, lesbian, or bisexual individuals go through a developmental process regarding their sexual identity. There is a similar developmental process for the professional who chooses to come out in the work place (Rochlin, 1979).

The first stage is the *professional gay*. After coming out, gay, lesbian, and bisexual professionals may be very conscious of their sexual identity. They begin to assert who they are and take on the responsibility of educating the world. Gay, lesbian, or bisexual persons can become enmeshed in their own sexual identity, seeking ways to be both visible and active in matters relating to gay, lesbian, and bisexual people. Typically, they begin to organize such gay, lesbian, and bisexual activities as educational programs for students and staff; events, socials, and rallies with outside speakers and entertainers; and gay, lesbian, and bisexual support groups for students and/or staff. Because of their high visibility and outspoken manner, professional gays can be perceived as threating to their colleagues. Whereas gay, lesbian, or bisexual professionals may feel that matters and conversation relating to sexual orientation are virtually absent in the work place, their heterosexual counterparts at times may feel bombarded with the number of times gay, lesbian, and bisexual issues are raised. As a result, the professional gay can begin to feel isolated as he or she sees colleagues begin to distance themselves.

Stage two is the *gay professional*. During this stage, other professionals may also be very conscious of their gay, lesbian, or bisexual colleague and begin to treat him or her as the gay expert. This often includes asking the colleague to chair committees focusing on the gay, lesbian and bisexual community, or to deal with all the gay students who are experiencing difficulty. It also means giving him or her responsibility for most or all of the training dealing with gay, lesbian, and bisexual issues. As a result, gay, lesbian, and bisexual professionals are seen solely as representatives of the gay or lesbian community. Their ability to serve any other part of the college community is minimized.

Stage three is labeled the *professional who is gay*. Though their sexual orientation is known, gay, lesbian, or bisexual professionals are successful in integrating their identities in the work place. They are seen as valuable resources involving gay, lesbian, and bisexual matters, but no longer are their abilities to serve the entire campus population minimized as in stage one. They speak freely about those people in their lives who are important to them. They may also have pictures of their significant others on their desks as do their heterosexual colleagues. And, depending on the work environment, they may bring their significant others to social gatherings.

For heterosexuals, gays, lesbians, and bisexuals alike, visibility is imperative if any education and role modeling is to take place. Gay, lesbian, and bisexual student affairs professionals need to be encouraged to be visible on our campuses. One lesbian professional said it this way:

> ... I remind them that our visibility as respected professionals is an important key to reducing homophobia and discrimination in our society. The closet keeps us hidden from others, but most tragically it keeps us hidden from ourselves. And when we come to fully know and love ourselves as we are, we then become able to present ourselves proudly in a world that desperately needs to understand us. (Marinoble, 1989, p. 8)

Certainly, interaction with visible and proud gay, lesbian, or bisexual faculty or staff can provide enormous opportunities for students who have not yet had such an experience. This exposure is beneficial not only to our heterosexual students in breaking down stereotypes and myths but also to our gay, lesbian, and bisexual students. Role modeling is important for our students who are searching for adults who can better understand their experience of being gay, lesbian, or bisexual. If there are no visible gay, lesbian, or bisexual professionals on campus, students may perceive that it is not safe, that they are not valued; they may go underground, leave the institution, or, worse yet, not accept who they are.

Just as it is important to have visible gay, lesbian, and bisexual staff members, so is it important to have visible heterosexual supporters or allies. The gay, lesbian, or bisexual person may be in a situation that is nonsupportive and hostile. For this reason it is crucial that allies and supporters make themselves known in the work place. Visibility through conversation, confrontation of homophobia, and the development of policies that include rather than exclude are some ways supporters can be visible. Being aware of gender-neutral language, not always asking about marital status, and having "guest" appear on invitations as opposed to "spouse" are simple ways to create a more open and safe environment. We need to cultivate and nurture these relationships during the weeks, months, or years of coming out.

PARTNERSHIPS

What about the gay, lesbian, and bisexual person who has a partner? What role does the partner play in the work environment?

All of the issues involved with traditional couples are present, plus a host of concerns that are unique to gay and lesbian couples. Unlike heterosexual couples, particularly those who are married, there are no formal social supports to keep same-sex partners together. Families may not be supportive, employers may not be sensitive to the illness of a partner, and government and legal systems do not recognize gay and lesbian partnerships, although they still collect their taxes. Given the high divorce rate among heterosexual couples, whose unions receive considerable societal and legal support, it is a monument to the persistence and dedication of gay and lesbian couples that their relationships survive and flourish in the numbers they do.

It is imperative that our employers understand the importance of gay and lesbian relationships by including these partners whenever heterosexual partners are invited. Gays, lesbians, and bisexuals need to feel as supported as their heterosexual counterparts in bringing their partners to social functions. If this action is perceived as blatant, then the level of homophobia present speaks for itself. We need to work toward an environment in which gay, lesbian or bisexual persons can have pictures of their partners on their desks and in which they, too, can openly converse about the special person in their lives. We need to begin working toward this goal so that our gay, lesbian, and bisexual colleagues can feel as fully integrated as their heterosexual counterparts. Respect comes when a gay, lesbian, or bisexual person comes out. Mutual respect, however, happens when allies are born because of this action.

As indicated in a recent issue of *Newsweek* (Salholz et al., 1990), as a result of previous marriages and increasingly through adoption, artificial insemination, surrogate parenting, and other circumstances, gay and lesbian couples are becoming parents. These nontraditional families join a host of other nontraditional families in the 1990s. The American family today is quite different than many expect. Part of what we need to do as professionals is insure that we have educated ourselves to the variety that exists in family life in America and take appropriate steps to be sensitive to the issues these differences present. Child care, flex time, and other amenities need to be granted to the gay, lesbian, or bisexual parent just as they are to the heterosexual parent.

Coming out is a process that impacts people in profound ways. Beyond the considerations already mentioned, the gay, lesbian, and bisexual professional may also ponder the following:

1. Do you have a confidant or a built-in support group of people? Because many gay, lesbian, and bisexual professionals feel isolated in the work place, it is important to lessen this isolation by having a support person or support network. These persons will perform a valuable service to the gay, lesbian, and bisexual person who is searching for acceptance in the work environment.

2. What is your knowledge base? How much do you know about gay, lesbian, and bisexual history, culture, and psychosocial development? Knowing more about who you are as a gay, lesbian, and bisexual can provide support, perspective, and stronger self-esteem. This type of self-education can be accomplished through reading gay, lesbian, and bisexual literature, magazines, and newspapers. These can be found in a gay or lesbian bookstore or a women's bookstore. If these are not available, the Lambda Rising bookstore (1625 Connecticut Avenue, NW, Washington, DC, 20009; 202-462-6969) offers a catalog from which you may mail order gay, lesbian, and bisexual titles and films. Gay film festivals are offered in some areas, and some video stores carry gay, lesbian, and bisexual movies. Some colleges and universities offer courses focusing on gay, lesbian, and bisexual topics. You can also join a support group that offers a social network in the community in which you live. There are also religiously based groups for gays, lesbians, and bisexuals, such as Dignity (Catholics), Integrity (Protestants), and Am Tivka (Jews) as well as the Metropolitan Community Church and Unitarian Church. Professional conferences are also a place to network and find support from other gay, lesbian, and bisexual colleagues. The *Gayellow Pages* and *Gaia's Guide* are books that provide information on bookstores, groups, gay resorts, and other useful information to tap into the gay, lesbian, and bisexual community. (See chapter 13 for information on these and other resources.)

3. What are the consequences of not coming out to those who are important to us? Often we visualize the consequences of coming out to people and anticipate the possible losses. However, the loss experienced by our family, friends, and ourselves by never sharing who we are also limits the depth and richness those relationships might otherwise provide.

LEGAL ISSUES

Most gays, lesbians, and bisexuals do not place much trust in the "system." Given our legal system or our college and university policies that brand gays, lesbians, and bisexuals as criminals and deviants, it is no wonder that trust is minimal. The legal system has been one of the strongest sources of institutionalized oppression for gay, lesbian, and bisexual people. Only two states, Wisconsin and Massachusetts, prohibit discrimination solely on the basis of sexual orientation. Several other states have executive orders that prevent discrimination in state positions but are not binding on private enterprise. "Despite continued litigation, the courts have consistently ruled that Title VII of the Civil Rights Act of 1964 does not offer protection to gays claiming employment discrimination in the private sector" (Schmitz, 1988, p. 55). Federal legislation is pending in both the House of Representatives and the Senate, but passage is not imminent. Fourteen states, 16 counties, and 64 municipalities provide legal protection of varying degrees against gay, lesbian, and bisexual discrimination (Leonard, 1989). In most instances, on the state and local levels such legislation is usually a part of the broader civil rights legislation that was passed in the 1960s and 1970s. Protection is similar to that provided by laws that prevent discrimination based on race, gender, ethnic or religious background, disability, or age.

Additionally, some employers have extended such protection as part of affirmative action statements. At best, the legal protection that exists is spotty. It is appropriate for anyone concerned about this dimension to consult legal counsel, their affirmative action office, or a private agency such as the American Civil Liberties Union.

Also of concern is the fact that 25 states and the District of Columbia still have sodomy laws that prohibit in some fashion sexual activity between consenting adults (National Gay and Lesbian Task Force, Privacy/Civil Rights Project, 1990). By its nature, this legislation is difficult if not impossible to enforce. It does, however, serve the social purpose of prohibiting same-sex relationships. Such laws can and do result in harassment, intimidation, and institutionalization of homophobia.

Given the nature of our society, it is unlikely that federal legislation rectifying this situation will occur soon. In addition, the conservative nature of judicial appointments during the Reagan years, demonstrated in a number of recent cases decided by the courts, lends little hope of a judicial solution to discrimination based upon sexual orientation. Although legislative and judicial solutions need to be pursued, it appears that in the immediate future protection is more likely to come on the local level and be based on the decisions of individual employers.

One bright note exists: For gay, lesbian, and bisexual people and their allies, the ability to educate and pursue nondiscrimination legislation is protected under the First Amendment's guarantee of freedom of speech. Legally, all can be advocates of same-sex relationships and be protected for such action. Unfortunately, as with most forms of discrimination, the burden falls upon the victim to prove discriminatory acts. The necessity of supporting legal defense organizations (e.g., Lambda Legal Defense Fund, the National Gay and Lesbian Task Force, and the American Civil Liberties Union), which provide support for such contests, is self-evident.

Even in situations where gay, lesbian, and bisexual persons enjoy some level of personal protection, few colleges and universities have taken the next step of recognizing same-sex relationships.

> [B]enefits accompanying employment and available to heterosexual partners have been generally denied to same-sex domestic partnerships, placing these couples and families in a disadvantageous position relative to nongay individuals. Employer-sponsored benefits include spousal coverage on health insurance, retirement or death benefits, child care, bereavement and sick leave. (Poverny & Finch, 1988, p. 16)

Gay and lesbian couples cannot have legally sanctioned marriages or the acknowledgement of common law marriages.

Besides the denial of spousal rights, most college and university campuses also have homophobic policies regarding live-in professionals. Married heterosexual partners are granted the right to live together in residential life positions and in faculty or married student housing. In fact, rarely are such couples even required to document the legal nature of their relationship. Yet these same privileges are denied to gay, lesbian, or bisexual partners. This arena, in particular, is a source of anger and frustration for many gay and lesbian professionals and subjects them to much strain, both emotional and financial. In addition, tuition remissions and waivers are often extended to heterosexual employees' families yet denied to gay, lesbian, and bisexual employees' families because the word *family* is defined in heterosexist terms. *Family housing* and *married student housing* are also terms prevalent on our campuses, and they exclude gay and lesbian couples in policy as well as semantics. Administrators need to begin to challenge how the word *family* is defined on their campus so that it reflects the realities of the larger society, which includes gay and lesbian couples.

Until legal recourse is more firmly established, contractual arrangements such as living wills, wills, and powers of attorney are the best options for gays, lesbians, and bisexuals. "Although the courts have been reluctant to address discrimination issues involving sexual orientation, the results of litigation have become increasingly costly to business, industries, and governmental units" (Poverny & Finch, 1988, p. 27). Though the costs are different for gay, lesbian, and bisexual professionals than for businesses, which colleges and universities are considered, elimination of homophobic laws and policies will benefit everyone.

EMPLOYMENT ISSUES

Job searches for the gay, lesbian, and bisexual professional can be a complicated and delicate process. Resumes and interviews are always a chess match: Which move made now will forestall an unwanted one later? Should you avoid placing any gay-, lesbian-, or bisexual-related experiences on your resume for fear that you may not be granted an interview? Yet if you do not include this experience, you negate your qualifications. It is a Catch 22. Perhaps what should come into question at this point are the ethical and moral standards of an institution that would not grant an interview if someone included gay, lesbian, and bisexual experiences on her or his resume.

Some gay, lesbian, and bisexual professionals create two resumes, one including their experiences with the gay, lesbian, and bisexual community and one that does not include that experience. Some gay, lesbian, and bisexual professionals feel that by not including the experience they may have a better chance at the job. Once in the job, they feel they can begin to make some changes. Other gay, lesbian, and bisexual professionals feel that this strategy only plays into the homophobia within the student affairs profession, that not including the gay, lesbian, and bisexual experience on the resume is self-defeating.

Interviewing provides the gay, lesbian, or bisexual with another interesting hurdle. To come out or not to come out: That remains the question. Each individual must rehearse and know what his or her game plan is for each job opportunity. How do gays, lesbians, and bisexuals find out if the environment is supportive of who they are? There is no substitute for gathering information regarding the institution in which you are interested. Does the institution have a nondiscrimination clause that includes sexual orientation? What are the personnel policies regarding diversity issues? What are the personal attitudes and knowledge base of the people with whom the gay, lesbian, or bisexual professional will be working? Is the atmosphere one of benign neglect or does the institution actively seek to support and celebrate the diversity inherent in its students and staff? Are there differences between 2- and 4-year, public and private, and religiously affiliated and sectarian institutions in terms of valuing diversity? What is known about a particular city and the resources it offers? What are the community resources? Gays, lesbians, and bisexuals may also consult progressive publications and organizations. Connecting with the informal gay network by contacting colleagues at other institutions who may have some information regarding the school at which you are interviewing can also be valuable. Individuals need to have questions prepared in advance to ask during a visit to campus regarding diversity issues in general and gay, lesbian, and bisexual issues on campus in particular.

Employers can make the interview process far less stressful for the gay, lesbian, and bisexual candidate. Employers can let each candidate know honestly the value of diversity on campus. When employers are not honest about the campus climate, the candidate may end up leaving the institution because he or she anticipated something quite different. Allow time for candidates to meet with student groups about which they may be interested in obtaining more information (e.g., gay, lesbian, and bisexual student group, African-American student group, Hillel, women's center).

Once hired by an institution, the gay, lesbian, or bisexual has more than the typical share of adjustments to a new job. If the individual came out during the interview or her or his gay, lesbian, or bisexual identity is known, she or he must be careful not to become the token or the expert. Too often people representing diversity are expected to deal with minority issues and special projects. It becomes an expectation, the reason they were hired. Such pigeonholing overlooks the gay, lesbian, and bisexual professionals' competency and knowledge. It is not the sole responsibility of gay, lesbian, and bisexual professionals to educate the world on these issues. Student affairs professionals must take responsibility for their learning about issues of diversity. They also must expand their definition of diversity: No longer does it include only people of color; it also includes gays, lesbians, bisexuals, women, disabled people, non-Christians, people from low socioeconomic classes, and people of different sizes and ages. Information needs to be provided regarding these groups of people for our staffs and students.

The following assessment tool, developed by Vernon Wall and Jamie Washington (1987), can enable the student affairs professional to assess the current climate on campus for gay, lesbian, and bisexual students and staff. It provides information on areas in which to initiate change or improve the campus environment in serving and welcoming this community of people. It also offers suggestions to all members of the campus community—students, staff, and faculty—who are interested in initiating such change.

Gay, Lesbian, and Bisexual Support Environment Assessment

1. __ T __ F   My campus has gay, lesbian, and bisexual student organizations supported by student government funds.

2. __ T __ F   My campus has gay, lesbian, and bisexual support groups through our counseling center.

3. __ T __ F   My campus has a gay, lesbian, and bisexual faculty/staff association.

4. __ T __ F   My campus has courses regarding gay, lesbian, and bisexual history and culture.

5. __ T __ F   My campus' affirmative action statement includes sexual orientation.

6. __ T __ F   My campus has a minority affairs office that includes gays, lesbians, and bisexuals as one of the groups they serve.

7. __ T __ F   My housing office has a clearly stated policy in the student handbook or conduct code that prohibits harassment and discrimination to minorities and includes gay, lesbian, and bisexual people.

8. __ T __ F   My housing office does not grant immediate room changes on the basis of sexual orientation, unless there is the presence of danger to the resident.

9. __ T __ F   I have openly gay, lesbian, and bisexual people on my professional staff.

10. __ T __ F   I have openly gay, lesbian, bisexual people on my student staff.

11. __ T __ F   There is a workshop each semester on gay, lesbian, and bisexual issues that is handled through our training program.

12. ___ T ___ F   We monitor publications, fliers, and handbooks to assure that they do not exclude gay, lesbian, and bisexual people by assuming heterosexuality.

13. ___ T ___ F   There is a policy that allows married couples to serve as hall director/area coordinators, and we extend this same policy to gay and lesbian couples.

14. ___ T ___ F   There is a strong commitment in our office to treat all people equally. This is as evident with our gay, lesbian, and bisexual population as it is with racial minorities.

15. ___ T ___ F   Gay, lesbian, and bisexual people find my campus community a relatively comfortable environment.

16. ___ T ___ F   Gay, lesbian, and bisexual people say that our housing office is a visibly supportive unit.

17. ___ T ___ F   When there is an office social, gay, lesbian, and bisexual colleagues are encouraged to bring their significant others or partners.

CONCLUSIONS

When each of us takes responsibility for our own educational process, gays, lesbians, and bisexuals will not be placed in positions in which their sexual orientation is highlighted. This self-education by heterosexuals will allow gays, lesbians and bisexuals to integrate their total identity fully. The question is not how gays, lesbians, and bisexuals manage all these issues but rather how everyone, heterosexuals included, manages this process in a way that celebrates everyone.

Our status as professionals does not negate the responses we may feel regarding gay, lesbian, and bisexual issues—ranging from anger or denial to acceptance and celebration. Fear arises from inaccurate and inadequate information. Student affairs professionals are often held back by this fear, which results in little to no action concerning gay, lesbian, bisexual issues. By soliciting resources such as books, videos, or names of supportive organizations and individuals, we can begin to reduce the fear. We need to examine the ways in which our colleges and universities have diminished the spirit and potential of our gay, lesbian, and bisexual colleagues. Chief executive officers, in particular, need to be willing to voice to their college or university community their commitment toward rectifying these problems. As the saying goes, "If you are not part of the solution, then you are part of the problem." Action, whether through a policy that includes sexual orientation, or a policy that refuses

ROTC or any other military group a place on campus until homophobic policies are rectified, needs to be taken.

Gay, lesbian, and bisexual professionals have paid a high price for being part of an almost invisible minority. Even though most will find a way to survive the prejudice that is often leveled against them, the educational system has the opportunity to transform the focus from mere survival toward integration, understanding, and enrichment (Olson, 1987).

REFERENCES

American heritage dictionary. (1975). New York: Houghton Mifflin.

Leonard, A. S. (1989). *Gay and lesbian rights protections in the United States.* Washington, DC: National Gay and Lesbian Task Force.

Levine, M. P., & Leonard, R. (1984). Discrimination against lesbians in the work force. *Signs, 9* (4), 187–197.

Marinoble, R. (1989). My closet door swings wide. *Empathy, 2,* 6–8.

Olson, M. R. (1987). A study of gay and lesbian teachers. *Journal of Homosexuality, 13* (4), 73–81.

Poverny, L. M. , & Finch, W. A. (1988). Integrating work-related issues on gay and lesbian employees into occupational social work practice. *Employee Assistance Quarterly, 4* (2), 15–29.

Rochlin, M. (1979). Becoming a gay professional. In B. Berzon (Ed.), *Positively gay* (pp. 159–170). Milbrae, CA: Celestial Arts.

Salholz, E., Clifton, T., Joseph, N., Beachy, L., Rogers, P., Wilson, L., Glick, D., & King, P. (1990, March, 12). The future of gay America. *Newsweek,* pp. 20–25.

Schmitz, T. J. (1988). Career counseling implications with the gay and lesbian population. *Journal of Employment Counseling, 25* (2), 51–56.

Wall, V., & Washington, J. (1987). *Gay, lesbian, bisexual support environment assessment.* Unpublished manuscript.

Chapter 11

BECOMING AN ALLY

Jamie Washington
University of Maryland—Baltimore County

Nancy J. Evans
Western Illinois University

As most writers and scholars in the area of oppression and multicultural education will concur (Friere, 1970; Katz, 1982), our language is imperfect and inherently "ism"-laden or oppressive. Therefore, clarifying terms is important. For the purpose of this chapter, the term most important to define is *ally*. According to *Webster's New World Dictionary of the American Language* (1966), an ally is someone "joined with another for a common purpose" (p. 41). This definition serves as a starting point to develop a working definition of ally as this term relates to issues of oppression. In this chapter, we will define *ally* as "A person who is a member of the 'dominant' or 'majority' group who works to end oppression in his or her personal and professional life through support of, and as an advocate with and for, the oppressed population."

The rationale behind this definition is that although an oppressed person can certainly be a supporter and advocate for his or her own group, the impact and effect of such activity are different on the dominant group, and are often more powerful when the supporter is not a member of the oppressed population. Understanding this notion is an important first step toward becoming an ally for any "targeted" or oppressed group. Given our definition, only heterosexual individuals can serve as allies of gay, lesbian, and bisexual people.

This chapter explores factors associated with becoming an ally of gay, lesbian, and bisexual individuals, including the importance of recognizing heterosexual privilege, motivations for becoming an ally, the practice of advocacy, what an ally should know, and positive and negative consequences of advocacy.

HETEROSEXUAL PRIVILEGE

The individual who decides to undertake the ally role must recognize and understand the power and privileges that one receives, accepts, and experiences as a heterosexual person. Developing this awareness is often the most painful part of the process of becoming an ally. Helms (1984) wrote about this stage of identity development for majority groups as it relates to racism, labeling it the disintegration stage. Although this theory is based on the development of Whites or European Americans as "dominants," there are some similarities with other dominant positions in this country. Some of these similarities exist around feelings of anger and guilt.

When heterosexual persons first learn that their gay, lesbian, or bisexual friends are truly mistreated on the basis of sexual orientation, they often feel anger toward heterosexuals and guilt toward themselves for being members of that group. This process can only happen, however, when persons have an understanding of sexual orientation and do not see it as grounds for discrimination, violence, or abuse. These feelings do not occur when the person still believes that gay, lesbian, and bisexual persons are sick sinners who either need to have a good sexual relationship with a person of the other sex or see a psychologist or a spiritual leader so that they can be cured. Such persons, who might be classified as being at the lowest level of development according to Helms' (1984) majority group identity model, are not yet ready to start down the ally road.

Some of the powers and privileges heterosexuals have that gay and lesbian, and in some cases bisexual, persons do not include:

- family memberships in health clubs, pools, and other recreational activities
- the right to legalized marriage
- purchasing property as a couple
- filing joint income tax returns
- ability to adopt children
- social activities on college campuses and in religious settings geared toward heterosexuals
- health insurance for one's life partner
- decisions on health-related issues as they relate to one's life partner
- assumption that one is psychologically healthy.

In addition to such tangible privileges of the heterosexual population, there are a great many other, not so tangible, privileges. One important intangible privilege is living one's life without the fear that people will find out that who one falls in love with, dreams about, makes love to, is someone of the same sex. This fear affects the lives of gay, lesbian, and bisexual persons from the day they first begin to have "those funny feelings" until the day they die. Although many gay, lesbian, and bisexual persons overcome that fear and turn the fear into a positive component of their lives, they have still been affected, and those wounds, even after healed, are easily reopened.

Coming to terms with the very fact that "as a heterosexual I do not experience the world in the same way as gay, lesbian, and bisexual people do" is an important step in the development of an ally. This awareness begins to move the heterosexual from being a caring, liberal person who feels we are all created equal and should be treated as such toward being an ally who begins to realize that although equality and equity are goals they have not yet been achieved, and that she or he has a role in helping to make these goals realities.

MOTIVATIONS FOR BECOMING AN ADVOCATE

What motivates heterosexuals to become gay rights advocates? There are certainly more popular and less controversial causes with which one can become involved. Since involvement in gay rights advocacy is a moral issue, moral development theory suggests some possible underlying reasons for such activity. Kohlberg (1984) hypothesized that moral reasoning develops through three levels: preconventional, conventional, and postconventional. At the preconventional level, moral decisions are based on what is good for the individual. Persons functioning at this level may choose to be involved in gay rights issues to protect their own interests or to get something out of such involvement (e.g., if this issue is particularly important to a supervisor whose approval is sought).

At the conventional level Kohlberg indicated that decisions are made that conform to the norms of one's group or society. Individuals at this level may work for gay rights if they wish to support friends who are gay, lesbian, or bisexual or to uphold an existing institutional policy of nondiscrimination.

Kohlberg's third level of reasoning involves decision making based on principles of justice. At this level the individual takes an active role to create policies that assure that all people are treated fairly, and he or she becomes involved in gay rights advocacy because it is the right thing to do.

Although Kohlberg focused on justice as the basis of moral decision making, Gilligan (1982) used the principle of care as the basis of her model of moral reasoning. Her three levels of reasoning are (1) taking care of self, (2) taking care of others, and (3) supporting positions that take into consideration the impact both on self and on others. Using this model, individuals at the first level become advocates to make themselves look good to others or to protect themselves from criticism for not getting involved. At the second level individuals reason that it is their role to "take care of" gay, lesbian, and bisexual students. The final perspective leads the individual to believe that equality and respect for differences create a better world for everyone, and he or she works to achieve these goals.

One could argue that the latter position in each scheme is the enlightened perspective that any advocate needs to espouse. We should, however, be aware that not every person is functioning at a postconventional level of moral reasoning and that arguments designed to encourage people to commit themselves to gay rights advocacy need to be targeted to the level that the individual can understand and accept. Kohlberg (1972) indicated that active involvement in addressing moral issues is an important factor in facilitating moral development along his stages. We can, therefore, expect that as people become involved in gay rights issues their level of reasoning may move toward a postconventional level.

ADVOCACY IN ACTION

Advocacy can take a number of different forms and target various audiences. Heterosexual supporters may focus some of their energy toward gay, lesbian, and bisexual individuals themselves. At other times the target may be other heterosexuals, and often strategies are focused on the campus community as a whole.

Advocacy with gay, lesbian, and bisexual people involves acceptance, support, and inclusiveness. Examples of acceptance include listening to gay, lesbian, and bisexual students in a nonjudgmental way and valuing the unique qualities of each individual. Support includes such behaviors as championing the hiring of gay, lesbian, and bisexual staff; providing an atmosphere in which gay, lesbian, and bisexual issues can be discussed in training or programming;

or attending events sponsored by gay, lesbian, and bisexual student organizations. Inclusiveness involves activities such as use of non-exclusionary language; publications, fliers, and handbooks that take into account sexual orientation differences; and sensitivity to the possibility that not everyone in a student organization or work setting is heterosexual.

Being an advocate among other heterosexuals is often challenging. Such a position involves modeling advocacy and support and confronting inappropriate behavior. In this context heterosexual supporters model nonheterosexist behaviors such as being equally physical with men and women, avoiding joking or teasing someone for nontraditional gender behaviors, and avoiding making a point of being heterosexual. Allies are spokespersons for addressing gay issues proactively in program and policy development. Confronting behaviors such as heterosexist joke telling; exclusion of gay, lesbian, and bisexuals either intentionally or by using language that assumes heterosexuality; discriminatory hiring practices; or evaluation of staff based on factors related to their sexual orientation is also part of the role of the advocate.

Advocacy in the institution involves making sure that issues facing gay, lesbian, and bisexual students and staff are acknowledged and addressed. This goal is accomplished by developing and promoting educational efforts that raise the awareness level and increase the sensitivity of heterosexual students, staff, and faculty on campus. Such activities include inviting speakers to address topics relevant to the gay, lesbian, and bisexual community; developing panel discussions on issues related to sexual orientation; including gay issues as a topic in RA training programs; and promoting plays and movies featuring gay themes.

Encouraging gay, lesbian, and bisexual student and staff organizations is also part of institutional advocacy. Such groups need to have access to the same campus resources, funding, and sponsorship as other student and staff organizations. Developing and supporting progay, prolesbian, probisexual policies are also a necessary aspect of advocacy. Antiharassment policies, antidiscriminatory hiring policies, and provisions for nonheterosexual couples to live together in campus housing are arenas that deserve attention.

THINGS YOU SHOULD KNOW AS AN ALLY

When dealing with issues of oppression, there are four basic levels of becoming an ally. The following examples relate specifically to being an ally to lesbian, gay, and bisexual persons.

- *Awareness* is the first level. It is important to become more aware of who you are and how you are different from and similar to lesbian, gay, and bisexual people. Such awareness can be gained through conversations with gay, lesbian, and bisexual individuals, attending awareness-building workshops, reading about gay and lesbian lifestyles, and by self-examination.
- *Knowledge/education* is the second level. You must begin to acquire knowledge about sexual orientation and what the experience is for lesbian, gay, and bisexual persons in this country. This step includes learning about laws, policies, and practices and how they affect lesbian, gay, and bisexual persons in addition to educating yourself about the gay and lesbian culture and norms of this community. Materials listed in chapter 13 in this book are a good starting place. Contacting local and national gay and lesbian organizations for information can also be helpful. Many such organizations are listed in chapter 13.
- *Skills* make up the third level. This area is the one in which people often fall short because of fear or lack of resources or supports. You must develop skills in communicating the knowledge that you have learned. These skills can be acquired through attending workshops, role playing situations with friends, developing support connections, and practicing interventions or awareness raising in safe settings, for example, a restaurant or hotel out of your home town.
- *Action* is the last but most important level. This is the most frightening step. There are many challenges and liabilities for heterosexuals in taking actions to end oppression of lesbian, gay, and bisexual people, and some are addressed in this chapter's discussion of factors that discourage advocacy. However, action is, without a doubt, the only way that we can effect change in the society as a whole; for, if we keep our awareness, knowledge, and skills to ourselves, we deprive the rest of the world of what we have learned, thus keeping them from having the fullest possible life.

In addition to the four levels in ally development, there are five additional points to keep in mind:

1. Have a good understanding of sexual orientation and be aware of and comfortable with your own. If you are a person who chooses not to identify with a particular sexual orientation, be comfortable with that decision, but recognize that others, particularly lesbian and gay persons, may see your stance as a cop out.

2. Talk with lesbian, gay, and bisexual persons and read about the coming out process. (The reference lists in chapters 1 and 2 and the resources listed in chapter 13 are good places to begin.) This is a process and experience that is unique to this oppressed group. No other population of oppressed persons needs to disclose to one's family and close friends in the same way. Because of its uniqueness, this process brings challenges that are often not understood.

3. As any other oppressed group, the lesbian, gay, and bisexual population gets the same messages about homosexuality and bisexuality as everyone else. Thus, there is a great deal of internalized heterosexism and homophobia. There are lesbian, gay, and bisexual people who believe that what they do in the "bed" is nobody's business and thus being an open lesbian, gay, or bisexual person to them would be forcing their sex practices on the general society, something that should not be done. It is, therefore, very important not only to be supportive, recognizing that you do not share the same level of personal risk as the lesbian, gay, or bisexual person, but also to challenge some of the internalized oppressive notions. You can help the lesbian, gay, or bisexual person to see himself or herself from a different, more positive, perspective.

4. As with most oppressed groups, there is diversity within the gay, lesbian, and bisexual community. Heterosexism is an area of oppression that cuts across, but is not limited to, race, ethnicity, gender, class, religion, culture, age, and level of able-bodiedness. For all of these categories, there are different challenges. Certainly, gay, lesbian, and bisexual individuals as members of these diverse populations share some common joys and concerns; however, issues often manifest themselves in very different ways in different groups, thus calling for different strategies and interventions. Some of these differences are discussed more fully in the chapter discussing gay and lesbian students of color.

5. It is difficult to enter into a discussion about heterosexism and homophobia without the topic of AIDS/HIV infection arising. Knowing at least basic information about the illness is necessary for two reasons: (1) to address myths and misinformation related to AIDS and the gay, lesbian, and bisexual community and (2) to be supportive of the members of the community most affected by this disease. Although we recognize that AIDS is a health issue that has and will continue to affect our entire country, the persons who live in the most fear and have lost

the most members of their community are gay, lesbian, and bisexual individuals. Accepting that reality helps an ally in his or her understanding of the intense emotion around this issue within the community.

These five points and the previous four levels of awareness provide some guidelines for becoming an effective ally. And although we recognize that these concepts seem fairly reasonable, there are some real challenges or factors that can discourage an ally from taking these steps.

FACTORS THAT DISCOURAGE ADVOCACY

Involvement in gay rights advocacy can be a scary and unpopular activity. Individuals who wish to take on such a role must be aware of and reconcile themselves to several potentially unpleasant outcomes. Some of these problems involve reactions from other heterosexuals, and some come from members of the gay, lesbian, and bisexual community.

An assumption is automatically made within the heterosexual community that anyone supporting gay rights is automatically gay, lesbian, or bisexual. Although such an identity is not negative, such labeling can create problems, especially for unmarried heterosexuals who might wish to become involved in a heterosexual romantic relationship. Heterosexuals also often experience derisive comments from other heterosexuals concerning involvement in a cause that is viewed as unimportant, unacceptable, or unpopular. Friends and colleagues who are uncomfortable with the topic may become alienated from the heterosexual supporter of gay rights or noticeably distance themselves from the individual. Difficulty may arise in social situations if the heterosexual ally is seen in the company of gay, lesbian, or bisexual individuals. Discrimination, either overt or subtle, may also result from getting involved in controversial causes. Such discrimination may take the form of poor evaluations, failure to be appointed to important committees, or encouragement to seek a position at a school "more supportive of your ideas."

The gay, lesbian, and bisexual community also may have trouble accepting the heterosexual ally. Often an assumption is made that such persons are really gay, lesbian, or bisexual but not yet accepting of their identity. Subtle or not so subtle pressure is placed on such people to come out or at least to consider the possibility of a non-heterosexual identity.

The gay, lesbian, and bisexual world is one that has its own language and culture. Heterosexual supporters can feel out of place and awkward in settings populated exclusively or mainly by gay men, lesbians, and bisexuals. Lesbians and gay men may be exclusionary in their conversations and activities, leaving the heterosexual ally out of the picture. Since most gay men and lesbians have had mainly negative experiences with heterosexuals in the past, the motives of heterosexuals involved in gay rights activities are often questioned. These experiences make it difficult for gay and lesbian people to accept that individuals will involve themselves in a controversial and unpopular cause just because it is "right."

BENEFITS OF BEING AN ALLY

Although the factors that discourage individuals from being an ally are very real, the benefits of being an ally are equally so. What are these benefits?

1. You open yourself up to the possibility of close relationships with an additional 10% of the world.
2. You become less locked into sex role stereotypes.
3. You increase your ability to have close and loving relationships with same-sex friends.
4. You have opportunities to learn from, teach, and have an impact on a population with whom you might not otherwise interact.
5. You may be the reason your son, daughter, sister, brother, minister, doctor, lawyer, teacher, mother, or father finally decides that his or her life is worth something and that he or she does not need to depend on chemicals or other substances to get through the day.
6. You may make the difference in the lives of adolescents who hear you confront antigay or antilesbian epithets that make them feel as if they want to drop out of junior high, high school, or college. As a result of your action, they know they have a friend to turn to.
7. Lastly, you can get invited to some of the most fun parties, have some of the best foods, play some of the best sports, have some of the best intellectual discussions, and experience some of the best music in the world, because everyone knows that lesbian and gay people are good at all these things.

Although the last statement is meant as a joke, there is a great deal of truth concerning the positive experiences to which persons open themselves when they allow themselves to be a part of and include another 10% of the population in their world. Imagine what it could be like to have had such close friends as Tennessee Williams, Cole Porter, Bessie Smith, Walt Whitman, Gertrude Stein, Alice Walker, James Baldwin, or Virginia Woolf.

Imagine the world without their contributions. It is possible for bisexual, lesbian, and gay people, as well as heterosexuals, to make a difference in the way the world is, but we must start by realizing the equity in our humanness and the inequity in the life experiences of bisexual, lesbian, and gay persons.

REFERENCES

Friere, P. (1970). *Pedagogy of the oppressed*. New York: Continuum.

Gilligan, C. (1982). *In a different voice*. Cambridge, MA: Harvard University Press.

Helms, J. (1984). Toward a theoretical explanation of the effects of race on counseling: A Black and White model. *Counseling Psychologist, 12*(4), 153–164.

Katz, J. (1982). *White awareness: Handbook for antiracism training*. Norman, OK: University of Oklahoma Press.

Kohlberg, L. (1972). A cognitive developmental approach to moral education. *Humanist, 6*, 13–16.

Kohlberg, L. (1984). *Essays on moral development: Vol. 2. Psychology of moral development: The nature and validity of moral stages*. New York: Harper & Row.

Webster's new world dictionary of the American language. (1966). Cleveland: World.

Chapter 12

INCLUDING BISEXUALITY: IT'S MORE THAN JUST A LABEL

Raechele L. Pope
University of Massachusetts at Amherst

Amy L. Reynolds
University of Iowa

"If one more person asks me how can I call myself a bisexual man and be in a monogamous relationship with a man, I'm going to scream."

"A close friend of mine once told me that she and a group of her lesbian friends held a mock funeral for a female friend (who had previously been involved with women) who had 'betrayed' them by getting married to a man."

"For a number of years I identified myself as a lesbian. When my relationship with a woman ended and I started dating men, most of my gay and lesbian friends quit calling. I felt as if I was no longer welcomed at the parties, socials, or political events. A few years later when I fell in love with a woman, a lesbian friend of mine said, 'We're glad you're back. We missed you.' I wanted to say, 'I wasn't the one who left.'"

"In my community there was a great deal of conflict and controversy about including the word bisexual *in the annual lesbian and gay pride parade. At a large community meeting to discuss the issue, a lesbian stood up and said to the bisexuals at the meeting, 'Can't you just be gay for the day?'"*

To be inclusive is difficult. It requires constant vigilance and an openness to both reminders and criticisms from others, particularly those who feel shut out or misunderstood. It demands the welcoming of ideas, behaviors, languages, styles, and people even when it is uncomfortable and seems cumbersome. To be inclusive requires changing from the common notion in this culture that difference is bad to a recognition, acceptance, and celebration of the full range of human diversity. True inclusion, for example, means involving all possibilities and people from the very beginning rather than adding them after the planning has been completed. Such late additions only provide the illusion of inclusion.

To be inclusive often means admitting mistakes, recognizing oversights, correcting them, and making a commitment not to make the same mistake twice. Exclusion can, and often does, occur even when one is attempting to be inclusive. To be inclusive is difficult, but it is not impossible.

This book was in its final editing phase when its editors recognized that few chapters actually addressed bisexual issues. This oversight needed to be corrected. An honest and healthy dialogue ensued over possible remedies: This chapter is the result of that dialogue.

The process that occurred during the conceptualization, writing, and editing of this book is representative of the current struggle for definition and understanding of bisexuality. Although bisexuality has been acknowledged since the early Kinsey studies on human sexuality, until recently there has been a paucity of literature. This lack of information and clear definition has led to myths, misinformation, and exclusion of bisexuality in both literature and the lesbian, gay, and heterosexual communities.

Although there is no one accepted definition of bisexuality, common to all is the description of individuals who connect with both women and men in terms of attraction, desire, and love (Hutchins & Kaahumanu, 1991; Klein, Sepekoff, & Wolf, 1990; Wittstock, 1990). One of the confusing aspects of bisexuality for many people is the diversity of possibilities (Hutchins & Kaahumanu, 1991; Wittstock, 1990). Some argue that bisexual individuals are people who are simultaneously attracted to both men and women. Others contend that bisexual people may experience sequential relationships with men and women. This type of bisexuality may mean that an individual spends some time in a gay or lesbian relationship followed by involvement in a heterosexual relationship or vice versa. Other individuals may self-identify as bisexual regardless of the gender of their current partner. It is this diversity and complexity of bisexuality that confuses, unnerves, and creates suspicion among lesbian, gay, and heterosexual people.

From this confusion and distrust stem many myths, misinformation, and missing information about bisexual people. There are stereotypes and biases that keep bisexual individuals marginal and make it difficult for them to find a supportive community (Fox, 1991; Hutchins & Kaahumanu, 1991; Wittstock, 1990). The nongay culture sees bisexual people as gay and, therefore, subjects them to homophobia and heterosexism. Meanwhile, in lesbian and gay communities, there is fear and distrust of what is often seen as the bisexual "choice." Many lesbian and gay people suspect individuals of choosing bisexuality as a means of maintaining heterosexual privileges. Ironically, the same notion that is used against lesbian and gay people—"it's only a phase"—is also used by gays and lesbians to dismiss and deny the significance of bisexual feelings and identity. In their efforts to combat homophobia and heterosexism, many gay and lesbian people often fight fiercely against the notion that sexuality is a choice, yet they resort to the tactics and thinking of the heterosexual community when challenging the existence of bisexuality. The ultimate irony is that if we truly believe in a sexual orientation rather than a sexual preference, choice is a moot issue.

Biphobia is alive and well and creates as many barriers as homophobia. Biphobia is prejudice based on the fear and distrust of bisexual people and feelings (Diehl & Ochs, 1989–1990; Wittstock, 1990). At the core of biphobia is the ultimate marginalizing question, "Does bisexuality really exist?" In the end, bisexual people often feel that they are balancing between two worlds and accepted by neither. This clearly complicates the formation of sexual identity in bisexual people. Golden (1987) believes that bisexuality may have more of a stigma than a lesbian identity. In fact, many bisexual women may publicly define themselves as lesbian and be strongly connected to the lesbian community (Schuster, 1987). The stigma and misinformation surrounding bisexuality creates internal barriers for bisexual individuals as well as interpersonal barriers between lesbian, gay, and bisexual people.

Gay and lesbian communities are grappling with how to talk about bisexuality as well as their own sexuality. Currently it seems that inclusion in some communities means adding bisexuality in name only. This is an important first step, yet it must be recognized that it is only a step in the process. The label *bisexual* is added to name the difference, but there is often no real exploration or discussion of what bisexuality actually means. The intention is good, but it falls short. These good intentions only mirror the lack of understanding and comfort in this culture with the full range of sexual feelings, behaviors, and identities.

Programming on college and university campuses around gay and lesbian issues also mirrors this same lack of comfort. Bisexuality is occasionally added to the title of a program or series of awareness events, but bisexuality is rarely discussed and almost never viewed as a truly integral component of the program. The assumption seems to be that "those people," that is, bisexual individuals, exist somewhere but are never present. This treatment leads one to question how students and staff who are dealing with being bisexual come to understand who they are.

Many believe that focusing on bisexuality and bisexual individuals dilutes and confuses opportunities to understand and educate about gay and lesbian people and heterosexism and homophobia. But when we assume that our minds can only comprehend limited complexity and multiplicity of meanings and identities, nature shows us that this thinking is false. We are confronted daily with innumerable varieties of flowers and plants, and we do not attempt to label them all roses for fear of complexity. We do not assume that the existence of one flower limits and minimizes the flourishing of another. The human mind is capable of embracing a multitude of truths. It is our fear that prevents us from venturing into this unknown place of acceptance and inclusion.

In order to recognize, accept, and truly celebrate bisexual individuals, there must be a willingness to challenge the notion of dichotomous sexuality and identity (Schuster, 1987). We must be willing and able to expand our world view and move beyond the either/or thinking that permeates our culture. It is not a matter of being gay or nongay. What is primary is that all people be allowed and encouraged to discover and embrace all of who they are. Until we can move to such acceptance, we have not truly allowed the full range of sexuality to be explored.

Klein (1978) suggested that to be fully human and complete, we must be willing to explore our sexuality. He contended that the foundation of the fear of gay and lesbian people (homophobia) is the fear of sexuality and intimacy. In this culture, we are taught that it is all right to be close and intimate with only some people, at certain times, and in particular ways. Such rules limit our intimacy and connection with other human beings. Somehow to be intimate is confused with being sexual. According to Klein, striving for unity with another person is central to our existence. We all are born with the potential for 100% intimacy with all people in our lives, yet because of certain cultural rules, we limit ourselves to being close to only a handful of people who meet our specific qualifications. Klein believes that healthy bisexuals are healthy not because they have the capacity to be sexually intimate with both genders but rather because of the openness and accessibility of their emotional intimacy. Klein's notions are inviting and offer us another way to view sexuality and intimacy.

Our task as human beings and as student affairs professionals is to create understanding and openness among all people. How can we move beyond tolerance, beyond including bisexuality in name only? This is not a simple question, and there are no easy answers. There never are. We do not intend to offer pat answers or transparent solutions. Such efforts insult the complexity of human sexuality. We will, however, offer our thoughts and ideas on creating environments that are more welcoming and inclusive of bisexual individuals. We recognize that changing ourselves and our environments takes time and we will make mistakes. The mistakes are part of the process and cannot be avoided. We must allow the process to unfold and be willing to take risks.

A beginning and crucial step, regardless of our sexual orientation, is acknowledging any discomfort and lack of information about bisexuality. We must be willing to invest time and energy in understanding bisexual individuals. It is only after we have made the commitment to challenge ourselves that we can begin the process of educating others.

In our programming and training we need to step back and create a new paradigm. Rather than just focusing on gay and lesbian people, we are charged with the tasks of broadening our definitions and of understanding the full continuum of sexuality. Undoubtedly, the creation of this new paradigm is very different from just adding bisexual people to the list of marginalized individuals. Angela Davis (1989), noted African-American political activist and teacher, said that in order to create a truly multicultural organization we must start from scratch: organizations that already exist must be disbanded. There is no way to add people of color after the fact and still create a multicultural organization. The norms have been established, the rules and procedures enacted. Her message is that just "adding people and stirring" keeps people marginalized and will not change the "flavor of the stew." Up until now, adding and stirring is what we have been doing with bisexual people. Perhaps it is time to disband gay and lesbian organizations and begin again with organizations that openly involve bisexual individuals from inception. We need to offer programs that examine the full range of human sexuality rather than reinforce the dichotomous notion of sexuality. These efforts may not only attract the interest and participation of more individuals but, in fact, may also include all those people who are currently participating but not being included or welcomed (bisexual individuals have participated and been leaders in the lesbian and gay movement from the very beginning but were not publicly identified or supported as bisexual).

We need to recognize that not all bisexuals look alike, act alike, or think alike. Bisexual individuals come in all colors, races, religions, abilities, classes, sizes, and political persuasions. We must not assume we know the sexuality of other individuals. We must not label the sexual orientation of others. Naming ourselves is one of our few fundamental rights, and it must be honored and protected.

We must speak out against intolerance and exclusion of bisexual people. When there is no bisexual voice being heard, we must ask why. We must recognize the silence and work to ensure that the void is filled. We must create an environment that welcomes all and diminishes none. Sometimes the most simple lessons are most easily forgotten. Supporting the rights of any group never inherently disadvantages another. Openly welcoming and involving bisexual individuals will not dilute the struggle against homophobia and heterosexism. It will strengthen it. We need to move beyond merely combating heterosexism and begin to challenge the core cultural beliefs that dichotomize and marginalize difference. Expanding our definitions and world views will create a foundation for true inclusion. This will be a difficult task. However, being inclusive can no longer be a matter of choice; it is about doing what is right, what is just, what is necessary, for all of us. It is difficult and it is possible.

REFERENCES

Davis, A. (1989, April). *Rethinking alliance building.* Paper presented at Parallels and Intersections: Unlearning Racism and Other Forms of Oppression Conference, Iowa City, IA.

Diehl, M., & Ochs, R. (1989–1990). Biphobia. *Empathy, 2,* 15–19.

Fox, A. (1991). Development of a bisexual identity: Understanding the process. In L. Hutchins & L. Kaahumanu (Eds.), *Bi any other name: Bisexual people speak out* (pp. 29–36). Boston: Alyson.

Golden, C. (1987). Diversity and variability in women's sexual identities. In Boston Lesbian Psychologies Collective (Eds.), *Lesbian psychologies: Explorations and challenges* (pp. 19–34). Urbana, IL: University of Illinois Press.

Hutchins, L., & Kaahumanu, L. (Eds.). (1991). *Bi any other name: Bisexual people speak out.* Boston: Alyson.

Klein, F. (1978). *The bisexual option.* New York: Arbor House.

Klein, F., Sepekoff, B., & Wolf, T. J. (1990). Sexual orientation: A multivariable dynamic process. In T. Geller (Ed.), *Bisexuality: A reader and sourcebook* (pp. 64–81). Novato, CA: Times Change Press.

Schuster, R. (1987). Sexuality as a continuum: The bisexual identity. In Boston Lesbian Psychologies Collective (Eds.), *Lesbian psychologies: Explorations and challenges* (pp. 56–71). Urbana, IL: University of Illinois Press.

Wittstock, M. (1990). The best of both worlds and still nothing. In T. Geller (Ed.), *Bisexuality: A reader and sourcebook* (pp. 26–33). Novato, CA: Times Change Press.

BISEXUAL ORGANIZATIONS

Bisexual People of Color Caucus/BiPol
584 Castro Street, No. 422
San Francisco, CA 94114
(415) 775–1990

East Coast Bisexual Network (ECBN)
Boston Lesbian/Gay Service Center
338 Newbury Street, 2nd Floor
Boston, MA 02115
(617) 247–6683

International Directory of Bisexual Groups
(obtainable through the Boston Bisexual Women's Network
c/o Boston Lesbian/Gay Service Center
338 Newbury Street, 2nd Floor
Boston, MA 02115)

National Bisexual Network
584 Castro Street, No. 422
San Francisco, CA 94114
(415) 775–1990

The North American Multicultural Bisexual Network
584 Castro Street, No. 441
San Francisco, CA 94114

BISEXUALITY RESOURCES

Bisexuality–News, views, and networking/The North American Journal on Bisexuality. Long Beach, CA: Gibbin. (PO Box 20917, Long Beach, CA 90801–3917; 213–597–2799).

Collins, L. E., & Zimmerman, N. (1983). Homosexual and bisexual issues. *Family Therapy Collections, 5,* 82–100.

Geller, T. (Ed.). (1990). *Bisexuality: A reader and sourcebook.* Novato, CA: Times Change Press.

Hill, I. (Ed.). (1987). *The bisexual spouse: Different dimensions in human sexuality.* McLean, VA: Barlina Books.

Klein, F., & Wolf, T. J. (Eds.). (1985). *Bisexualities: Theory and research.* New York: Haworth.

Maddox, B. (1982). *Married and gay: What happens when a gay man marries a lesbian?* New York: Harcourt Brace Jovanovich.

Paul, J. P. (1984). The bisexual identity: An idea without social recognition. *Journal of Homosexuality, 9,* 45–63.

Paul, J. P. (1985). Bisexuality: Reassessing our paradigms of sexuality. *Journal of Homosexuality, 11,* 21–34.

Chapter 13
RESOURCES

Shawn-Eric Brooks
University of California—Los Angeles

This chapter is devoted to providing resources to assist in addressing various issues relating to sexual orientation. Whether one's interest is in providing general information to students, staff, and faculty or in designing programs around sexual orientation issues, this chapter contains resources that will prove helpful. Note that the information contained in this chapter is not exhaustive of the subject of sexual orientation. These resources have surfaced as being particularly helpful to our colleagues who have trodden these roads before you.

Many thanks to all who responded to a request for resources to be included in this chapter.

GENERAL WORKS ON GAY, LESBIAN, AND BISEXUAL LIFESTYLES

If the statistics are accurate, about 1 out of 10 people identify themselves as homosexual. If you apply this statistic to persons in your life, you may be amazed at how many of your friends, family members, colleagues, and students identify with varied lifestyles. What are their issues, concerns, hopes, aspirations and dreams? Items in this section of the chapter provide information about various sexual orientations.

Abbott, S., & Love, B. (1972). *Sappho was a right on woman*. New York: Stein and Day.

Altman, D. (1973). *Homosexuality: Oppression and liberation*. New York: Avon.

Alyson, S. (Ed.). (1985). *Young, gay, and proud*. Boston: Alyson.

Baetz, R. (1980). *Lesbian crossroads: Personal stories of lesbian struggles and triumphs*. New York: Morrow.

Becker, C. (1988). *Unbroken ties: Lesbian ex-lovers*. Boston: Alyson.

Bell, A. P., & Weinberg, M. (1981). *Homosexualities: A study in diversity in men and women*. Bloomington: Indiana University Press.

Bell, A. P., Weinberg, M., & Hammersmith, S.K. (1981) *Sexual preference: Its development in men and women*. Bloomington: Indiana University Press.

Berzon, B. (1988). *Permanent partners*. New York: Dutton.

Blumenfeld, W., & Raymond, D. (1988). *Looking at gay and lesbian life*. New York: Philosophical Library.

Bode, J. (1976). *View from another closet: Exploring bisexuality in women*. New York: Hawthorne.

Brod, H. (Ed.). (1987). *The making of masculinities: The new men's studies*. Boston: Allen & Unwin.

Brown, H. (1976). *Familiar faces, hidden lives: The story of homosexual men in America today*. New York: Harcourt Brace Jovanovich.

Bullogh, Y. (1978). *Homosexuality: Past and present*. New York: Garland.

Clark, D. (1979). *Living gay*. Millbrae, CA: Celestial Arts.

Covina, G., & Galana, L. (Eds.). (1975). *The lesbian reader*. Oakland, CA: Amazon.

Cruikshank, M. (1981). *Lesbian studies: Women loving women*. San Francisco: Angel.

Cruikshank, M. (1982). *Lesbian studies: Present and future*. New York: Feminist Press.

Curry, H., & Denis, C. (1980). *A legal guide for lesbian and gay couples*. Berkeley, CA: Nolo.

Darty, T., & Potter, S. (Eds.). (1984) *Women-identified women*. Palo Alto, CA: Mayfield.

D'Emilio, J. (1983). *Sexual politics; sexual communities*. Chicago: University of Chicago Press.

Fast, J. (1975). *Bisexual living*. New York: Pocket.

Fisher, P. (1972). *The gay mystique: The myth and reality of male homosexuality*. New York: Stein and Day.

Fleming, M. C. (1989). *About courage*. Los Angeles: Holloway House.

Fricke, A. (1981). *Reflections of a rock lobster: A story about growing up gay*. Boston: Alyson.

Gordon, S. (1975). *You: The psychology of surviving. . . .* New York: Quadrangle/New York Times.

Hanckel, F., & Cunningham, J. (1979). *A way of life, a way of love: A young person's introduction to what it means to be gay*. New York: Lothrop, Lee, and Shepard.

Heger, H. (1980). *The men with the pink triangles*. Boston: Alyson.

Heron, A. (Ed.). (1983). *One teenager in ten: A testimony by gay and lesbian youth*. Boston: Alyson.

Humphreys, L. (1972). *Out of the closets: The sociology of homosexual liberation*. Englewood Cliffs, NJ: Prentice-Hall.

Hunt, M. (1977). *Gay: What you should know about homosexuality*. New York: Farrar, Straus, Giroux.

Jay, K., & Young, A. (1977). *Out of the closets: The voices of gay liberation*. New York: Jove.

Katz, J. (Ed.). (1976). *Gay American history: Lesbians and gay men in the USA*. New York: Crowell.

Klaich, D. (1974). *Woman plus woman*. New York: Simon and Schuster.

Klein, F. (1978). *The bisexual option: A concept of one hundred percent intimacy*. New York: Arbor House.

Kleinberg, S. (1980). *Alienated affections: Being gay in America*. New York: St. Martin's.

Kohn, B. (1980). *Barry and Alice: Portrait of a bisexual marriage*. Englewood Cliffs, NJ: Prentice-Hall.

Kus, R. (Ed.). (1990). *Gay men of alcoholics anonymous: Firsthand accounts*. Iowa City: Winter Star.

Lauritsen, J., & Thorstad, D. (1974). *The early homosexual movement*. New York: Times and Change.

Leavitt, D. (1986). *The lost language of the cranes*. New York: Bantam.

Loulan, J. (1987). *Lesbian sex and lesbian passions*. San Francisco: Spinsters/Aunt Lute.

Masters, W., & Johnson, V. (1979). *Homosexuality in perspective*. Boston: Little, Brown.

McNaught, B. (1981). *A disturbed peace*. Washington, DC: Dignity.

McWhirter, D., & Mattison, A. (1983). *The male couple*. Englewood Cliffs, NJ: Prentice-Hall.

Moses, A. (1978). *Identity management in lesbian women*. New York: Praeger.

Nieberding, R. A. (Ed.). (1989). *In every classroom: The report of the president's select committee for lesbians and gay concerns*. New Brunswick, NJ: Rutgers University Press.

Pharr, S. (1988). *Homophobia: A weapon of sexism*. Little Rock, AR: Chardon.

Pleck, J.H. (1984). *The myth of masculinity*. Cambridge, MA: Massachusetts Institute of Technology Press.

Ponse, B. (1978). *Identities in the lesbian world: The social construction of the self*. Westport, CT: Greenwood.

Rosen, D. (1974). *Lesbianism: A study of female homosexuality*. Springfield, IL: Thomas.

Russo, V. (1987). *The celluloid closet*. New York: Harper & Row.

Silverstein, C., & White, E. (1977). *The joy of gay sex*. New York: Crown.

Simpson, R. (1977). *From the closets to the courts*. New York: Viking.

Sisley, E. L., & Harris, B. (1977). *The joy of lesbian sex*. New York: Crown.

Spada, L. (1979). *The Spada report: The newest survey of gay male sexuality*. New York: New American Library.

Stekel, W. (1950). *Bisexual love*. New York: Emerson.

Vida, G. (1978). *Our right to love: A lesbian resource book*. Englewood Cliffs, NJ: Prentice-Hall.

Wolf, D. (1979). *The lesbian community*. Los Angeles: University of California Press.

Wolff, C. (1977). *Bisexuality: A study*. London: Quartet.

COMING OUT—A FAMILY AFFAIR

The term *coming out* refers to a process that homosexuals progress through; moving from pre-identification through homosexual identification to positive integration and celebration of homosexuality in one's life. The process can sometimes be quite difficult, not only for the individual experiencing same-gender attraction but also for the individual's family and friends. Resources in this section relate to the process of coming out and issues that family members encounter when someone comes out.

Black, G. G. (1985). *Are you still my mother? Are you still my family?* New York: Warner.

Borhek, M. (1979). *Coming out to parents: A two-way survival guide for lesbians and gay men and their parents*. New York: Harcourt Brace Jovanovich.

Fairchild, B. (1975). *Parents of gays*. Washington, DC: Thunderbolt.

Fairchild, B. (1979). *Now that you know: What every parent should know about homosexuality*. New York: Harcourt Brace Jovanovich.

Muchmore, W., & Hanson, W. (1977). *Coming out right: A handbook for the gay male*. Boston: Alyson.

Mueller, A. (1987). *Parents matter: Parents' relationships with lesbian daughters and gay sons*. Tallahassee, FL: Naiad.

Rafkin, L. (Ed.). (1987). *Different daughters: A book by mothers of lesbians*. Pittsburgh: Cleis.

Silverstein, C. (1977). *A family matter: A parent's guide to homosexuality*. New York: McGraw-Hill.

Stanley, J. P., & Wolf, S. J. (1980). *Coming out stories*. Boston: Persephone.

COUNSELING ISSUES

These works deal specifically with counseling gay and lesbian clients.

Berzon, B., & Leighton, R. (Eds.). (1979). *Positively gay*. Milbrae, CA: Celestial Arts.

Boston Lesbian Psychologies Collective. (1987). *Lesbian psychologies: Explorations and challenges*. Urbana, IL: University of Illinois Press.

Clark, D. (1977). *Loving someone gay*. Millbrae, CA: Celestial Arts.

Clark, D. (1987). *The new loving someone gay*. Berkeley, CA: Celestial Arts.

Coleman, E. (Ed.). (1988). *Integrated identity for gay men and lesbians.* New York: Harrington Park.

Finnegan, D. G., & McNally, E. G. (1987). *Dual identities: Counseling chemically dependent gay men and lesbians.* Center City, MN: Hazeldon.

Gonsiorek, V.C. (Ed.). (1982). *Homosexuality and psychotherapy: A practitioner's handbook of affirmative models.* New York: Haworth.

Griffin, P. (1988). *Strategies for addressing homophobia in physical education, sport, and dance,* 101 & 102. Two parts available from Pat Griffin, 105 Totman Bldg., University of Massachusetts, Amherst, MA 01007

Kus, R. (Ed.). (1990). *Keys to caring: Assisting your gay and lesbian clients.* Boston: Alyson.

Moses, A., & Hawkins, R. (1982). *Counseling lesbian women and gay men.* St. Louis: Mosby.

Stein, T., & Cohen, C. (1986). *Contemporary perspectives on psychotherapy with lesbians and gay men.* New York: Plerrum.

Weinberg, C. (1972). *Society and the healthy homosexual.* New York: Anchor/ Doubleday.

Woodman, N., & Lenna, H. (1978). *Counseling with gay men and women: A guide for facilitating positive lifestyles.* San Francisco: Jossey-Bass.

SPIRITUALITY, RELIGION, AND HOMOSEXUALITY

Sexual attitudes, taboos, and practices have, for centuries, been used by dominant groups within our society to keep others subordinate. Nowhere has this been evidenced as greatly as it has within the religious arena. Whatever organized religion does not understand, it excludes. Homosexuality is no exception. Items in this chapter examine the gay and lesbian lifestyles as they relate to spirituality and the movement toward inclusion within organized religions.

Beck, E. T. (Ed.). (1982). *Nice Jewish girls: A lesbian anthology.* Trumansburg, NY: Crossing.

Blumenfeld, W. J., & Raymond, D. (1988). *Looking at gay and lesbian life.* Boston: Beacon.

Boswell, J. (1980). *Christianity, social tolerance, and homosexuality.* Chicago: University of Chicago Press.

Boyd, M. (1984). *Take off the masks.* Philadelphia: New Society.

Boyd, M. (1986). *Gay priest: An inner journey.* New York: St. Martin's.

Brod, H. (Ed.). (1988). *A mansch among men: Explorations in Jewish masculinity.* Freedom, CA: Crossing.

Brown, J. R., & Butwill, N. (1973). *Religion, society, and the homosexual.* New York: MSS.

Clark, J. M. (1987). *Gay being, divine presence: Essays in gay spirituality.* Las Colinas, CA: Tangelwud.

Curb, R., & Manaham, N. (Eds.). (1985). *Lesbian nuns: Breaking silence.* New York: Naiad/Warner.

Day, D. (1987). *Things they never told you in Sunday school: A primer for the Christian homosexual.* Austin: Liberty.

Diament, C. (Ed.). (1989). *Jewish marital status.* Northvale, NJ: Jason Aronson.

Edwards, G. (1984). *Gay/lesbian liberation: A biblical perspective.* New York: Pilgrim.

Flood, G. (1986). *I'm looking for Mr. Right but I'll settle for Mr. Right Away: AIDS, true love, the perils of safe sex, and other spiritual concerns of the gay male.* Atlanta: Brob House.

Fortunato, J. E. (1982). *Embracing the exile: Healing journeys of gay Christians.* New York: Harper & Row.

Fortunato, J. E. (1987). *AIDS, the spiritual dilemma.* San Francisco: Harper & Row.

Glaser, C. (1988). *Uncommon calling: A gay man's struggle to serve the church.* San Francisco: Harper & Row.

Gramick, J. (Ed.). (1983). *Homosexuality and the Catholic church.* Chicago: Thomas More.

Hanigan, J. P. (1988). *Homosexuality: The test case for Christian sexual ethics.* New York: Paulist.

McNaught, B. (1981). *A disturbed peace: Selected writings of an Irish Catholic homosexual.* Washington, DC: Dignity.

McNeill, J. (1988). *Taking a chance on God.* Boston: Beacon.

McNeill, J. (1988). *The church and the homosexual.* Boston: Beacon.

Nelson, J. B. (1978). *Embodiment: An approach to sexuality and Christian theology.* Minneapolis: Augsburg.

Nugent, R. (Ed.). (1983). *A challenge to love: Gay and lesbian Catholics in the church.* New York: Crossroad.

Pennington, S. (1978). *But Lord they're gay: A Christian pilgrimage.* Hawthorne, CA: Lambda Christian Fellowship.

Pennington, S. (1985). *Good news for modern gays: A progay biblical approach.* Hawthorne, CA: Lambda Christian Fellowship.

Perry, T. D. (1987). *The Lord is my shepherd and He knows I'm gay.* Austin: Liberty.

Roscoe, W. (Ed.). (1988). *Living the spirit: A gay American Indian anthology.* New York: St. Martin's.

Ruether, R. R. (1985). *Women-church: Theology and practice of feminist liturgical communities.* San Francisco: Harper & Row.

Scanzoni, L., & Mollenkott, V. (1978). *Is the homosexual my neighbor? Another Christian view.* San Francisco: Harper & Row.

Sherwood, Z. (1987). *Confessions of a gay priest.* Boston: Alyson.

Spong, J. S. (1988). *Living in sin? A bishop rethinks human sexuality.* San Francisco: Harper & Row.

Thompson, M. (Ed.). (1987). *Gay spirit: Myth and meaning*. New York: St. Martin's.

Uhrig, L. J. (1986). *Sex positive: A contribution to sexual and spiritual union*. Boston: Alyson.

Wolf, J. G. (Ed.). (1989). *Gay priests*. San Francisco: Harper & Row.

Woods, R. (1988). *Another kind of love: Homosexuality and spirituality* (3rd ed.). Ft Wayne, IN: Knoll.

Zanotti, B. (Ed.). (1986). *A faith of one's own*. Trumansburg, NY: Crossing.

DIVERSITY WITHIN THE GAY, LESBIAN, AND BISEXUAL COMMUNITY

When we celebrate diversity we generally focus our attention on issues such as race, religion, disabilities, age, and sexual orientation. One of the unique things about sexual orientation is that it runs through every other diverse population. Items in this section represent some of the celebration of diversity that exists within the gay, lesbian and bisexual community.

Adelman, M. (Ed.). (1986). *Longtime passing: Lives of older lesbians*. Boston: Alyson.

Atkinson, D.R., & Hackett, G. (1988). *Counseling nonethnic American minorities*. Springfield, IL: Thomas.

Balka, C., & Rose, A. (1989). *Twice blessed: On being lesbian, gay, and Jewish*. Boston: Beacon.

Beam, J. (1986). *In the life: A Black gay anthology*. Boston: Alyson.

Beck, E. (1982). *Nice Jewish girls: A lesbian anthology*. Boston: Persephone.

Berger, R. (1982). *Gay and gray: The older homosexual man*. Urbana, IL: University of Illinois Press.

Bulkin, E., Pratt, M., & Smith, B. (1984). *Yours in struggle*. Brooklyn: Long Haul.

Carballo-Dieguez, A. (1989). Hispanic culture, gay male culture, and AIDS: Counseling implications. *Journal of Counseling and Development, 68*, 26–30.

Carrier, J. M. (1989). Gay liberation and coming out in Mexico. *Journal of Homosexuality, 17* (3&4), 225–252.

Chan, C. S. (1989). Issues of identity development among Asian-American lesbians and gay men. *Journal of Counseling and Development, 68*, 16–20.

Chuney, C., Kim, A., & Lemeshewsky, A. (Eds.). (1987). *Between the lines: An anthology of Pacific/Asian lesbians*. Santa Cruz, CA: Dancing Bird.

Churchill, W. (1971). *Homosexual behavior among males: A cross-cultural and cross-species investigation*. Englewood Cliffs, NJ: Prentice-Hall.

Clark, C. (1986). *Living as a lesbian*. Ithaca, NY: Firebrand.

Hill, I. (Ed.). (1987). *The bisexual spouse: Different dimensions in human sexuality*. McLean, VA: Barlina Books.

Lorde, A. (1988). *A burst of light*. Ithaca, NY: Firebrand.

Loiacano, D. K. (1989). Gay identity issues among Black Americans: Racism, homophobia, and the need for validation. *Journal of Counseling and Development, 68*, 21–25.

MacDonald, B. (1983). *Look me in the eye: Old women, aging, and ageism*. San Francisco: Spinsters.

Moraga, C., & Anzaldna, G. (Eds.). (1980). *The bridge called my back*. Boston: Persephone.

Newman, L. (1988). *A Letter to Harvey Milk*, Ithaca, NY: Firebrand.

Pres, C. (1985). *Considering motherhood: A workbook for lesbians*. San Francisco: Spinsters/Aunt Lute.

Ramos, J. (Ed.). (1987). *Copaneras: Latina lesbians*. New York: Latina Lesbian History Project.

Ross, M. W. (1989). Gay youth in four cultures: A comparative study. *Journal of Homosexuality, 17* (3&4), 299–314.

Schilenberg, J. (1985). *Gay parenting*. Garden City, NY: Anchor.

Scott, J. (1978). *Wives who love women*. New York: Walker.

Smith, M. J. (Ed.). (1983). *Black men/White men: A gay anthology*. San Francisco: Gay Sunshine.

Watanabe, T., & Iwata, J. (1987). *The love of the samurai: A thousand years of Japanese homosexuality*. London: GMP.

Williams, W. (1985). *The spirit and the flesh: Sexual diversity in American Indian culture*. Boston: Beacon.

Vacha, K. (1985). *Quiet fire: Memories of older gay men*. Trumansburg, NY: Crossing.

GAY AND LESBIAN LITERATURE

The following items are recommended gay and lesbian literature.

Aaab-Richards, D. (1987). *Tongues untied*. London: Gay Men's.

Berg, A. (1983). *Making love*. New York: Ballantine.

Brown, R. (1973). *Rubyfruit jungle*. New York: Bantam.

Bulkin, E. (Ed.). (1980). *Lesbian fiction: An anthology*. Boston: Persephone.

Falk, R. (1975). *Women loving*. New York: Random House.

Gearhart, S. (1980). *The wanderground: Stories of the hill women*. Boston: Persephone.

Guy, R. (1976). *Ruby*. New York: Viking.

Hamilton, W. (1977). *Coming out*. New York: Signet.

Hanscomb, G. (1982). *Between friends*. Boston: Alyson.

Hansen, J. (1970). *Fadeout*. New York: Henry Holt.

Hobson, L. (1975). *Consenting adults*. Garden City, NY: Doubleday.

Kopay, D., & Young, P. (1977). *The David Kopay story*. New York: Arbor House.

Ortiz-Taylor, S. (1980). *Faultline*. Tallahassee, FL: Naiad.

Rees, D. (1982). *The milkman's on his way*. London: Gay Men's.

Reid, J. (1976). *The best little boy in the world*. New York: Ballantine.

Rule, R. (1981). *Outlander*. Tallahassee, FL: Naiad.

Russ, J. (1980). *On strike against God*. New York: Out and Out.

Sarton, M. (1975). *Mrs. Stevens hears the mermaids singing*. New York: Norton.

Shockley, A. (1981). *The Black and White of it*. Tallahassee, FL: Naiad.

Stockton, C. (1986). *Lesbian letters*. San Francisco: Heron.

Walker, A. (1977). *Men loving men*. San Francisco: Gay Sunshine.

Warren, P. (1974). *The front runner*. New York: Morrow.

Warren, P. (1976). *The fancy dresser*. New York: Morrow.

White, E. (1982). *A boy's own story*. New York: New American Library.

PROGRAMMING RESOURCES

The following items are recommended for use in programming around the issues of gay, lesbian, and bisexual awareness.

Alternatives: A Game of Understanding
  PO Box 1050
  Amherst, MA 01004-1050
  (413) 546-4523

Opening Doors to Understanding and Acceptance: A Guide to Facilitating Workshops on Lesbian, Gay, and Bisexual Issues
  Contact: Kathy Obear, Human Advantage
  6 University Drive, Suite 125
  Amherst, MA 01002
  (413) 584-0812

Human Rights Foundation, Inc. (1984). *Demystifying homosexuality: A teaching guide about lesbians and gay men*. New York: Irvington.

MOVIES/VIDEOS—NONFICTION

Additional information on the availability of these films can be obtained from the Lambda Rising Bookstore, 1625 Connecticut Avenue, NW, Washington, DC 20009 (202-462-6969).

As Is
Before Stonewall
Life and Times of Harvey Milk
Pink Triangles
Stick, Stones, and Stereotypes (Equity Institute, Amherst, MA)
Teenagers and Homosexuality (University of Minnesota, Minneapolis)
We Bring a Quilt
What If I'm Gay? (ABC Afterschool Special)

MOVIES/VIDEOS—FICTION

Additional information on the availability of these films can be obtained from the Lambda Rising Bookstore, 1625 Connecticut Avenue, NW, Washington, DC 20009 (202-462-6969).

By Design
Consenting Adults
Desert Hearts
First Dance
In a Shallow Grave
Law of Desire (Spain)
Making Love
Maurice
My Beautiful Launderette
Parting Glances
That Certain Summer
Tidy Endings
Torch Song Trilogy
Truth About Alex
Women in Love

THE FUND FOR HUMAN DIGNITY

The following publications are available through the Fund for Human Dignity, 666 Broadway, Suite 410, New York, NY 10012 (212-529-1600):

About Coming Out: Twenty Questions About Homosexuality
Sobre El Asunto De Darse A Conocer Como Homosexual
Answers to a Parent's Questions About Homosexuality
Who's Behind the Gay Rights Movement?
Are There Gay People Working in My Business? Answers to Employer's Questions
National Gay and Lesbian Task Force's Corporate Survey
What Can Gay People Do About the Media?
Bridges of Respect: Creating Support for Lesbian and Gay Youth
And God Loves Each One: A Resource for Dialogue About the Church and Homosexuality
Community Center Starter Packet
Gay Switchboard Packet
Military/Security Clearance Packet
Gay/Lesbian Prisoner's Support Packet
Police (Training) Packet

JOURNALS AND MAGAZINES

Ache (A Journal for Black Lesbians)
PO Box 6071
Albany, CA 94706
(415) 824-0703

The Advocate (National Gay Newsmagazine)
22761 Pacific Coast Highway, Suite 234
Box 8991
Malibu, CA 90265

BGM (Black Gay Men)
PO Box 9391
Washington, DC 20005
(202) 232-5796

Gay Community News
62 Bereley Street
Boston, MA 02116
(617) 426-4469

Blackout (Black Gays and Lesbians)
19641 West Seven Mile
Detroit, MI 48219

Christopher Street (A Gay Newsmagazine)
60 West 13th Street
New York, NY 10011

Common Lives/Lesbian Lives
PO Box 1553
Iowa City, IA 52284

Communication (Monthly for Lesbian and Gay Clergy and Religion)
PO Box 436, Planetarium Station
New York, NY 10024
(212) 595-2758

Conditions (A Magazine of Writing by Women)
PO Box 56, Van Brunt Station
Brooklyn, NY 11215

Journal of Counseling and Development
Special issue on Gay, Lesbian, and Bisexual Issues in
Counseling, *68*(1) September/October, 1989.

Journal of Gay/Lesbian Psychotherapy
1721 Addison Street
Philadelphia, PA 19146

Journal of Homosexuality
CERES

San Francisco State University
San Francisco, CA 94132
(415) 338-1137

Lambda Rising Book Report
1625 Connecticut Avenue, NW
Washington, DC 20009
(202) 462-6969

Lesbian Connection (A Resource Guide)
Ambitious Amazons
PO Box 811
East Lansing, MI 48823

Lesbian History Archives
PO Box 1258
New York, NY 10001

Lesbian Voices
Jonick Enterprises
PO Box 2066
San Jose, CA 95109

New York Native (Gay Newspaper)
PO Box 1475
New York, NY 10008

Outlines (Chicago Monthly Paper)
Lambda Publications
1300 West Belmont, Suite 3
Chicago, Illinois 60657

Out/look (National Lesbian and Gay Quarterly)
PO Box 460430
San Francisco, CA 94114

Outweek (Gay Newsmagazine)
159 West 25th Street
New York, NY 10001

The Pyramid Periodical (Quarterly for People of Color)
PO Box 1111, Canal Street Station
New York, NY 10012

Swan (For Older Gay Men)
4864 Luna, No. 191
Phelan, CA 92371

USA Gaze (Newspaper)
9 North 4th Street, No. 212
Minneapolis, MN 55401

TRAVEL GUIDES

Travel guides provide listings of numerous places of interest throughout the nation and throughout the world for lesbians and gays. The following travel guides are available at most gay and lesbian bookstores. If you don't have access to a bookstore, they can be ordered through Malibu Sales, PO Box 4371, Los Angeles, CA 90078-4371 (800-333-5433).

Bob Damron's Address Book
Gaia's Guide (Lesbian Tour Guide)
Gayellow Pages: United States and Canada
Inn Places
Our World (International Gay Travel Magazine)
Places of Interest to Women
Spartacus

GAY AND LESBIAN ORGANIZATIONS

Affirmation: United Methodists for Lesbian and Gay Concerns
   PO Box 1021
   Evanston, IL 60204
   (708) 475-0499

Affirmation: Gay and Lesbian Mormons
   PO Box 46022
   Los Angeles, CA 90046
   (213) 255-7251

AIDS Coalition to Unleash Power (ACT-UP)
   496-A Hudson Street, Suite G-4
   New York, NY 10014
   (212) 533-8888

Alliance for Gay and Lesbian Artists in the Entertainment Industry
   PO Box 69A18
   West Hollywood, CA 90069
   (213) 273-7199

American Association of Physicians for Human Rights
   Box 14366
   San Francisco, CA 94144

American Civil Liberties Union (ACLU) Lesbian and Gay Rights Project
   132 West 43rd Street
   New York, NY 10036
   (212) 944-9800

American College Personnel Association (ACPA) Standing Committee on
Lesbian, Gay, and Bisexual Awareness
  c/o AACD
  5999 Stevenson Avenue
  Alexandria, VA 22304

American Foundation for AIDS Research (AmFAR)
  40 West 57th Street, No. 406
  New York, NY 10019
  (212) 719-0033

American Baptists Concerned
  870 Eire Street
  Oakland, CA 94610
  (415) 465-8652

American Psychological Association Committee on Lesbian and Gay
Concerns
  1200 17th Street, NW
  Washington, DC 20036

Asian American Lesbian and Gay Men's Coalition
  Box 2337
  Philadelphia, PA 19103
  (215) 849-4612

Association of College and University Housing Officers (ACUHO)—
I Committee for Lesbian, Gay, and Bisexual Concerns
  c/o Central Support Services Office
  Jones Tower, Suite 140
  101 Curl Drive
  Columbus, OH 43210-1195

Association for Gay, Lesbian, and Bisexual Issues in Counseling
  Box 216
  Jenkintown, PA 19046

Association of Gay and Lesbian Psychiatrists
  1721 Addison Street
  Philadelphia, PA 19046

Association of Lesbian and Gay Psychologists
  2336 Market Street, No. 8
  San Francisco, CA 94144

Black and White Men Together
  PO Box 148, Ansonia Station
  New York, NY 10023
  (212) 222-9794

Brethern/Mennonite Council for Lesbian and Gay Concerns (BMC)
  PO Box 65724
  Washington, DC 20035
  (202) 462-2595

Catholic Coalition for Gay Civil Rights
PO Box 1985
New York, NY 10159
(718) 629-2927

Center for Homophobia Education
PO Box 1985
New York, NY 10159

Concerned Insurance Professionals for Human Rights
Box 961996
Los Angeles, CA 90069-9006

Conference for Catholic Lesbians
PO Box 436, Planetarium Station
New York, NY 10024

Dignity (An Organization for Gay and Lesbian Catholics)
National Office:
Room 413
755 Boylston Street
Boston, MA 02116
(617) 267-5646

Directory of Homosexual Organizations and Publications
Homosexual Information Center
4758 Hollywood Boulevard, Suite 208
Hollywood, CA 90028

Education in a Disabled Gay Environment (EDGE)
PO Box 305, Village Station
New York, NY 10014
(212) 246-3811, ext. 292

Friends for Lesbian and Gay Concerns (Quaker Gays and Lesbians)
PO Box 222
Sumneytown, PA 18084

Gay Activists Alliance
PO Box 2, Village Station
New York, NY 10014

Gay American Indians
Box 2194
San Francisco, CA 94080
(415) 621-4716

The Gay Employment Protection Project
PO Box 24565
Los Angeles, CA 90024

Gay and Lesbian Advocates and Defenders
PO Box 218
Boston, MA 02112
(617) 426-1350

Gay and Lesbian Democrats of America
114 15th Street, NE
Washington, DC 20002

Gay and Lesbian Parents Coalition International
PO Box 50360
Washington, DC 20004
(703) 548-3238

Gay Married Men's Association
PO Box 28317
Washington, DC 20038
(703) 548-3238

Gay Parents Legal and Research Group
Box 1723
Lynwood, WA 98036
(206) 774-7464

Gay Public Health Workers
c/o Herbert
1801 Clysdale Place, NW
Washington, DC 20013

Gay Rights National Lobby
Box 1892
Washington, DC 20013
(202) 546-1801

Gay Teachers Association
Box 435, Van Brunt Station
Brooklyn, NY 11215

Gay Veterans Association
346 Broadway, No. 814
New York, NY 10013
(212) 787-0329

High Tech Gays
PO Box 6777
San Jose, CA 95150

Institute for the Protection of Gay and Lesbian Youth
Murray Hill
PO Box 1401
New York, NY 10156

Integrity (An Organization for Gay and Lesbian Episcopalians)
National Office:
Rev. Ron Wesner
5014 Willows Avenue
Philadelphia, PA 19143

International Advisory Council for Homosexual Men and Women in
Alcoholics Anonymous
    PO Box 90
    Washington, DC 20044
    (202) 544-1611

International Gay Information Center
    PO Box 2, Village Station
    New York, NY 10014

Jewish Lesbian Daughters of Holocaust Survivors
    PO Box 6194
    Boston, MA 02114

Lambda Legal Defense
    666 Broadway
    New York, NY 10012

Latin American Lesbians and Gay Men's Coalition
    c/o Reyes
    562 Guerrero, No. 1
    San Francisco, CA 94110

Lesbian and Gay Associated Engineers and Scientists
    PO Box 4247
    San Francisco, CA 94101

Lesbian and Gay Caucus of the Democratic National Committee
    1742 Massachusetts Avenue, SE
    Washington, DC 20003

Lesbian and Gay People in Medicine
    c/o American Medical Students Association
    1910 Association Drive
    Reston, VA 22091

Lesbian Mothers National Defense Fund
    PO Box 21567
    Seattle, WA 98111

Metropolitan Community Church
    National Office:
    PO Box 5570
    Los Angeles, CA 90055

National AIDS Network
    2033 M Street, NW, No. 800
    Washington, DC 20036
    (202) 293-2437

National Association of Black Lesbians and Gays
    19641 West Seven Mile
    Detroit, MI 48219
    (313) 537-0484

National Association of Lesbian and Gay Alcoholism Professionals
204 West 20th Street
New York, NY 10011
(212) 713-5074

National Association of People With AIDS
2025 Eye Street NW, No. 415
Washington, DC 20006
(202) 429-2856

National Association of Student Personnel Administrators (NASPA)
Network for Gay, Lesbian, and Bisexual Concerns
1700 18th Street, NW, Suite 301
Washington, DC 20009
(202) 265-7500

National Coalition of Black Gays
Box 57236, West End Station
Washington, DC 20037
(202) 387-8096

National Federation of Parents and Friends of Gays
5715 16th Street, NW
Washington, DC 20011
(202) 726-3223

National Gay and Lesbian Task Force
1517 U Street, NW
Washington, DC 20009
(202) 332-6483

National Gay Task Force
National Office:
Room 506
80 Fifth Avenue
New York, NY 10011

National Gay Rights Advocates
540 Castro Street
San Francisco, CA 94114
(415) 863-3624

National Gay Youth Network
PO Box 846
San Francisco, CA 94101

National Lawyers Guild, Gay Caucus
558 Capp Street
San Francisco, CA 94110
(415) 285-5066

NETGALA (College and University Alumni/ae Associations)
1442 1442 Q Street NW
Washington, DC 20011

New Ways Ministry
    4012 29th Street
    Mt. Rainier, MD 20712
    (301) 277-5674

Parents and Friends of Gays (International Directory)
National Federation of Parents and Friends of Gays
    5715 16th Street, NW
    Washington, DC 20011
    (202) 726-3223

Parents and Friends of Lesbians and Gays
    Box 24565
    Los Angeles, CA 90024
    (213) 472-8952

Presbyterians for Lesbian and Gay Concerns
    c/o James Anderson
    PO Box 38
    New Brunswick, NY 08903

Salsa Soul Sisters
    Box 1119, Stuyvesant Station
    New York, NY 10009
    (212) 384-2668

SIGMA (Sisters in Gay Ministry Associated)
    10 Almay Road
    Rochester, NY 14616

Task Force on Gay Liberation, American Library Association
(Social Responsibilities Round Table)
    Box 2383
    Philadelphia, PA 19103
    (212) 382-3222

Unitarian Universalists for Lesbian and Gay Concerns
    25 Beacon Street
    Boston, MA 02108
    (617) 742-2100 ext. 522

United Church Coalition for Lesbian and Gay Concerns
    18 North College Street
    Athens, OH 45701
    (614) 593-7301

Universal Fellowship of Metropolitan Community Churches
    5300 Santa Monica Boulevard, No. 304
    Los Angeles, CA 90029
    (213) 464-5100

Women's Legal Defense Fund
2000 P Street, NW, No. 400
Washington, DC 20036

World Congress of Gay and Lesbian Jewish Organizations
PO Box 18961
Washington, DC 20036